PELICAN BOOKS
A719
PATTERNS OF INFANT CARE IN AN
URBAN COMMUNITY
JOHN AND ELIZABETH NEWSON

John Newson was born in London in 1925. He was educated
at Bancrofts School, South-West Essex Technical College,
and University College, London, reading first physics and
mathematics, and later psychology. He has been lecturing and
doing research at the University of Nottingham since 1951,
specializing in child psychology and statistics. His other
research interest is the early development of perceptual
abilities.

Elizabeth Newson was born in London in 1929. She was
educated at the Mary Datchelor School and University
College, London, where she read psychology. After teaching
infants for a year in Nottingham, she joined the Nottingham
University psychology department as a research student in
1952, and has been doing research ever since; she is now a
University Research Fellow, sponsored by the Nuffield
Foundation. Her earlier research work was concerned with
the perceptual and conceptual basis of the process of learning
to read.

John and Elizabeth Newson met at University College and
were married in 1951. They have three children – one boy and
two girls – between the ages of three and nine. They regard
having young children of their own as an indispensable professional qualification, and a necessary and effective counter-
balance to the study of child development as they encounter it
in learned journals. For recreation they escape with their
children rather than from them, and their favourite pastime
is sailing small boats in Suffolk.

JOHN AND ELIZABETH NEWSON

PATTERNS OF INFANT CARE

in an Urban Community

Penguin Books
Baltimore · Maryland

Penguin Books Ltd, Harmondsworth, Middlesex, England
Penguin Books Inc., 3300 Clipper Mill Road, Baltimore 11, Md, U.S.A.
Penguin Books Pty Ltd, Ringwood, Victoria, Australia

—

First published by George Allen & Unwin Ltd 1963
under the title *Infant Care in an Urban Community*
Published in Penguin Books 1965

Copyright © George Allen & Unwin, 1963

—

Made and printed in Great Britain
by Richard Clay & Company, Ltd,
Bungay, Suffolk
Set in Monotype Times New Roman

Dedicated with gratitude

to the 709 Nottingham mothers who shared
with us their experience of babies in the
first year of life

and to the babies themselves

CONTENTS

TABLES

9

ACKNOWLEDGMENTS

Many people have been concerned, directly or indirectly, in the preparation of this book and the carrying out of the investigation which it describes. Our first acknowledgment must be to the City of Nottingham Health Department, and particularly to the Medical Officer of Health, Dr William Dodd, and his staff, who most kindly put at our disposal the experience and skill of the Health Visitors. To the Health Visitors themselves we are especially grateful: it is no exaggeration to say that the survey could not have been made without their tireless and continuing help.

We are indebted to the Sir Halley Stewart Trust for their kindness in making a contribution towards the original costs of production of this book.

When we tried to number the friends and colleagues who have helped us with their comments, criticism, encouragement and advice, we found that their names would fill several pages; we hope that those we do not mention here will include themselves among the many to whom we offer our thanks. To Len Chaloner, F. Le Gros Clark, Dr Ann Dally, Daisy Hogg, Mabel Holmes, Dr E. L. Loewenthal, Keith and Gillian Newson, Alison Paechter, Rosalind Palmer, Professor W. J. H. Sprott, Dr Christopher Wardle, and to others who listened patiently and argued vigorously, our warmest gratitude.

Finally, we should like to thank our children, Roger, Carey and Joanna, who are tolerant of the busyness of our life; and who, by involving us so deeply with themselves, have taught us more than we could ever otherwise have known of the complexities of infant care in an urban community.

NOTE – For obvious reasons, all names of mothers and their children have been changed, although some attempt has been made at verisimilitude: for instance, Nottingham names have been replaced by Nottingham pseudonyms, Irish by Irish, etc. Occupations given are accurate except in a very few cases where the occupation is so rare in the community that the informant might be identifiable; here a closely comparable job has been substituted. In one case certain minor details, of no significance to the content, have been altered for the sake of anonymity.

INTRODUCTION

This book is the report of a research project aimed at discovering how infants are being reared in England at the present time. The information which it presents was derived from home interviews with more than 700 mothers of one-year-old children, during which they answered questions about how they had handled their babies during the first year of life.

As every parent knows, there is not, and probably never has been, any shortage of opinions about how babies 'ought' to be brought up. The young mother, from the moment it is known that she is expecting a child, becomes fair game: neighbours, relations and friends, each one an authority on the subject, are all delighted to share with her their superior knowledge. Once her child is born, the barrage of advice continues – much of it conflicting, some of it self-contradictory, and a fair proportion accompanied by the implicit corollary that failure to carry it out will give deep offence to the adviser. The bewildered mother now turns to the 'experts' for the pronouncement of science; only to find that Dr X at the clinic is at singular variance with her own Dr Y, who disagrees with his partner, Dr Z, who opposes the health visitor, who contradicts what the midwife said. Perhaps she had better get a good book on the subject; well, here we have Dr Spock, Dr Gibbens, Sir Truby King, Dr de Kok, Mrs Cuthbert and *Good Housekeeping*: all different – pay your money and take your choice.

Infant handling in Britain today is still a subject on which many different specialists use the full weight of their professional authority to back up their private prejudices concerning what is good and what is bad in the care of young children. In the face of the conflict which results, intelligent parents are rapidly forced to the conclusion that the experts know little more about the matter than they do themselves.

The truth is, of course, that in the present state of knowledge there is not a sufficient body of well-substantiated evidence about the facts and consequences of child rearing on which to base sound practical advice to parents. There is no lack of theoretical speculation, but so far very few theories of child rearing have been subjected to the inconvenience of being reconciled with the empirical evidence. Whatever the reason may be for this unfortunate state of affairs, the situation can hardly have arisen simply because the subject has no importance: indeed, it is probably because it has such immense importance that the professional advisers and pseudo-experts have flourished in such profusion.

Thus it is not the purpose of this book to give advice to anxious parents. Rather, we are trying to find out what parents actually *do*, what sources of advice do influence them, how they actually feel about their children and how they react in practice to all the situations which naturally arise in the handling of a young baby. The study which we have undertaken has a certain value simply as a descriptive sociological investigation. We hope it may also make a small contribution towards providing that foundation of empirical evidence upon which a deeper understanding of child development must be based.

PART ONE

THE PRACTICE OF INFANT CARE

CHAPTER ONE

BIRTH IN PROSPECT AND RETROSPECT

In this investigation we are primarily concerned with the ways in which mothers handle their infants during the first year of life, but it is impossible to study this period in complete isolation. A mother's behaviour towards her baby is bound to reflect her own very personal feelings and attitudes. In part, these stem from her own childhood experiences, the kind of family life she has herself known, her relationships with her own parents and siblings, and the experience she has already had in caring for young children. Her feelings for the baby will be influenced, too, by her present situation: how long she has been married, how far her marriage is a success, how well she is adjusted to the roles of wife and mother, how many other children she has, how much work she has to do, how much money there is available, and so on. To what extent the reactions of her particular baby match up to her expectations will be another important factor in her attitude towards him. Obviously, much will depend upon whether it is her first child.

It is often not realized that, for the country as a whole, a very large number of first (legitimate) babies are in fact conceived out of wedlock. The figures for 1957 showed that, of fertile women, one in five was already pregnant by the time she married. The fact that Nottingham had an illegitimacy rate of 9 per cent,[1] which was nearly twice the national average, probably indicates that quite a large number of marriages in our sample were precipitated by the girl becoming pregnant, and this must obviously be taken into account. Although we

1. City of Nottingham, *Annual Report of the Health Services*, 1959; see also Virginia Wimperis, *The Unmarried Mother and her Child* (Allen and Unwin, 1960).

did not ask the mothers whether their babies were in fact desired and planned for, the subject did often come up in conversation, and our impression was that many babies, especially in the larger families, were more welcome in retrospect than in prospect. It is certainly true in Nottingham that any mother with two or more young children will encounter again and again the standard conversational condolence: 'But you wouldn't be without them *now*, dear, would you?'

Mrs Machin, wife of a foundry worker and the mother of four children, gave us an exceptionally candid and revealing account:

'They've all of them bin a surprise – I never wanted none of them, and specially this last one. And I don't mind admitting, I've taken pills and pills, but I never got shut of none of 'em yet. Now with Janice – I was two months with her, and then I made a show, and I went to the doctor, and she said "I'm afraid you've had a miscarriage" – course, I didn't tell her I'd been taking pills! But then I didn't have one again, so I goes back to the doctor, and she examines me, and she says, "Well, it's still there, you're lucky!" Oh dear! [laughed]. But once I knew she was a girl, I was glad I'd got her. But I don't want no more.'[1]

Mrs Lievesley, an engine-driver's wife, had five children. She had 'had to get married' nineteen years ago, and she hadn't wanted this baby either.

'We didn't want none of 'em, come to that. They was all accidents. But we was *really* surprised to see Vicky, because we was using something before her.'

Of course, not all pregnancies are unwanted, and the wife who continues into her late twenties without having a child is certainly not likely to receive unqualified social approval.

1. Madeline Kerr also noted a preference for *ex post facto* contraception; see *The People of Ship Street*, p. 83 (Routledge and Kegan Paul, 1958). A particularly interesting case study project on attitudes towards family planning is reported by Pauline Shapiro, 'The Unplanned Children', *New Society*, 1 November 1962.

We did find some mothers who had succeeded in bearing a child only after great difficulty, or even at some personal risk, and it was clear that having a baby meant a very great deal to them. Mrs Frearson, who had been neglected by her own mother and used as a pawn in family quarrels, was the proud and tender mother of two children; but to achieve this she had had to undergo a series of six operations during the first twelve years of her married life, and her first long-hoped-for pregnancy had ended in a miscarriage. Mrs James, a lively young woman of twenty-three, had a slipped disc; her first baby had been born prematurely and died after a few hours, and she had been told then that she mustn't have any more children.

'They said I couldn't stand the weight of carrying. Well – I was *determined* to have a baby, so I said to Jack, "We'll just go ahead and have one, and we won't tell anyone or ask anyone's advice." So we did. I never saw any doctor or clinic or anyone right through until I called the midwife when he started. He was ten pounds, and twenty-four inches long. Oh, it was fine, I wouldn't have missed it for the world. . . . But we had to keep waking the midwife up with cups of tea, I was her fifth in forty-eight hours.'

Mrs James was hoping to have another baby to complete her family, and, judging by her strength of purpose, she probably will. She has little faith in doctors' forebodings.[1]

All these various attitudes towards pregnancy are associated with the fact that the arrival of a first baby involves a big change in the life of most women. A number of subtle social influences are at work which assist her in acquiring her new role of mother long before the baby is born. Many a prospective mother has noticed how her relationship with other mothers changes as the fact of her pregnancy becomes more apparent. Neighbours who have children begin to smile at her in a new way, and her slightest inquiry after the welfare of other babies will be warmly welcomed and eagerly

1. When following up this family, after this chapter was completed, we found that Mrs James had indeed achieved a second healthy baby.

encouraged. It is almost as if she had been admitted to membership of an exclusive club, the existence of which she had scarcely been aware of previously. In motherhood she will find she has a new interest which she is able to share with women in all walks of life, including those with whom she would otherwise have almost nothing in common. Even women of an older generation, whose children have long since grown up, will expect her to be interested in their own nostalgic reminiscences. The ritual surrounding the arrival of a baby seems to provide the lowest common denominator of essential womanhood.

In broader perspective, these subtle changes which the expectant mother experiences in her relationships with other people are probably a reflection of deeper and more pervasive cultural pressures through which society seeks to prepare a woman for the role of motherhood. In our society, as in many others, the birth of a first child is more than a biological event. It carries overtones of a ceremonial rite whereby a young woman is initiated into the established matriarchy. Like the acquisition of a wedding ring, the bearing of the first (legitimate) child confers enhanced status. And, as with most rites of passage, whether they concern a tribal initiation into manhood or an English boy's admission to his public school peer group, the prestige of the initiated is maintained by the tradition of ordeal by pain and suffering: a slowly changing tradition, which we will discuss in more detail presently.

In a more primitive state of society one would expect the new mother to be influenced most strongly by older and more experienced mothers, generally those who belong to her own kinship group, and in particular her own mother and her elder sisters; but the conditions of modern life have done much to alter this. For one thing, these older women are not generally present in the same household. It is true that the housing situation does force a certain proportion of young married couples to set up their first home together in the house of parents, but this is generally regarded as an unfortunate and temporary expedient rather than as something which reflects the natural order. Although the influence of the maternal grandmother is still surprisingly strong, factors such as rehousing, geographical dispersion and social mobility are progressively weakening her traditional authority in this vital sphere. A still more important factor is that in our society the whole business of birth and child care has become a matter of special medical concern. There are, of course, very important reasons for this, and it has indeed been suggested that the advance of civilization may be measured by the decline in the infant mortality rate; but the fact that one of the maternal grandmother's chief roles – her chief source of authority, in fact – is being steadily taken over by the doctor, the midwife and the health visitor may have far-reaching cultural repercussions.

Not unexpectedly, some grandmothers are reluctant to give up their traditional function as mentor and adviser, and this is probably responsible for the scarcely veiled hostility with which the advice of the midwife or health visitor is sometimes received. One maternal grandmother in our sample was determined to show her daughter that she knew better than the midwife. Mrs Donovan was a woman of generous and imposing proportions, who from first to last dominated the interview; her daughter and son-in-law, a lorry-driver, lodged with her, and were plainly well under her thumb. After the birth of the baby, we were told, the midwife said, before leaving them for the night, 'Now you are NOT to give that baby ANYTHING'. The baby cried; 'all that stuff she'd swallowed', Mrs Donovan explained. She told her daughter that the other lodgers had to be considered, the baby couldn't cry all night, and she was going to give it some cinder-water. Her daughter faint-heartedly protested, 'Oh, Mum, the midwife said . . .', but Mrs Donovan was adamant. She got a cup of water, plunged into it a red-hot poker, strained the liquid, and gave the baby two and a half teaspoonsful of it. The baby vomited black mucus, and slept all night. 'Haven't you ever heard of cinder-water?' Mrs Donovan asked us with scorn. 'Well, I'm surprised they don't teach you *that* at the University.' The interviewer asked, 'and what did the midwife say?' 'Huh,' said Mrs Donovan, 'she never knew'.

Among the older and more experienced mothers, the feeling was sometimes expressed that the health visitors were scarcely competent to advise, not being married themselves. In actual fact, many health visitors are married, but their critics either did not realize this or conveniently forgot it for the purpose of the argument. The wife of a lorry-driver, a cheerful and attractive slattern, now pregnant with her fifth child, told us she never went to the clinic, though it was barely 300 yards from her door.

'*They*'re no good. Well, just look at them. A lot of old maids, not a married one among them. *They*'ve never had any children. They don't know what it's like.'

Mrs Dodds had the same complaint, and added:

'Well, you see people of every nationality there. Well, it's not that I've anything against foreigners, but all the babies have to be undressed, and I think they pick up things.'

On the other side of the picture, there were, of course, insecure, less experienced, or socially isolated mothers who would have been completely at sea without the friendly advice and counsel of the people at 'the welfare'. Yet another lorry-driver's wife had nothing but praise for both the midwife and the health visitor.

'We get a lot better looked after than we were years ago – I mean clinics and everything, where you can go and get advice and all that sort of thing, I mean, they couldn't get that years ago, could they? I mean, if I was ever in doubt about Jane, I used to be straight up to the clinic – I always used to go – and Miss H. used to come and see me; and she's a very nice woman, you can talk to her and discuss things with her.'

It is characteristic of life in modern civilized countries that people growing up in them tend to be sheltered and insulated from some of the more fundamental and dramatic experiences which life has to offer. Thus people often have little acquaintance with sexual behaviour, great physical suffering, insanity or death, unless or until they themselves become intimately involved. The same is true of childbirth. Only a few women have the opportunity of witnessing the birth of a child before they themselves have a baby, and very few indeed before they are themselves pregnant. Thus childbirth tends to be regarded as a mysterious and awesome event surrounded by a veil of secrecy. Furthermore, what they come to know about it by way of casual conversation is frequently not at all reassuring. Often, it seems, those who have most to say on the subject tend to give the most lurid and sensational accounts, and to find some kind of perverse satisfaction in retailing vivid descriptions of abnormally difficult births and of unusual complications to young women about to give birth themselves. It is therefore not surprising that some women approach their first confinement in a state of nervous anxiety arising largely from their own misconceptions and ignorance. If they then have the misfortune to be attended by unsympathetic doctors or nurses who merely regard them as unsatisfactory patients, what could be an exciting and memorable experience becomes an unhappy time to be forgotten as quickly as possible. The effect of this kind of attitude on the part of the hospital staff can be demoralizing even for an experienced mother. Mrs Wheeler, who came into hospital for the birth of her fourth baby, told us:

'Well, I was really disgusted about the whole business. I was in the ward, and they kept asking me if I was having pains yet, and I said I had them in my legs, in my thighs, which is where I do get them. They said nonsense, you don't have them in your legs. I said, "Well, I do." But they took no notice. Then all of a sudden the baby's head had come, and I shouted, and of course they came running, and said, "Why didn't you *say* you were having pains?" Then the sister was ever so cross, and they took the baby away, and I didn't see her till six o'clock next morning. I didn't know if it was a boy or a girl, I didn't know if it was dead. Oh! I went through such agony of mind that night. Well – these things you just have to forget.'

Fortunately, there are today several indications of a much more enlightened attitude towards this whole problem. The most obvious of these is the provision of special classes for pregnant mothers. These 'relaxation classes' are usually provided in conjunction with ante-natal clinics, either at welfare centres or at the hospitals, but some are also now being organized by general practitioners, who can ask for a health visitor to attend their own weekly clinics. The classes themselves are partly educational and partly practical. They dispel ignorance by explaining in some detail the normal course of labour and what the mother can expect to happen at each stage, and they also teach her how to relax and to regulate her breathing and exertions so as to cooperate to the fullest extent in the delivery of the baby, thus making the whole process as natural, easy and painless as possible.

From our survey we discovered that, of mothers expecting their first baby, about 41 per cent had done relaxation exercises. Most of these had in fact attended the relaxation classes, but a very small minority had read one of the appropriate books[1] and had undertaken the exercises on their own initiative. We also found that those who had done the exercises were more likely to have a positive attitude in remembering the subsequent birth. This, of course, may not be a simple relation of cause and effect, since it may well be that those mothers who take the trouble to attend the relaxation classes are more likely to be well adjusted towards the whole matter of childbirth anyway. However, the general consensus of opinion among these mothers was that the exercises had been a great help.

Our results showed that 60 per cent of all legitimate births were home births; hospitals took 27 per cent, Nottingham's one maternity hospital 11 per cent, and the remaining 2 per

1. e.g. Helen Heardman, *A Way to Natural Childbirth* (E. and S. Livingstone, 1954).

Grantly Dick Read, *Revelation of Childbirth* (3rd edition, Heinemann, 1955).

cent were taken by private nursing homes. If, however, we consider first births alone, only 26 per cent take place at home, and the maternity hospital takes a much higher percentage (40 per cent). Unless there are special reasons for hospitalization being desirable, it is not easy in Nottingham to book a National Health hospital bed for second or third births. There are considerable class differences shown here, and these will be discussed later.[1]

Of course, the mother's attitude to childbirth will also depend upon what happens during the course of her particular confinement. Inevitably, some births are more difficult than others, and complications do occur. Unfortunately also, some doctors and nurses still treat the natural childbirth movement with amusement and even contempt, thus undoing much of the morale-building which has been patiently achieved through relaxation classes.

Our general impression, after many conversations on the subject, was that hospitals are the chief offenders in allowing morale to weaken; this should not be inevitable, but is obviously likely to happen in an institution unless considerable effort is made to avoid it. Too often we heard complaints of the impersonal atmosphere of the labour ward, of a sense of the conveyor-belt, and, especially, of being left alone, sometimes for two or three hours, during the first stage of labour, that 'loneliest time in a woman's life', as it has been called. For the woman at home, there is none of this; she has the comforting familiarity of her own bed, or her own fireside until she reaches the second stage; some familiar person – her husband, her mother or a neighbour – will probably be there to sit with her and to rub her back; and, above all, there will be the midwife, who will have examined her several times during her pregnancy, and with whom, therefore, she already has a personal relationship. The midwife may be rushed off her feet; she may, in fact, have to dash back and forth between confinements; but she always seems able to provide that touch of intimacy, of real friendliness, which is of the greatest support to a woman in labour, and which

1. Pp. 164–8.

so often seems to be lacking in the institution. To the midwife, Mrs Smith is 'Mrs Smith', instead of the impersonal 'now, mother' of the hospital, and Mr Smith is a real person with real needs and anxieties, instead of simply an intruder. Because of this personal touch, and probably because of the familiarity of her surroundings, the mother finds the home midwife approachable in a way that the busy sister of a hospital ward perhaps is not. Mrs Wilcox, rushed into hospital after a difficult home birth, had her baby taken from her and could not find out why. A diffident nineteen-year-old, no one seems to have made any attempt to reassure her.

'Well, I don't really know what it was. Every time I asked them . . . you can't get to know anything in there. You know, I kept asking what were the matter, and she said she didn't like the sound of his cry. She said he was screaming. Well, I don't know, they wouldn't tell me no more. I didn't even know he was on the danger list until they took him off – they'd had him christened. I don't know what was wrong with him, I don't know to this day.'

The midwifery profession seems to be in the forefront of medical opinion in having moved on in its objectives, from making childbirth painless by simple loss of consciousness to the more positive goal of giving women the real happiness in childbearing which is possible. The widespread use of analgesics rather than general anaesthetics has assisted this aim by helping to free women from the tension which itself creates pain, while allowing them to use their energies creatively. The conference convened in 1960 by the Royal College of Midwives[1] saw nothing absurdly idealistic in asking themselves the question: 'Are we doing all we can to ensure mothers the supreme pleasure that having a baby can offer her, or has something of the pleasure been lost to the mother of today as a result of our clinical approach and our concentration upon her as a patient?' For those who still doubt that childbirth can be, not only a fulfilling, but also

1. Royal College of Midwives Conference on Human Relationships in the Care of Mother and Baby: at Oxford, March 1960.

an intensely pleasurable experience, we found plenty of evidence that many mothers find a deep joy in the actual process of giving birth.

The questions we asked were: 'How did you get on? Did you have a good time?'; and from the mother's answer we assessed her attitude as 'positive', 'not very positive', or 'negative'. On this rather arbitrary classification, most fell in the category 'not very positive', and their comments were generally variations on the theme 'It was all right':

'It was all right, I suppose. You soon forget about it, don't you?'

'Oh, I had a very good time really. It's not a thing you'd *want* to do, is it, but mine was a very good birth.'

'Having babies is easy to me, I just have 'em and it's over and done with.'

Only about 10 per cent could be classified as showing a really negative attitude, and almost all of these had had abnormal labours.

Miner's wife:
'It was my worst yet.'

Van driver's wife:
'Ooh, I thought I was dying' [laughed].

University lecturer's wife:
'As far as I'm concerned, they can give me all the anaesthetic they've got. I just don't want to know anything about it, I think all that stuff about the joy of birth is a lot of nonsense.'

Roughly a fifth of the mothers showed a positive attitude:

Machine operator's wife:
'Oh, I had a wonderful time over him. Yes, it was really a birth where – well, I should *love* it all over again. You know, I could remember every part of it. His was a wonderful birth.'

27

Engineer's wife:

'People said it would be awful, but really it was a thrill – it was a real sensation – I've never known anything like it.'

Chief clerk's wife:

'Well, I wouldn't say I enjoyed it, that it was a great *joy* to me; of course, it wasn't very comfortable, but it was a marvellous experience, there's no doubt about it – oh yes – in fact I'm quite looking forward to having another one. I saw him before he was actually born, I was very fortunate, because above the bed there was this huge arc light, and of course you could see everything reflected there – it was just by chance, but it was very nice.'

Minister's wife:

'It's a natural function to me, and I treat it as such. *Oh* – it's marvellous – yes – yes.'

It is worth noting that many of these positive mothers had in fact had abnormal or rather difficult labours but had found the experience very rewarding none the less; while there were some who could not be classed as positive towards this birth, owing to its abnormality, but who obviously had potentially positive attitudes. Mrs James, the wife of a shop manager, whom we have already mentioned as having had her baby against medical advice, said:

'Oh, it was fine, I wouldn't have missed it for the world. His shoulders were very broad, though, and he had to be pushed back again, and so I got torn; but I wouldn't have missed even that.'

Mrs Bolton, an optician's wife, gave birth to twins after a breech labour:

'I don't think anyone could say they *enjoyed* it. It was the only confinement I've *witnessed* of the lot; it was interesting, but it was a relief when it was all over.'

When the birth took place at home, a friend or relative was frequently present in the room at the actual moment of birth. This was true of 43 per cent of all home births, but in no single case was a lay person present when the birth took place in hospital or nursing home; we have no information as to how many mothers, if any, in fact ask to have their husbands with them during hospital labours.

The non-medical helpers at home births were fairly evenly divided into three groups: close female relatives, husbands and neighbours. Our figures here apply only to those who were present throughout the birth of the baby; in most home births there will be a lay person present during the earlier part of labour, but in more than half of our sample they leave the room before the final stage. At 15 per cent of home births, a neighbour was present; at 13 per cent, the husband was with his wife; and at 15 per cent, the woman's mother, mother-in-law or sister was there. Mothers outnumber mothers-in-law by two to one; and together they outnumber sisters in the same proportion. It is an interesting reflection upon the geographical dispersion of the extended family that the neighbour has taken over the mother's traditional place at her daughter's confinement, and is there more than twice as often. Where the woman's mother *is* present, it tends to be a first birth, and often the daughter is living in the mother's house at the time; usually in these cases a move to a separate dwelling takes place during the following year.

Since the proportion of lay people present throughout home labours was so high, it seemed useful to correlate this factor with the woman's attitude towards the birth. No significant difference in attitude is found according to whether a friend or neighbour is or is not present. Where we did find a difference, however, was in the woman's memory of the birth if her husband had been there. Thirty-six per cent of these mothers spoke of labour as a pleasurable or exciting experience, as compared with only 20 per cent of those who had been attended by a friend or relative. It is probable, of course, that the mother who wants her husband with her during labour already has a rather positive attitude towards birth; many mothers did, however, specifically mention their husbands as having contributed in large part to the happiness of the occasion. Nobody mentioned other relatives or friends in this way.

'Well I didn't really think I'd want him, but the midwife believes in it, she got him in, and really, I was ever so glad.'

'Oh I always have him there – I wouldn't have a birth without him.'

'I really think it brought us closer together, and he thinks so too.'

Although we did not often have the chance to ask the father for his views, there was plenty of evidence that he, too, found the birth of his children a moving experience:

'It was the first time he's been there – oh, it was a great experience for him. He wished he'd been there at the others.'

'He's always there; he likes to see 'em born, gives him a thrill, you know, sort of.'

'No, he wouldn't stop wi' me – I wanted him to. He saw a film of a birth after; and he said "I wish I'd stopped with you now", but I told him it was too late now, I'm not having any more.'

– and for Mr Johnson, an unemployed miner, the whole process of birth was fascinating; he told us:

'I've seen everything: I've seen a breech birth, I've seen a normal birth, and now I just want to see a sincerian birth; and I *shall*, I'm *determined*.'

On the whole, then, our general impression of the mothers' attitudes to childbirth, as described by them in retrospect, is that, for an important minority, birth is remembered as an occasion of great joy and physical satisfaction; for a somewhat larger number, it is a time of absorbing interest and excitement; and a still larger number at least derived a sense of achievement and fulfilment from an experience which they thought well worth the physical discomfort involved. It should perhaps be mentioned here that the vast majority of mothers (93 per cent) were fully conscious at the time of birth, and obviously preferred it that way. More than one mother also expressed some regret that she was unable to see her own baby being born.

CHAPTER TWO

FOOD AND COMFORT: BREAST, BOTTLE AND DUMMY

It is a common practice for a doctor or midwife to encourage a mother to put her infant to the breast as soon as possible after the birth. This is partly because the sucking of the baby acts as a positive stimulus assisting the return of the uterus to its normal size. Although the physiological mechanism is rather complicated, the physical effect upon the mother is quite immediate and definite. As one mother put it, when the baby first sucks it makes your toes curl up.

Obviously mothers are encouraged to breast feed for the sake of the baby as well, and a high proportion of mothers do begin the baby's feeding by this method. Four days after birth, 83 per cent of mothers are either breast feeding or at least still making some attempt to do so. However, it is clear from what they say that a large number of them only do this because they believe or have been told that it is expected of them. They have little intention of carrying on once they get out of hospital, or once things get back to normal at home. Thus after two weeks, by which time the mother will have come home or the midwife will have given up her daily visits, the proportion still breast feeding is down to 60 per cent; and, by the time the baby is a month old, about half the mothers will have given up breast feeding completely.

'I fed him myself just when he was born – you have to do, you know – well, they like you to feed them because of you having milk fever or anything like that, you see. But your milk soon goes when you get up and you're doing your work. But I wouldn't have gone on with it anyhow.'

'I did for a while in hospital – you always have to try, you know.'

32

'The midwife's a one for the breast feeding, she won't let you bottle feed.'

'Of course, while the nurse was here I had to.'

If so many mothers have weaned to the bottle before the baby is a month old, how long do the others continue with breast feeding? So as to be able to compare our results with those of previous workers, we classified all these mothers according to whether they were still breast feeding at one month, at three months and at six months. The result of this analysis is presented in Table 1. We have given separate

TABLE 1

Mothers still breast feeding babies at various ages

Samples (see p. 268 f.)	1 month	3 months	6 months
	%	%	%
Health visitor sample (corrected)	53·5	28·5	13·0
University sample (corrected)	39·5	21·1	8·9

figures for the Health Visitor and University samples because there is some discrepancy between them. In particular, the difference between the proportions still breast feeding at one month is statistically significant, and therefore cannot be ignored. Presumably it has arisen because the mothers tended to give a somewhat more 'favourable' account to the health visitors.[1] If she is feeling slightly on the defensive, it is, after all, easy to imagine a mother saying 'about a month' when she really means three weeks.

The discrepancy between samples is, however, of little importance when we come to compare our results with those from previous surveys.[2] This is done in Table 2. As these

1. This research problem is discussed on pp. 269 and 272–4.

2. R. M. Dykes, *Illness in Luton* (Leagrave Press, Luton, 1950). Population Investigation Committee, *Maternity in Great Britain* (O.U.P., 1948). J. Spence *et al.*, *1,000 Families in Newcastle upon Tyne* (O.U.P., 1954). A. L. Ross and G. Herdan, 'Breast Feeding in Bristol', *Lancet*, 1951, I, p. 630.

earlier investigations also used health visitors as interviewers, we have only included our health visitor sample for comparison. The fact that stands out clearly is that our sample shows a considerably reduced percentage of mothers breast feeding at each age.

TABLE 2

Proportions of mothers still breast feeding at various ages: surveys compared

	1 month	3 months	6 months
	%	%	%
Luton (1945)	—	57	39
National Survey (1946)	60	42	30
Newcastle (1947–8)	78	48	31
Bristol (1947–8)	67	44	32
Nottingham (1959–60)	54	29	13

If we can assume that Nottingham is not very peculiar in this respect, the most obvious inference is that breast feeding in general is on the decline. These earlier surveys were undertaken more than ten years before ours, and at a time when many foods were still rationed. People then were undoubtedly more conscious of the relationship which exists between wise feeding and health in times of austerity. In 1945, promoting the health and welfare of infants was still considered part of the war effort, and the mother who was able to feed her baby herself was actually saving food, nominally for her own consumption, but in fact to eke out the rations of the whole family. By 1960, however, what we ate was no longer a matter of constant concern for the housewife. Shops were well stocked, and most families had enough money coming in to buy all the food they needed. Pre-packaged and processed foods were commonplace, and, in particular, all kinds of artificial foods for babies were readily available and widely advertised.

Why do they stop?

It is a commonly held belief, particularly among the middle classes, that large numbers of working-class mothers give up breast feeding early in order to return to work. The facts as we found them are quite otherwise, and the stereotype of the working mother getting back to the factory as soon as possible after the birth can be discounted as a factor in the decline of natural feeding, even in this city of traditionally high employment for women. By the time the child is twelve months old, less than 2 per cent of mothers are yet back in full-time work, and no difference is shown between the occupational classes. Twelve months after the birth, again, less than 8 per cent even have part-time jobs; and most of them involve either 'outwork' in the home or a few hours' work in the evening.

In the broader perspective, it is clear that a necessary precondition of any large-scale decline in breast feeding is the availability and cheapness of suitable artificial or substitute foods, feeding bottles, teats and the means of sterilization. With higher material standards of living, including running water, efficient sanitation and a modern stove, it requires little effort to take the necessary hygienic precautions; and, in a more affluent society, the total cost of artificial feeding is no longer an important consideration. In an underdeveloped country, alternatives to natural feeding are inconvenient and impracticable;[1] with the material assets of civilization, the inconveniences of bottle feeding are so diminished as to be almost non-existent, and it is breast feeding for which a positive effort has to be made: and this is particularly true where, as we found, civilization has

1. F. Le Gros Clark has pointed out that 'those who are accustomed to see cow's milk as simply a natural "bridge" from the breast to solid foods have not grasped the full extent of the problem. Most of the peoples of the world have still practically no milk but mother's milk; and for several hundred thousand years at least the human stock seems to have had no domesticated milk herds.' F. Le Gros Clark, 'The Weaning of the Human Child', in *Nutrition*, Summer 1953.

brought with it excessive feelings of modesty towards the exposure of the breast during feeding.

Although the mother who early resorts to artificial foods is now among the majority, she is still likely to feel a certain amount of guilt at denying her baby what in magazine articles for women is often called 'his birthright'; and this is reflected in the reasons she first gives for her action. We asked every mother: 'Did you have any special reason for not breast feeding/stopping when you did?' The answers to this question were, as we expected, highly stereotyped, most of them variations on the theme that the milk wasn't good enough, or that there wasn't enough of it.

'I had plenty of milk, but it wasn't any good.'

'My milk all went to water.'

'It just wasn't satisfying him, and he was losing weight, so when he was two days old [sic] I put him on the bottle, and asked the doctor for the tablets to stop it, like.'

'I tried for two days, but it wasn't any good. It looked like sour milk, actually. She wasn't getting any satisfaction from it.'

'I had too much milk, and I think it's apt to pull you down a bit.'

'I think it was too rich for him.'

'It looked too thin.'

The introductory straight question was followed by what we regarded as a probe question: every mother who had breast fed even for one day only was asked, 'Did you enjoy feeding the baby?' followed, if necessary, by a supplementary question, on the general lines of 'Do you think you'd have stopped anyway, even if you'd had enough milk?'

The replies to these questions were revealing. Over and over again, we found, the physical reasons at first given were cover for underlying attitudes which were, as so many mothers now admitted, quite sufficient reason in themselves for changing to the bottle. These ranged from a vague sense of the inconvenience of breast feeding, frequently connected with considerations of modesty, through an often-expressed feeling of real embarrassment, to a deep-seated revulsion from the whole process, often quite inexplicable to the mother herself.

Departmental manager's wife:
'I've had great arguments about breast feeding. Well, with a bottle you know exactly what you're giving them. I've seen people who breast feed, they feed the baby and half an hour later it cries and they give it a bit more, and then it's sick because it's had too much. With a bottle, at least they can cry it out afterwards and you know they've had enough. I don't think I'm the sort of mother who really likes it, anyway, so perhaps it's lucky I couldn't.'

Haulier's wife:
'I think really it's all very old-fashioned, that. Well, with a bottle you can put 'em down and think, well, you've had your quarter of a pint. You know how much they've had. I couldn't get peace of mind by the breast.'

Bricklayer's wife:
'Your clothes never seem clean at all, like – always wet through. I had a job getting rid of it. It's not that I don't reckon it's good for babies – it's just that it ties you down a bit, you can't go out. You've got to be back for the hour. You can't do it in the park, can you? And it was warm last year, we was often down the park, and you could just take a napkin and a bottle with you.'

House-painter's wife:
'I don't like to breast feed them. I mean it's if you go into company, I don't think it's right, you see. I've never breast fed any of them longer than a fortnight. And then they didn't use to wake up, it made your breasts hurt you a lot. And I thought the best thing to do was to get these tablets and put her on the bottle. Doctor said, "All right, mother, if that's what you want you can have it."'

Twist-hand's wife:

'Oh yes – it was nice, but . . . I used to feel a bit conscious though, you know – I don't know why, I think all mothers do really. The children used to ask things. But it's only natural really.'

Iron-works labourer's wife:

'I thought this time I'd ask the doctor to give me some tablets to swill it away and it'd be all right then; and she did that; but I think the midwife wasn't too well pleased about it. I don't like it anyway, cause – you know – kids get older – you know – they notice more, and they think more, and they *say* more. I don't like doing it in front of them.'

Lorry-driver's wife:

'To tell you the truth, my little girl [two and a half] used to stare at me, and that put me off it – it embarrassed me.'

Lorry-driver's wife:

'Enjoy it? No, not really. Well, really . . . I found it most embarrassing, to tell you the truth – I do, I always have done. I'm all right when I'm on my own, but if there's anyone in and it's feeding time, you feel a little bit – well, you don't really know what to say – whether to go out of the room, or to say, well, it's feeding time, *you* go out, or what – I never, like, what you call *enjoyed* it, no.'

Machine operator's wife:

'My husband's a bit funny about breast feeding – he says it's dirty, *he* does.'

Toolsetter's wife:

'Well . . . well, I know it's a silly thing, but I just never have been able to bring myself to do it – I don't know why, but I just can't – I feel a sort of disgust for it; I do, I know it's silly, I know it's stupid, because I was breast fed, but it's just something that I don't like.'

Each of these answers had been preceded by a stereotyped reply of the 'physical reason' type quoted earlier.

The reasons given by the mothers in the University sample[1] were analysed in some detail. Taking mothers who had breast fed for less than two weeks (that is, for not more than a few days after the midwife or hospital lost contact with them), we found that 72 per cent of them began by giving some reason connected with the quantity or quality of their milk: that they had never had enough or that it had decreased on getting up, that it had been too thin to satisfy the baby or too rich to be digested, or that for some other reason it had 'not suited the baby'. Many of these mothers had already weaned the child to the bottle by the time it was two days old, on the grounds that they 'didn't have enough milk'; one gathered that after two days' attempt at breast feeding (by which time one would hardly expect the milk to be secreted in great quantity) honour was felt to have been satisfied. Twenty-four per cent gave other physical reasons for not breast feeding, mostly of a much less questionable nature: they had inverted nipples or had suffered from breast abscesses, the baby could not or would not suck, there had been separation of mother and baby during the first two or three weeks owing to illness or the baby's prematurity, or breast feeding had been abnormally painful. The remaining 4 per cent – all the wives of white-collar or professional workers – admitted at once that they had made a decision from the start not to breast feed.

On analysing the answers given by these mothers to the probe questions, we found that 55 per cent had not wanted to breast feed, and would not have gone on anyway. Twenty-eight per cent said that they would have liked to have breast fed; the remaining 17 per cent were undecided, or our information was inadequate. While it is clear from these figures that 'not enough milk' is often the public excuse for a private attitude, it is also plain that some mothers genuinely fail in lactation and may be genuinely disappointed and upset at their inability to breast feed. Several had made

1. The University sample alone was used here, since information beyond the first 'stereotype' answer was not always available in the Health Visitor sample.

intensive efforts to keep their milk, but without effect; some had taken immense trouble to breast feed, and were happily successful. One who had shown especial persistence was Mrs Barra, the Nottingham-Scots wife of a Polish steel-erector. Her baby was a month premature, and had been kept in the premature baby unit at the hospital for three weeks. Mrs Barra had returned home immediately after the baby's birth; but while in bed she expressed her milk and sent it up to the hospital for him, and, once on her feet again, she attended the hospital every three hours in order to feed him herself. She was able to retain her milk, and fed the baby for nine months; it was no surprise to hear her answer the question, 'Did you enjoy feeding the baby?' with a firm 'Ooh, yes! I don't think there's anything nicer!'

Where a mother had truly attempted feeding, without success, the reality of her disappointment was usually very obvious. Mrs Piercy, the wife of a crane repairer, felt that it was very unfair: her sister had fed each of her children for *three years*.

'My milk was ever so watery, and after about four days it just went. I never can keep it, I never have. Oh, I used to pray to keep my milk.'

Some mothers remembered breast feeding as a time of unhappiness and frustration:

Cabinet-maker's wife:
'She didn't seem to be able to suck properly – to get the nipple in her mouth, you know. Yes, I can remember lots of tears being shed over Janie.'

Salesman's wife:
'My milk just went off gradually. I drank gallons to try and keep it . . . I used to cry when I couldn't feed her.'

Mrs Williamson, the wife of a miner, kept her milk for long enough to know what she was missing when she had to stop.

'I'd have liked to 've breast fed her, you know, because – well – I can't explain it to you really – she was just so little, and you like to feel her lips to you, kind of thing, and – well – yes, I would, really.'

Of the mothers who fed their babies for more than a fortnight, 66 per cent had actively enjoyed the experience. We did not ask what particularly they had liked about breast feeding, but many of them told us. While a few simply emphasized the pleasure of feeling that they were doing the best thing for the baby ('they come on a lot nicer on the breast'), very many tried, like Mrs Williamson, to describe the emotions of tenderness which had been engendered by the act, and a sense of closeness with the baby which they felt could not be achieved by bottle feeding. Some of them (and it was not those who had read the psychology books) thought that the close tie between mother and baby that was experienced during breast feeding was not merely a momentary pleasure, but persisted into later childhood.

Shop manager's wife:
'I don't like bottle feeding – I don't think it's fair to the baby. Because when you breast feed them – you know – there seems . . . an extra something between you; you feel more . . . as one, shall we say. It was a disappointment not to be able to longer – oh it *was* – I didn't want to stop feeding him, I didn't like that at all. Oh, I think it's terrible when people won't feed their babies, just for convenience. And when you *can* feed them yourself – oh, it's lovely – there's nothing quite so nice – when they just lay there and you feel that closeness to you; well, I suppose you can hold them close with the bottle, but it's not the same somehow. I do think that when you feed them yourself you get a . . . a *bond* between you – it's a wonderful thing, I can't explain it.'

Clerk's wife:
'Yes, I did enjoy it – I think it's nice if you can do it, definitely. I don't know, I think you feel a closer tie with your child really – of course, I couldn't feed the other one at all, I had an abscess, and I notice the difference with these two really.'

Motor mechanic's wife:

'Oh *yes* – I think they love it too, they seem to be part of you somehow, you know. I fed her as long as I could (seven months). My milk just went, there was nothing in it, it was too thin. Otherwise I would have gone on until I could have ... until I started her on solids.'

Mrs Beeching's family spanned two generations; at fifty, she was the oldest mother we interviewed. She had four children, widely spaced; the eldest was twenty-nine, and the next in age to the baby thirteen. She and her husband, a cycle-packer, were somewhat taken aback at having parenthood thrust upon them once more, just as they were settling down to being grandparents, and in many of her answers she showed her consciousness of the differences between methods of upbringing now and when her first child was born. For the first time, Mrs Beeching found herself unable to breast feed.

'I *do* like it, you can cuddle them down, you know, like. I mean, with a bottle I feel like a woman with two left arms. I don't seem to get *near* enough. Course, it's just what you get used to, I suppose – but then you see, I've never had a bottle before when I've finished my breast feeding. Same as over Stephen (older sibling), I had a lot of milk even when he was ten months old, and I was still feeding. I went off to the doctor, it was a fresh one, and I told him I'd like some tablets to take the milk away; and he give me a dirty look through his glasses and said, "How old is the child?" – you know, I could just read his thoughts, "here's another one wants to jack up"; and I told him, and he said, "Good heavens, woman, he should have been off months ago!" [she laughed]. Talk about turncoats, men are! Well, of course it *was* a long time, I mean compared to what they do today – I mean, about three months and they think they've done a marvellous job.'

'A marvellous job' – and with many mothers there was a very definite sense of duty attached to breast feeding, combined with a certain amount of shame if they did not continue when it was possible to do so. Mrs Beeching's scorn for mothers who gave up early was echoed by Mrs Marcham, the wife of a shop assistant. She had breast fed for seven months.

'It just went off on me. I would have gone on if I could, for about a year, I should imagine. I think it's a good thing, I do definitely. I don't see why mothers should get rid of it. I think it's just idleness with them, most of them, I do honestly.'

Others had done their best to breast feed in spite of their dislike of the process.

Vehicle-builder's wife:
'It never appealed to me at all, but, you know, with your first . . . I wanted – I thought, well I'll do everything I can, you know. I tried breast pumps and everything.'

Maintenance labourer's wife:
'Well – I don't like it really, but it's for the baby's benefit, so of course you do it. I would definitely have gone on if I'd had it.'

'To me it was just another job – I felt it was worth while,' said a university lecturer's wife, who had continued breast feeding for eight months although she found no special pleasure in it; and the wife of a sales clerk showed a little embarrassment at what she clearly felt to have been a failure on her part.

'I think I'm inclined to shirk that a little bit, I don't know why; I felt ashamed of myself afterwards. I didn't seem to get the hang of it very well – I don't know if it'd improve as you have more children, I think you get into the swing better. He was very slow . . . in that sort of a state you're still a bit low yourself, and I think you're inclined to – you know – take the easiest way out; and as a result I didn't keep it up for very long [one month]. I'm afraid to admit it was just plain laziness on my part.'

One or two mothers had the rather negative attitude that breast feeding was desirable mainly from the point of view of the mother's own health.

Lorry-driver's wife:
(Did you enjoy feeding the baby?)

'Well, it didn't bother me – I wish I could have breast fed her really, because I had a lot of trouble with my milk, I had to have a breast pump on them you know, and it was worse having that than it would have been feeding the baby; I mean, it's not very nice. I would have fed her for a bit I think, because I think it's better for you if you can get rid of your milk that way.'

With few babies being fed to the point of exhaustion of the milk supply, 'getting rid of your milk' is naturally a preoccupation for mothers who wish to stop. The reader will already have noticed several references to 'tablets from the doctor', and the free availability of stilboestrol or hex-oestrol to mothers who ask for it cannot be ignored as a factor in the decline of natural feeding. It appears to be common knowledge that a mother can ask her doctor for tablets to 'swill away your milk', as Nottingham women say, and the use of the drug seems to be more the rule than the exception, even among mothers who are supposedly stopping breast feeding because they 'haven't enough milk'. This may be partly because of a very widespread dislike of supplementary feeding, or 'doing it half and half'. We never heard of a case in which the doctor refused to cooperate with the mother by prescribing the drug; and this further amenity of civilization must do much to encourage the would-be bottle feeder who would otherwise be deterred by the discomfort and inconvenience of engorged breasts. The point was well made by a forty-year-old mother, wife of a coal packer, who had five children, the first born seventeen years earlier.

'I wouldn't have fed any of them if I'd known what I know today; I always had a lot of pain, but I thought you

44

had to breast feed to get rid of your milk. I didn't know you could take something. Well, they didn't bother with you in them days, did they?'

To sum up the breast feeding situation as we found it: while 83 per cent of mothers are breast feeding at four days after birth, only 60 per cent are still doing so by a fortnight, and a further 10 per cent give it up during the following fortnight. Only about one in ten mothers continue for as long as six months, the age which is commonly taken by medical and psychiatric opinion as the 'normal' time to wean from the breast. Seventy-two per cent of the mothers who stop within the first fortnight give as their reason the failure or unsuitable quality of their milk; on further questioning, it appears that 55 per cent of all those who stop within this period would not have breast fed longer in any case. Breast feeding is generally considered more inconvenient and more 'messy' than bottle feeding, and for many mothers modesty and feelings of distaste form the major factor in their preference for the artificial method. Supplementary feeding, widely advocated by the baby books as a means of continuing breast feeding for as long as possible where there is a failing milk supply, is much disliked and not often resorted to for more than a week or so. The availability of drugs to make the changeover as quick and pleasant as possible must also be considered a factor in the general decline of breast feeding. The wish to return to work does not seem to have any bearing on the question.

It is likely that the widespread feeling of embarrassment at the exposure of the breast for feeding, which appears to be mainly a working-class attitude, has a very close connexion with the rise over the last fifteen years of the breast as a sex symbol.[1] It was, indeed, hardly possible that a part of the body so constantly emphasized as a major means of erotic stimulation and a major component of sexual display could remain unaffected by the shame which still attends

1. A full discussion of this topic will be found in E. J. Dingwall, *The American Woman* (Duckworth, 1956).

sexual function. The young woman, taught from adolescence to use her breasts as perhaps her most potent weapon in sexual competition, may almost inevitably come to feel that there is little difference between exposing her breasts in feeding her baby and uncovering them in the most blatant sexual invitation. It is perhaps revealing that some women were embarrassed even in front of their husbands, very many were disturbed by their older children's interest, and two at least, although breast feeding for the child's good, were careful to stop 'before he begins to know' – the inference apparently being that it is safe to have this intimate relationship with a baby for just so long as he is unconscious of it. It may be significant that in the United States, where the cult of the breast is even more obvious, breast feeding seems to be still less popular than it is here; one recent survey in New England [1] found that 60 per cent of all mothers never even attempted to feed their babies themselves.

One practical implication of these general findings is that it is necessary to be extremely cautious in using the duration of breast feeding as a valid measure of maternal feeling. The mother who feeds her baby for 'the recommended six to nine months' is a statistically rare phenomenon in Nottingham today; and it is clear that to take early weaning from breast to bottle as an indication of maternal rejection, an interpretation often made in psychiatric practice, is to assume a cultural context which no longer exists. Psychiatric interpretation too often tends to work within the cultural framework of the therapist himself, so that a judgment which might be valid within his own social class may have no reference at all to the habits and expectations at a different economic level. In this chapter we have discussed the breast-feeding habits of a representative cross-section of the population; but infant feeding is a part of human behaviour which is markedly affected by occupational class, and we shall discuss these differences later on.

1. R. R. Sears, E. Maccoby, and H. Levin, *Patterns of Child Rearing* (Row, Peterson and Co., 1957).

The routine of feeding

Whether the mother breast feeds or bottle feeds, there still remains the question of scheduling: of deciding how often to feed the baby, how much he should be allowed to take at any one time and how far the schedule itself should be kept to if the baby demands otherwise. It is common knowledge that 'expert' opinion on this question has in recent years altered considerably. During the twenties and thirties, feeding according to the clock at set intervals was almost invariably advocated, and the emphasis was upon strict regulation of the child's food intake according to external standards laid down by medical specialists. With the trend towards greater permissiveness in general in the handling of infants, there has more recently been a change in orientation; the aim is no longer to force the child by a strict habit-training programme to fit into an arbitrary schedule, but rather to allow him gradually to regulate his own needs so that ultimately he falls into a reasonably regular routine of his own making. Where, twenty-five years ago, the baby was expected to conform to a preconceived pattern of behaviour, more recently published textbooks of child care emphasize that individual infants may differ in their requirements, that these differences should be respected and that it may be necessary for the mother to vary her practices according to her particular child's natural rhythms and variations in appetite. There has thus been a gradual trend towards what is usually referred to as 'demand feeding'.

However, this term is to some extent ambiguous. The degree of self-regulation which a 'demand-fed' baby in London or New York is in fact allowed, for instance, is likely to differ very considerably from that enjoyed by, say, the Balinese infant. In many pre-literate societies, babies are never to be heard crying. They are picked up immediately they show signs of distress, and may be put to the mother's uncovered breast casually and automatically, just to see whether suckling will pacify the child. As a consequence, there are no set times for feeding: the child is left to take exactly the amount he requires, as and when he feels like it. Children may even be carried by the mother in such a position that they can reach to the breast and suck without any manoeuvring into position by the mother. Thus the only limit to the child's feeding is that governed by the mother's capacity to secrete milk. Under modern conditions of urban civilization, few women can be quite as casual as this about breast feeding. For one thing, the mother's own life will almost inevitably itself be regulated by the clock: in particular, meals may have to be prepared for husband and children coming home from work and from school and having to return at a fixed time; and she may have other duties and commitments which make it difficult for the baby's demands always to be put first. The mere necessity of unfastening a possibly complicated arrangement of dress and brassière makes feeding more of a business than it is in a more primitive society (the decision to breast feed in the first place may have involved the woman in a radical overhaul of her wardrobe, since in many dresses it is simply not possible to expose the breast); and the considerations of modesty, already referred to, may make her feel that she must withdraw from the family circle into a room apart. In short, breast feeding has come to be a much more deliberated activity; and true demand feeding, in the sense that the infant's first stirring of desire is immediately and automatically satisfied, is unlikely to occur in the modern urban setting.

In fact, although demand feeding is usually at least mentioned in the more 'modern' baby books, the practice is rarely recommended without reservations. It may, for instance, be suggested that a mother can only attempt demand feeding if she has no other children and few household responsibilities; alternatively, it may be implied that demand feeding is just a name for a flexible schedule to help the baby to develop his own natural rhythm of feeding. In addition, where self-regulation is advocated, the writer will usually throw a sop to the schedulists by assuring the mother that, even if she does let the child decide his own feeding times to start with, all normal babies will naturally 'settle down' to a regular four-hourly routine within a few weeks at most. When individual babies fail to settle to a convenient and regular pattern of feeding, or take a long time over learning to sleep through the night without 'demanding', a problem is deemed to exist; the implication is that it is probably due to mismanagement on the part of the mother. Thus, despite a rather grudging concession to the baby's needs as an individual and not a stereotype, there remains the general underlying assumption that routine in itself is, almost in a moral sense, good for babies, quite apart from considerations of the mother's convenience; and that failure to provide regularity in the life of the infant may have serious though unspecified consequences, particularly in relation to the child's later character development.

A point worth noticing is that demand feeding is nearly always discussed in connexion with breast feeding rather than bottle feeding; this probably only reflects the fact that those giving advice usually still accept prolonged breast feeding as the norm. In the young baby, bottle feeding entirely on demand may be frowned on medically, since, while it is generally agreed that 'you can't overfeed a breast-fed baby', artificial feeding is a very different matter. In addition, the preparation of a bottle for a tiny baby takes time and effort, so that it is that much more difficult for the bottle-feeding mother to meet his sporadic demands. A mother may also object to the wastage of milk left after a short feed, or to the time expended in making up feeds in small quantities. On the other hand, if there are other people around to help, demand feeding may be made more possible by the use of the bottle, since the job can be delegated; and, by the time the baby is about three months old, demand feeding by bottle becomes very simple indeed: with the use of lightweight, unbreakable bottles, the feed may be propped on the pillow, and the baby becomes not only self-regulated but self-fed. Whatever may be the views of the psychologist on such deprivation of bodily contact, it is certain that the baby's ability to manipulate the bottle himself is seen as a real advantage by the busy mother, and allows demand feeding where it might otherwise not be possible. The practice is frowned on officially, however, and bottle props do not seem to be available in this country at the time of writing, as they are in the United States.

Of the advice more directly available to the mothers in our investigation, as opposed to that given in the textbooks, we can only give a general impression based on their own comments. The usual hospital practice seemed to be a rather strict scheduling, which occasionally gave the impression of routine run mad;[1] one or two individual members of nursing staff were sometimes quoted as suggesting a more flexible approach once the mother returned home. Midwives seemed to be individualists: each had her own theory, some favouring a very rigid schedule, some preferring complete self-regulation by the baby, while others fell between the two extremes. Mothers had the impression that doctors in general were authoritarian and strict in their advice on feeding routine; it was occasionally mentioned with some surprise that a particular doctor favoured feeding the baby when it was hungry. The health visitors were said by the University sample mothers to be rather non-committal in their attitude to what the mothers did: 'do what is most convenient to you', 'follow your own instinct' was the prevailing tone of the advice quoted. It must be emphasized that these remarks refer to what the mothers *believe* to be the medical attitudes, and not necessarily to the attitudes as they in fact are; but, for practical purposes, the first may be more important than the second.

In investigating the mothers' own attitudes to feeding routine, we attempted to distinguish between different methods by introducing a four-fold classification showing

1. One mother reported that her baby had regularly refused to be woken at the official hospital feeding times. Instead of being allowed to feed him when he was ready for it, she was told to express her milk at the 'correct' times; a nurse then fed this breast milk to the baby by bottle when he woke. The whole relationship thus spoilt for her, it is small wonder that this young woman abandoned breast feeding immediately upon her return home.

the degree of strictness of scheduling: rigid to clock/flexibly rigid/flexible/demand. 'Rigid to clock' indicated that the mother kept strictly to fixed times of feeding, that she would make the baby wait until the correct time, and that she would wake him if he was asleep when the clock said he should be feeding. 'Flexibly rigid' meant in practice that she would not wake him if he was sleeping, but that she would make him wait until within a quarter of an hour or so of the set time. 'Flexible' denoted a certain degree of allowance made for variability of need; the baby might be fed if he cried up to an hour before feeding time, but not earlier, or a substitute (usually sweetened water) might be given. Some effort was thus made to keep to routine, but the baby's most urgent demands were responded to. 'Demand' feeding meant that the baby was fed as and when he wished; substitutes would sometimes be given if he cried very much earlier than usual (for instance, more than two hours before the next feed was expected), but if he refused them he would be allowed a milk feed, however little time had elapsed since the last feed; and many mothers followed the principle of offering food first in response to crying – 'My mother said to try feeding her first when she cried, then if she didn't want it you'd know it was something else'. The method of introducing the question was left to the interviewer, but various probe questions were suggested, such as 'If the baby was asleep, did you wake him for his feed?'; 'If he cried before the normal time, did you feed him?'; 'What did you do if he didn't seem hungry?'. It was stressed that the point to look for was whether the routine was decided by the baby or the mother; thus, in the not unusual case of the baby who, given complete freedom to choose his own feeding times, had put himself on to a regular four-hourly routine, the child would obviously have to be classed as demand-fed rather than 'rigid to the clock'. The Health Visitor and University samples yielded comparable results, and Table 3 shows corrected values for the combined total sample.

It thus appears that, within the limits of these verbal definitions, the overwhelming majority of mothers in our sample believe in and practise demand feeding, or at least use a schedule with a high degree of flexibility. There is no difference in scheduling between breast feeders and bottle feeders: whether they feed their babies naturally or artificially, these mothers are equally responsive to what they interpret as demands for food, however this may disturb the regularity of routine. In this, they seem to be following (or, perhaps one should say, leading) the current trend of psychological advice. Only 6 per cent are attempting to impose an arbitrary and rigid schedule of feeding, and it is a little ironical to find that many of these are doing so because they are trying to follow textbook advice and happen to have rather old textbooks.

TABLE 3

Proportions of mothers adopting different types of feeding schedules

Demand	Flexible	Flexibly rigid	Rigid to clock
53%	22%	19%	6%

We thought it possible that some mothers might change in the degree of their responsiveness towards first babies and later babies, especially since people who approve of stricter scheduling often claim that demand feeding is only possible with first babies. We found a slight but consistent trend in the reverse direction: the tendency was for mothers to become more flexible and less routine-conscious with second and later babies. The difference is small and not statistically significant, but we can at least say that there is no evidence at all to suggest that mothers have to give up demand feeding as their families increase. This is confirmed by the comments of the mothers themselves, not one of whom said that they had become stricter with second or later babies.

Cabinet-maker's wife:

'With Jane I was very routine-minded. I went to the clock. If she was asleep, I woke her up. But I changed my mind over Paul; I was more relaxed from the start, having had one, I suppose. You don't worry so much.'

Miner's wife:

'I used to ask my mother, and I used to read these books, and it just came to me gradually. My mam said give it to her when she wanted it, they all did, everybody told me that, but the books didn't say that, they said to give it to the hour . . . Well, when she was very young, you know, a few weeks old, I'd go straight to the hour – even if it was ten minutes, I wouldn't let her have anything. I didn't know really then, I just used to read books and that; but when she got a bit older I used to let her have it when she wanted it.'

Labourer's wife (interviewer's report):

'Mrs Kevan is interesting for her complete changeover from extreme rigidity in feeding to extreme demand. With her first child, Maureen, she kept strictly to the clock, never fed her a minute early. Maureen used sometimes to cry for an hour or more before a feed, was never satisfied, was always "mardy", and at three is still a grizzly child. As a result of this experience, Mrs Kevan decided that rigid feeding was not sensible, and has gone to the other extreme: Billy has always been fed the moment he cried for food, and even at twelve months has no set meals, only oddments given him throughout the day, sometimes from the plates of his parents; she says "He's almost always got something in his hand – a biscuit or chocolate or something – and the bottle's always on tap for him." He drinks two pints of milk a day, but otherwise his diet is inadequate.'

Weaning

Many specialists in child development attach a great deal of importance to the process of weaning. Historically, this emphasis is most obviously attributable to the influence of Freud and his followers. In psychoanalytic theory it is held that breast feeding provides the infant with intense sensual pleasure, and it is suggested that he becomes extremely reluctant to relinquish these first pleasures of the oral body-zone. In consequence, weaning is considered to be a potentially traumatic experience, which may have unfortunate after-effects in the child's later character development. Whatever the historical reason, the subject of weaning receives a good deal of attention in manuals of infant care, and the reader is given the impression that weaning is a difficult and delicate operation which the mother must approach with circumspection. The usual assumption is that most mothers will breast feed for a minimum of six months, and the main problem is taken to be that of weaning from the breast to the cup. It is true that in our sample only about 2 per cent of infants were weaned from the breast, without giving a bottle, before six months of age; but, as we noted in the previous section, only 12 per cent of mothers are still breast feeding at six months. Furthermore, a quarter of these mothers who continue breast feeding beyond six months do not wean straight to the cup at all, but have an intervening period of bottle feeding. The majority of mothers (60 per cent) have changed to the bottle before the baby is four months old, *and* are still giving the bottle at a year. It follows that the problem of weaning direct from breast to cup is one which is faced by only 11 per cent of all mothers, and this includes the 1 per cent of our sample who were still breast feeding at the time of the interview.

Thus, as the term has been traditionally used, our questions about weaning were only appropriate for a mere 10 per cent of the population. We did ask these mothers what difficulties they had experienced and how the child had reacted; but for most of them it had all been quite straightforward, and the only point of interest that emerged was that a few babies had apparently weaned themselves without any persuasion from the mother, by refusing the breast spontaneously.

For the great majority of the population, then, it is clear that the process of weaning must be considered from two different points of view, in that there are two separate and distinct stages which may each have some special significance. The first of these is the transition from breast feeding to bottle feeding; the second, the stage at which the child is required to give up the bottle for good.

It should be noted that, for a very large proportion of the babies now under discussion, this first change occurs before the infant is six weeks old. This is an important consideration. The effects of weaning must always be considered in relation to the age of the child, and it is fairly obvious that a six-week-old baby is not able to appreciate the significance of a change of this kind in the same way as a baby of six months. A child at six months has already established some kind of social relationship with its mother as a distinct individual, and any dramatic change in her behaviour will naturally interfere with this social relationship. Put at its simplest, the child *understands* that its mother is withholding something, and the mother knows this. The infant of less than six weeks, on the other hand, may resent the change in the process to which he has become accustomed, and may show his feelings by refusing the new method of feeding; but his resentment is diffuse, perhaps bewildered, and is unlikely to be canalized into a direct attack upon his relationship with his mother.

Thus, with a six-weeks' infant, the only problem of importance to the mother is that the child should settle down to the new method of feeding as smoothly and happily as possible. Sometimes, of course, there is a period of trial and error, during which it is discovered that the baby will accept or digest one kind of artificial food more readily than another, or there may be difficulty in finding the right size or shape of teat; but in general we rarely found any indication, from what the mothers said, that the changeover from breast to bottle was difficult to accomplish. To the question 'Did the baby mind?', a reply very frequently given was that he preferred the bottle. We did encounter a small number of cases of prolonged feeding problems, but it would be extremely difficult to attribute the majority of these to any attempted change in the mode of feeding the baby: most of them appeared to have existed from birth. Some children seem naturally inclined to suck less strongly than others, or to take less milk at a feed.

Mrs James was sure that the fact that the midwife had given Anthony Ovaltine when he was four hours old spoilt him for breast feeding; anyhow, he refused the breast consistently for the first month, and then went on to refuse the bottle. All milk had to be given by spoon from the start, which she found extremely time-consuming and tiring; she therefore put him on to solid foods at three weeks, and this was successful. She went on trying him with the bottle every now and then during the months that followed, and finally persuaded him to accept it at the age of ten months; at the time of the interview he was regularly having at least two bottles a day.

Mrs Firth's baby had been a very slow feeder from the start, sucked weakly and was soon satisfied, though she cried soon after she had been put down. Test weighing after a fortnight showed that she was often not getting more than half an ounce in twenty minutes. Mrs Firth changed to bottle feeding, and fed entirely on demand, but said she could not remember the child ever taking more than four ounces at a time. She is still a very poor eater.

In investigating the reaction of children to the second stage of weaning, when the bottle is finally given up for good, we were unable to obtain very much direct information. The reason is simple. At the time of the interview, when the babies were a year old, 69 per cent of them were still using a bottle regularly at least once in twenty-four hours. Of the remaining 31 per cent, we have already noted that 11 per cent had never been given one, so that, at the age of twelve months, only 20 per cent had been completely weaned *from the bottle*. This finding is particularly interesting in view of the fact that the most usual advice given to mothers is that they should persuade the baby to give up the bottle by nine or ten months at the latest. It indicates that weaning from the bottle does not follow the pattern that is assumed to be desirable and normal for weaning from the breast. In particular, weaning from the bottle bears little or no relationship to the time at which the baby begins to have solid foods. The most usual time for the introduction of solids is at about three months, and certainly the great majority (80 per cent) have started mixed feeding by five months. By a year, most babies are to some extent sharing in the meals provided for the rest of the family. Thus, in many cases, the bottle is being used continuously to the point at which it has become merely a convenient receptacle to drink from. Most usually at this age, it will be used for a milk drink before going to sleep at night, but it may also be used for orange juice and, very frequently, for milky tea. In many homes it is available all day, and the child simply reaches for it when he is thirsty; in such a situation, its advantages over a cup are obvious. The main point that emerges from these findings is that weaning to a diet consisting predominantly of solid foods is normally being accomplished without the baby being asked to relinquish the pleasures of sucking.

Dummies

Apart from the high level of permissiveness during the weaning period, a very large number of babies are provided with ample opportunities for non-nutritive sucking. Our main question on the use of dummies (otherwise known as 'comforters', 'pacifiers' or, in this part of the world, 'titties') was designed to discover how many mothers had given their child a dummy at any time during the first year of life. As might be expected, fewer mothers were prepared to admit this to health visitors than to the University interviewer.[1] Of the Health Visitor sample, 63 per cent said they had used a dummy; of the University sample, 72 per cent. On this evidence, and remembering that some mothers may also be prevaricating to the University interviewer, a very conservative conclusion would be that at least 72 per cent of children have a dummy at some time during their first year. Most of these children in fact have a succession of dummies to replace those lost or worn out; the habit will usually be started dur-

1. See pp. 272-3.

ing the first few months, and 50 per cent of all the children in our sample still have a dummy at a year. While many mothers are beginning to think of 'breaking him off it' at this age, most are prepared to let the child have it so long as he feels the need of it. It appears that in this country the dummy industry is big business. It should be mentioned here that many babies are given a variation on the dummy known as a 'dormel' or a 'dinky feeder', according to the make used. This consists of a very small glass container with a rubber teat, into which is put about a teaspoonful of rose-hip syrup, sweetened water, medicine or other liquid. While this is not strictly 'non-nutritive sucking', dummies, too, are commonly dipped in rose-hip syrup, golden syrup, sugar or glycerine, and we have therefore included these variations in the same category.

As may be imagined, comments on the question 'Has he ever had a dummy?' varied widely, from indignation among some middle-class mothers that the question should have been asked at all, to blessings on an invention that could give a baby so much comfort and his mother so much peace. The dummy is in fact fast gaining ground in middle-class homes (see Chapter 9), partly, perhaps, as the result of some vigorous campaigning by authorities appealing to the middle classes: notably Dr Spock (whose views on dummies were given some prominence in the *Observer* when parts of his book on child care were serialized in 1958[1]) and Mrs Anne Cuthbert, late mothercraft columnist of the middle-class quality magazine *Housewife*.[2] We may yet see the dummy become respectable; but, so far, middle-class mothers still tend to hide it from their friends and from the doctor. A cross-section of the comments that were made is given below.

Sales representative's wife:

'*No*! I can't bear the things, can you? Oh, they look dreadful. And they're so unhygienic, always on the floor. Well,

1. Benjamin Spock, *Baby and Child Care* (Bodley Head, 1958 edition).
2. See, for instance, Anne Cuthbert, 'Babies Should be Happy', *Housewife*, February 1960, Vol. 22, No. 2.

since he's been crying such a lot at night – my neighbour suggested giving him a dummy. Oh! – I said to her – that is the very *last* thing I should ever do. Horrible things.'

Company director's wife:

'Oh, I disapprove of them. I think it spoils the shape of their mouths, don't you agree?'

Sales clerk's wife:

'I think they're dirty things.'

Foundryman's wife:

'I think we made a mistake in giving him that, because I don't think he really needed it, and now it's a habit we've got to break him from.'

Engine-driver's wife:

'It's a godsend at night, but I don't like to see kids with it stuck in their mouths.'

Bricklayer's wife:

'I think they *look* awful. I don't like to see them with 'em when they're out, do you? But they're a comfort to them. You'd give them anything sometimes, wouldn't you, eh? With this one I would. *Always* crying, you know.'

Labourer's wife:

'We tried him with a dummy, but he wouldn't take it. We tried everything – syrup, sugar, jam on it, everything, but he didn't want it.'

Baker's wife:

'All my children but one had dummies, and *he* still sucks his thumb at thirteen.'

Lorry-driver's wife:

'I mean, when they're teething I do think it's a little bit of comfort to them then – I mean she used to cry . . . I mean, when we first had her, it was a fortnight of misery – cry, cry, cry – and I kept saying, I'm not going to give her a dummy – but in the end, of course, we had to do it, it was the only way we could get a bit of peace . . . [At nine months]: One day the doctor came in; he says, Oh, she sucks a dummy does she? he said, You want to chuck that on the back of the fire, he said, straight away, he said, she doesn't need that. Let her cry, he said, she'll get over it. Well she was poorly, she was full of cold, and she'd got diarrhoea, it was her teeth the doctor said. She broke out all in this rash, and she was crying nearly all the time; and I thought, Well, I must stick it out, she's not going to have it today. But in the end I had to give it to her – it was the only way.'

Father:

'Well, there's no point in them crying if you can avoid it. Course there's not!'

Coal-heaver's wife:

'It's a comfort – it's like cigarettes – I have my cigarette, why shouldn't he have his dummy?'

Civil engineer's wife:

'He uses it when he's going to sleep, and if it's a comfort to him I don't see any reason to stop it – I mean, after all, he's still a baby. In fact, Susan – now she had a dummy, and to be quite candid Susan had the dummy at night-time, going to bed, till she was exactly three years of age; and when she was three I thought it was time she stopped, so I told her it had gone – and it didn't seem to worry her, I could probably have stopped it sooner – no trouble at all. After all, they are only babies till they go to school, aren't they?'

Doctor's wife:

'Oh, I'd advise anyone to give their baby a dummy. It's just a little comfort after all, what's the harm?'

To summarize briefly the findings presented in this chapter, the general picture shows, in the language of clinical psychology, a high degree of oral permissiveness, although not by traditional means. While breast feeding seems to be declining at a rate which many will find alarming,[1] the early change to bottle feeding is combined with a responsiveness to the baby's demands which may make the whole feeding situation more satisfying to him than was the breast feeding by schedule which was until recently the generally recommended practice. For the majority of children, the traditional emphasis on weaning as a traumatic experience seems to be misplaced in view of the extension well into the second year of oral gratification by sucking; and, in so far as the term 'oral gratification' must include dummy sucking (a topic unaccountably neglected by the psychoanalyst), this period may continue up to the age of three or four.

1. Particularly, perhaps, in view of recent findings that breast feeding ensures a very low ingestion of strontium in comparison with bottle feeding. See E. Widdowson, J. Slater, G. E. Harrison and A. Sutton, 'Absorption, Excretion and Retention of Strontium by Breast-fed and Bottle-fed Babies', *Lancet*, 1960, Vol. II, p. 941.

CHAPTER THREE

EATING AND SLEEPING

On the whole, infants today are very well fed. As part of the interview we asked the mothers to tell us everything their babies had been given to eat or drink during the previous twenty-four hours. In carrying out the pilot survey, we had found that the mothers were well able to remember the diet for the previous day quite clearly and accurately, and we therefore decided that a direct factual question about the food given to the infant on one particular sample day would yield the most reliable information on what the child had actually eaten, as opposed to what the mother liked to think of as a 'typical' diet. There are good days and bad days in most families' diets, and by using this method it was hoped that the lavish Sunday dinners and the scratch lunches of Monday wash-day would cancel each other out.

In the subsequent analysis, we noted whether the total diet for a complete day was deficient in vitamin C, in protein, or in both. Bearing in mind that this was just one specimen day, the results of this analysis were extremely reassuring. Less than 7 per cent were deficient in vitamin C, less than 7 per cent in protein, and only $\frac{1}{2}$ per cent were deficient in both at once. We also found that 65 per cent of these children were still receiving a pint or more of milk a day. Our general impression, however, was still more positive. In the majority of cases, the diet was not simply adequate: it could better be described as abundant. The food was suitable, well varied and appetizing, and it was often comparatively expensive. As we have already seen, at one year these children were usually sharing in the meals prepared for the rest of the family; but, where the adult fare happened to be unsuitable that day, special alternative dishes were usually provided for the baby. It seems no longer to be the case that father, the breadwinner, has the meat while the children make do with potatoes and gravy; while many were not yet sharing in the family joint (on the grounds of lack of teeth), these children would normally have had egg, cheese or some other source of protein, at some time during the day, in addition to the vegetables and meat juices of the main adult meal. There was widespread use of the special tinned baby dinners and puddings – one baby (the child of a grocery manager) was getting through thirty tins a week – and it was also obvious that the mothers bought many little delicacies especially for the baby. Altogether, we had the impression that, at a time when families in Britain are probably feeding better, and more wisely, than ever before,[1] one-year-old babies are getting their fair share of the generally increased prosperity.

It is perhaps worth noticing here that many babies in this area, particularly where their fathers eat out at midday, are introduced early to 'high tea'. For a large number of babies, as for their mothers, midday dinner is a mere snack, and tea, when the 'mester' comes home from work, is the main meal of the day. An inquiry into the children's dinner-time diets alone would thus give extremely misleading results, as can be seen from this extract from an interview in one of the poorest homes:

What did he have for his breakfast?

'I fried up some potatoes; and then he had a bit of bread and butter and a bottle of tea.'

And for his dinner?

'He had chips, and some more bread and butter, and another bottle of tea.'

What did he have for tea?

'Sausages and Yorkshire pudding and potatoes and cauliflower and turnips and gravy. We have us tea when mester comes home, you see. And then he had another bottle of tea, like.'

1. W. S. Crawford Ltd, Market Research Division, *The Foods We Eat* (Cassell, 1958).

The baby whose main meal is tea usually also has an earlier snack at four o'clock or thereabouts, typically of biscuits and milk or milky tea. Where midday dinner is the child's main meal, it is common for potted meat or custard to be provided at teatime, as well as the usual bread and butter and cake; and these children benefit additionally from the high-tea custom, in that they are likely still to be up when father is having his evening meal and to be fed from his plate with titbits of meat or bacon. This extra source of protein foods, which seems considerable enough to be mentioned frequently by mothers, is a privilege probably only enjoyed by the youngest child.

Most children of this age are given some sort of snack either at mid-morning or in the afternoon; most commonly, this consists of biscuits and a drink of some sort – fruit juice, milk, tea or milky coffee. As we noted in the last chapter, many babies have unrestricted access to their bottle of milk. The penny bar of chocolate (about $\frac{1}{2}$ oz.) is very usual, often given during an afternoon walk to the shops; and, on the housing estates especially, the one-year-old, particularly if he has older brothers and sisters, is already beginning to establish a conditioned response to the ubiquitous chimes of the ice-cream van.

To complete our picture of the children's diet, we asked whether vitamin supplements were given. The basic supplements used for babies are those supplied by the Health Service on production of vitamin coupons, to children under two years: at the time the survey was taken, these consisted of concentrated orange juice, subsidized and costing five-pence for a six-ounce bottle, and cod-liver oil, which was free. In addition, some commercial preparations such as rose-hip syrup (vitamin C) and Adexolin (vitamins A and D) were obtainable from the clinics at a reduced price.

Thirteen per cent of our informants said that they gave no vitamin supplements at all, one or two of them on principle:

'No, I don't get that. Well, it's like these vitamins they give you when you're pregnant – well, they don't do you any good. Well, I never took them, and I had an easy time. They're better off wi'out 'em.'

Eighty per cent said they gave extra vitamin C to their children: 58 per cent used the Welfare orange juice,[1] and 22 per cent other preparations – rose-hip syrup, blackcurrant syrup, Haliborange and so on. We included among the 22 per cent those mothers who made sure that their children had fresh fruit or tomato juice every day and who stated this in answer to the question on supplements. The 58 per cent also includes mothers who gave their children both Welfare orange juice and other vitamin C supplements. In addition, there were a very few mothers (not represented in these figures) who mentioned as vitamin C supplements various products which in fact contain little or no vitamin C: in particular, orange-flavoured squashes and 'milkman's orange juice'.[2]

Vitamin A and D supplements were less popular, and there was a discrepancy between the answers given to the health visitors and those given to the University interviewer. Thirty per cent of mothers told the health visitors that they used the Welfare cod-liver oil, and 31 per cent that they bought other preparations, such as branded cod-liver oils, halibut oil or Haliborange, Adexolin, or some similar product. Of the University sample, 21 per cent reported using Welfare cod-liver oil and 27 per cent bought commercial preparations. The health visitors are naturally identified with the product which they themselves are largely responsible for recommending and distributing, and since vitamin A preparations in general are much less attractive than the orange juice (many mothers have a strong dislike of the fish-oils on account of their smell) this discrepancy is to be expected. It must also be remembered, in interpreting all of these figures, that mothers have no doubts as to what is recommended policy on

1. Since this time, the price of Welfare orange juice has been raised to 1s. 6d., and consumption has dropped accordingly.
2. Which? (Consumers' Association Ltd), 1960, reported finding no vitamin C at all in the United Dairies orange drink, compared with 10 mg. per fluid oz. in the juice of fresh oranges and 56 mg. per fluid oz. in Welfare orange juice.

vitamins, and that therefore all the proportions given are likely to be exaggerations of the truth.

Perhaps it is also an indication of increased prosperity, and the consequent ability of most families to provide a varied menu, that we had comparatively few reports of feeding difficulties at one year. We asked mothers: 'What do you do when you prepare something for him and he won't eat it?' For the great majority, this situation appeared to present no problems. While the dinner-table may become a battle-ground later on, the mother of the year-old infant is in general very permissive towards his likes and dislikes, and refusals to eat are usually met with equanimity. At this age, the situation seems to carry none of the moral overtones which later impel the mother to insist that the older child should eat up what has been placed before him. More than four fifths of the mothers gave replies which we classified as 'unconcerned'; typical examples are 'just leave it'; 'get him something else'; 'wait till he feels like eating'; 'throw it down the lavatory or give it to the cat'. We were frequently told that the situation did not often arise; and it is probably true that children of this age are not so inclined to make a fuss over eating as are children in other age groups. Perhaps this in part reflects the mothers' own refusal to make an issue of any non-cooperation at this stage; most one-year-olds have not yet learned the use of self-starving as a weapon against the mother. More positively, at twelve months the child is just beginning to use a spoon for himself, so that mealtimes, at this age probably more than at any other, are pleasurable to him for the opportunities they provide for new kinds of manipulative play: eating is thus not only physically satisfying but a highly interesting occupation.

Less than 10 per cent could be classified as 'mildly concerned' about their one-year-olds' feeding; in this category, a fair amount of persuasion was resorted to, games were invented to help the child eat, and so on.

'If he doesn't want his tea you c'n, like, play with him, and he'll take it then. We do do that – we pretend it's a puffer-train or something like that, we can get him to eat it that way.'

A very few mothers were 'anxious' in this respect: that is to say, meals were a series of battles to 'get the food down'. Frequently in these cases the child's first year showed a history of feeding difficulties, whether caused by the mother's own anxieties or by the child's temperament it was hard to tell; it often seemed a case of mutual exacerbation.

'It always takes hours. I told them at the clinic, and they said, "Well, she's always been like that, what do you expect?" I've never known a child like it.'

'He's going through a faddy stage at the moment. I must admit that I'm inclined to lose my temper sometimes – I suppose it's only natural. He must be taught that food is not to be played with, it's there to be eaten, and he's got to get on with it, even though he *is* only a year old.'

Both of these were the mothers of first babies; and several more experienced mothers said that they had learned by trial and error not to be anxious over feeding.

'I just give her something else.'
(You don't try and get her to eat it?)
'Oh no, that's another lesson I've learned. I did it with the eldest girl and, oh dear, it made her a bag of nerves. I used to cry over her – I took her to the doctor – I got in a real stew; and she was no better off. It's only this last year that she's really beginning to eat well. You see, I *tried* to force her; but it was no good – she wouldn't eat it in the end. This one, I just let her please herself; she's doing a lot better for it, I must admit. I wouldn't force her – not again.'

The one-year-old's sleep

The amount of time spent by her baby in sleep, and the time which she herself spends in persuading him into this state, is apt to be a big preoccupation for the mother during the first year or so of the child's life. Up to the time that toilet training replaces it as the major topic of domestic conversation, the extent of her baby's sleep, as it compares with that of other babies she knows, or perhaps with some arbitrary standard supplied by her imagination or by the baby book, is a subject for pride, or else for worry, irritation or shame. When we come to discuss the habits and expedients which are evolved by mothers in dealing with bedtime and wakefulness, the first necessity is, then, to examine the hard facts of sleep: how many hours of the day does the twelve-months child spend asleep, and how far do babies differ in their needs?

For the adult, sleep requirements may not be at all the same thing as the actual amount of sleep taken. The baby of one year, however, normally has ample opportunity to sleep if he wishes to, and once asleep he will be given every encouragement to remain so until he is satiated; for the purposes of this inquiry, therefore, we have taken the number of hours' sleep any individual baby needs as being synonymous with the number of hours he actually spends asleep.

To obtain this estimate, we decided to use factual and specific questions about the amount of sleep taken on one sample day: as in the case of sample diets, we believed that this approach would be less likely to produce biased or 'optimistic' answers than would a request for information on the baby's 'normal sleep'. We therefore concentrated on the twenty-four hour period ending at the time the baby woke on the morning of the interview. The mothers were asked what time the baby had been put to bed the night before, how soon after that he fell asleep, whether he had woken in the night and for how long, what time he had finally woken in the morning (many babies of this age wake early, have a bottle, and then sleep again for another hour or two, often in their mother's bed), and how much time he had spent in actual sleep, as distinct from 'resting' or 'in his pram', during the previous day. Various check questions were asked as necessary, to make sure that the times we were being given were indeed sleeping times and not simply periods of inactivity or crying in pram or cot. We finally asked whether the sleeping pattern reported was in fact normal for the child in question.

It very often happened that the mother prefaced her remarks on bedtime by the qualification 'well, he was a bit late last night'. Very seldom were we told that last night's bedtime had been 'a bit early'. We gathered that this was the mother's way of covering herself against possible criticism of the child's late bedtime. In analysing sleeping times, therefore, we ignored this type of remark and included all actual times given, except where a definite reason was given for the child's lateness – that he had been ill or suffering from teething pains, for example, or that the family had been out for the day and had returned late. Similarly, information as to waking periods during the night had to be incorporated into the analysis at our discretion. Thus, the child who was 'a bit wakeful last night', and who normally woke at night twice or more in the week, would be included in the analysis; whereas the baby who had spent a couple of hours 'screaming with his teeth' would be excluded. Some babies habitually woke and cried or were given attention for an hour or two most nights, and these of course were not excluded. Occasionally, the mother was unsure of the baby's sleeping times for the previous day, although this did not often happen. For various reasons, then, we finally had to set aside about 5 per cent of the sample, where the information available was incomplete or atypical for the baby concerned; but on the subject of sleep it seems unlikely that such exclusions could seriously distort the overall picture.

The analysis (random sample only) showed that, at the age of twelve months, these children took an average of 13·6 hours' sleep during the twenty-four-hour period. Of this total, again on average, just under twelve hours' sleep was taken at night, and the remainder during the day. There were, of course, wide individual differences, which will shortly be discussed, but these figures seem to fit in reasonably well with the findings of other research workers, as distinct from the 'normal sleep requirements' given by the baby books.[1] The average sleeping times found by some earlier investigations, together with our own figures, are presented in Table 4.

TABLE 4

Hours spent daily in sleep at various ages

Author	Age of subjects	Average sleeping time	Number of subjects
Kleitman and Engelmann[2]	3 weeks	14·9 hours	10
Kleitman and Engelmann	3 months	14·9 hours	19
Kleitman and Engelmann	6 months	13·7 hours	16
This survey	12 months	13·6 hours	476
Kleitman, based on various studies[3]	2 years	13 hours	
	5 years	11·5 hours	

Wilkinson, in reviewing these studies,[4] has pointed out that the figures for infant sleep requirements are somewhat surprising: they clearly contradict the common assumption that very young infants normally spend nearly all their time in sleep. It is true that books of advice to mothers tend to give the impression that babies only fail to remain quietly asleep when there is some definite physical reason for this. If the baby fails to 'settle down', the mother is encouraged to look for some special cause of discomfort: perhaps he is still hungry, has indigestion, is too hot or too cold, or needs a nappy change. Only extremely rarely is it suggested that wakefulness between feeds is normal and that crying may be an indication of boredom. 'Goodness' in a very young baby

1. The *Ostermilk Baby Book*, for instance, more widely read than any other among these mothers, states: 'It is generally accepted that a baby of from one to three months should sleep nineteen hours out of the twenty-four. From three to six months, the hours of sleep should be eighteen, and from six to nine months, sixteen hours.'

2. N. Kleitman and T. G. Engelmann, 'Sleep Characteristics of Infants', *Journ. Applied Physiol.*, 6, 1953, pp. 216–82.

3. N. Kleitman, *Sleep and Wakefulness*, pp. 166–70 (Chicago, 1939).

4. R. T. Wilkinson, 'How much sleep do we need?', *Listener*, Vol. LXV, No. 1659, p. 70.

is usually taken to be synonymous with his ability to sleep for long periods without waking; every mother is familiar with the neighbourly inquiry 'Is he a good baby?' (i.e. is he at least comatose for most of the time?) – to which the answer of perfection appears to be 'Oh yes, he's ever so good. I hardly know I've got him.' Furthermore, the aim of 'good' baby management seems to be to produce 'good' babies. The novice mother is frequently led to believe that experienced and capable mothers and professional baby nurses develop a special competence in handling young babies in such a way that they naturally become 'good' – that is to say, make few attention demands. Mothers are exhorted to be calm, gentle but firm; above all, they are told not to pick the baby up unnecessarily. On the other hand, the baby must not be left to cry unnecessarily: the secret lies in knowing where to draw the line. The general implication is, of course, that babies who are wakeful and therefore demanding are probably like this because they have been 'spoiled'. An altogether simpler hypothesis, and one which mothers may find much less guilt-provoking, is that on the whole young babies sleep a good deal less than is commonly supposed.

It is also true that some babies naturally require a lot more sleep than others. Our figures certainly indicate very extensive individual differences in the sleep requirements of one-year-olds. From the complete distribution of sleeping times, we found that a few babies were reported as regularly taking as little as nine hours' sleep in the twenty-four, whereas, at the other extreme, one or two babies seemed to need as much as eighteen hours a day. The range of individual differences is thus so large that some babies appear to require literally twice as much sleep as others.

In view of this very wide variation in amounts of sleep, it was not altogether surprising to find that there were considerable individual differences in the times at which babies sleep. Only about 5 per cent of these babies had no daytime nap, but some had as little as fifteen minutes and some as much as five hours. With one-year-olds, the most usual practice was to put them to bed either before or after the midday meal, but some babies normally had rests at both times. The most usual time for going to bed in the evening appeared to be around 7 p.m., but 31 per cent are put to bed before 6.30, and a small number (5 per cent) after 9.30. A few of these actually went to bed at the same time as the parents. In these figures for late bedtimes, we have not included a proportion of children who habitually started their night's sleep in the living-room, on the sofa or in the pram, and were transferred to their cot after some hours' sleep: the times given refer to the hour at which the child settled for the night's sleep, wherever that might be.

Despite the fact that 'good' babies are supposed to sleep right through the night from an early age, most parents know from experience that having young children usually means having at least a proportion of disturbed nights. At twelve months, although the majority of these children were said by their mothers normally to sleep through the night, 35 per cent of all mothers reported that they had woken at some time during the night preceding the interview, and in almost all of these cases it had been necessary for one of the parents to get up to the child. Again, at the time of the interview a fair number of babies (16 per cent) were reported still to be waking regularly every night, and more were waking at least twice a week. Between 60 per cent and 70 per cent of mothers (depending on whether they were talking to the University interviewer or the health visitor) claimed that their babies now woke at night less than once a week.

We found that 60 per cent of the babies were still sleeping in the parents' bedroom at a year. Fourteen per cent shared a room with some other person, usually a sibling, or with several siblings, and only 26 per cent were sleeping in a room alone. Obviously a shortage of accommodation may be a big factor in this; but we believe that the figure is too high to be entirely accounted for by physical overcrowding in these families. At this age, and remembering that there are likely to be other toddlers in the family (some of whom also sleep in the parents' room), most parents have to be prepared to get up to their children at night occasionally at least; and one suspects that, even when a spare room is available, many parents find it practically convenient to have the child in the same room, for their own comfort and to avoid disturbing other members of the family. The possibility of one child disturbing another is also the usual reason for some babies (8 per cent) starting their night's sleep in the living-room with the parents; the constant hum of conversation or television is less likely to wake the baby than is the more intermittent noise of other children in the house or in the street outside.

'All these kiddies in this little house, y'see – if they make a noise and wake him up, y'see – so we keep him down here while they're awake.'

A negligible number of children officially slept in the same bed as parents or siblings; almost all babies seem to have their own sleeping place, at least until they grow too big for their cot. A fair number of the wakeful babies, however, as we shall see, often or occasionally spend part of the night in the bed of the parents, or sometimes an elder sister, having been taken in as a quick and certain means of comfort. Many more come into their parents' bed in the early morning for a cuddle, a romp, 'a bit o' love', and perhaps another hour's sleep.

Getting the baby to sleep

A variety of methods was used in getting the children to settle down to sleep at night. While many mothers began by saying that they simply tucked the baby up and left him, further questioning elicited that a large number of these babies were tucked up with a bottle or dummy to suck. Forty-three per cent in fact take a bottle or dummy, or both, to bed with them, and *in addition* about a third of all babies are soothed and made sleepy before being put in their cot by being given a warm drink from a bottle on the mother's lap. The relaxing sequence of sucking and satiation ending in sleep, the child's first real comfort experience after birth, thus still persists as the basic method of inducing sleep at twelve months. Some mothers did a good deal more by way of actively helping the child to fall asleep; the following responses are typical of methods which we classified under the heading 'active soothing'.

Printer's cutter's wife:

'I always have to get her to sleep before I take her up. I rock her on my lap and give her a bottle. Because if not, she'll be awake till ten o'clock walking up and down her cot. I mean, someone said to me, "Leave her, she'll drop to sleep"; but not Kathryn, no, we tried her one night, and it was ten o'clock and she was still walking up and down the crib. So we always get her to sleep first.'

Clerk's wife:

'I don't do anything special to him, but I stay in the room and tidy up, and just talk to him a bit. I think he likes to know I'm there. I don't leave him till he's off.'

Teacher's wife:

'I lie down on my bed and pretend to go to sleep too, or sometimes I sing to him. It usually takes about quarter of an hour.'

Miner's wife:

'Her dad stands by her and rocks her crib for her. He spoils her really, but he won't hear her cry.'

Van-driver's wife:

'My big girl [ten] always has him in her bed till he goes off to sleep. I think he's company for her too. We move him when we go to bed.'

B.R. linesman's wife:

'John [sibling, twelve] sits with him on his lap and watches the television, and that usually makes him drop off in no time. If it doesn't, well he's got his bottle and he's happy there, and we just wait till he's really off. *I* don't have to do a thing.'

Labourer's wife:

'I stay with him and stroke his head. They say you

shouldn't do, but when you've got more than one you've got to do what you can, or yóu'd have them all waking up.' (This interview was interrupted by threats to the two older girls, six and three, of a smack, a hiding, a strap, if they woke the two-year-old.)

Mothers are probably aware that many authorities would regard soothing to sleep as an obvious example of spoiling the child; and this is reflected in the fact that there was a significant difference between the Health Visitor and University samples. Fifteen per cent reported 'active soothing' to the health visitors, as opposed to 23 per cent to the University interviewer. Despite the discrepancy, we may still conclude that the mothers who in practice do nothing at all to get the child to sleep beyond laying him down and tucking him up are much in the minority at this age.

The topic of bedtime was pursued further by asking: 'What do you do if he won't sleep, or cries after you've left him?'; and this was followed by the check question: 'And if he goes on crying?' Answers of the type 'It never happens' were ruled out by asking the mother if necessary to consider the hypothetical case of such a situation occurring that evening.

There seem to be two main patterns of behaviour in response to the baby who refuses to sleep. Some mothers take a firm line: they may or may not start with attempts at re-settling the child, but if he persists in wakefulness they will leave him to cry himself to sleep. One or two of them go further, and actively punish the child for failing to sleep, but this is not very frequent. The second, more indulgent group of mothers may allow the baby to cry for a short period (ten minutes at most), in the hope that he will fall asleep; but if he persists they go to him, and either soothe him in one of the ways already described until he sleeps, or may finally bring him downstairs to rejoin the family. Some of this group go to the child immediately he starts crying; with some he never starts crying in the first place, since they habitually soothe him and stay with him until he is asleep; and in some cases the mother does not attempt to soothe the child, but immediately brings him downstairs if he does not seem ready for sleep.

The general pattern of the first group, then, is to take a firm stand against indulgence, and, following the generally recommended practice, to let the child cry itself to sleep, once the mother has satisfied herself that there is nothing physically wrong. Typically, the situation is seen as a clash of wills, in which the mother must be victorious if she is not to 'lay up trouble for herself' and 'make a rod for her own back'. Only 11 per cent of mothers, however, are prepared to follow this strong-minded policy.

Sales clerk's wife:

'I did want to go up to him, but at the same time it can become a regular habit, and it might go on for months. And of course you can't always let them rule the roost like that, even though they *are* so tiny. They've got a certain amount of will of their own, and I think they do learn, even if you are inclined to think it seems hard-hearted at the time.'

Postman's wife:

'Well – she was very good for the first eight months. Then when she was eight months she seemed as if she wouldn't go down when I put her in the crib. So I told the clinic about it, and they told me to just leave her, to let her cry it out. Well, that's what I do do, you see. A fortnight ago I'd have had to bring her down every night, and I thought I didn't want to have the same trouble with her as I had with the little boy. So I stuck it out and let her cry it out. Some nights I'm harder than others. Two hours is the longest I've left her, I think.'

Cycle-assembler's wife:

'If he really won't go off and he's really tired, and he just won't go, his dad smacks his bottom. His daddy goes up to him because he takes more notice of him than me. His daddy shouts at him and puts him down and smacks his behind, and that's it.'

76

The second group (89 per cent), more weak-willed or more sympathetic to their children, according to one's point of view, make only the most perfunctory gesture towards discipline before responding to the child's wishes.

Machine-operator's wife:

'If she starts crying, I know she'll not go off so I bring her right down. Because she shouts so – folks'd think I'm killing her. I tried it, like, thinking she might go off, but oh dear! folks'd pass – we've got a pub up here, you see – and they'd look up. It sounds terrible. I don't know about other people, but *myself* I don't like to hear 'em cry. Because I think there's something wrong somewhere, you see.'

Miner's wife:

'I wouldn't let her cry in her cot. It's not wise – it upsets them. If they get to sleep crying, I don't think they sleep sound. If they're crying hard there must be something wrong.'

Sales clerk's wife:

'I don't think it would do him any harm *really* – but I don't like to hear them cry. I'm a bit soft with him. I don't like to admit it really, but I wouldn't leave him a minute, silly, isn't it?'

Machine-operator's wife:

'We stay by his cot and just rub his head a bit. Well, I think that stops him from getting nervous – I mean, if you leave them to cry in the dark I think they do tend to get a bit nervous. I've never let them cry or lie upstairs screaming. We don't pamper them, but we just don't let them scream for the sake of screaming.'

Her husband added:

'You don't know what damage you're doing to a child's mind when you leave them to cry on their own. Well, I was never left to cry on my own, see. If he goes to bed and he's not ready to go, we don't like to . . . if he cries, we'd sooner have him down than see him upset himself by crying.'

Because bringing the child downstairs seemed more indulgent than other forms of soothing, and because the authorities (doctors, baby books and health visitors) seem to unite in deploring this practice, we thought it worthwhile to isolate the proportion of mothers who admit to allowing it. Here, not surprisingly, we found a discrepancy between the two samples. Fifty-nine per cent of the University sample said that they brought the baby downstairs if he cried; only 41 per cent were prepared to tell the health visitors that they did. The clinic attitude seems unambiguous on this point, and indeed many of the mothers of the University sample showed some feeling of guilt in making the admission; so that the true figure may well be above 59 per cent. We may take it, then, that the great majority of mothers are far more lenient over bedtime than they are generally advised to be, and that well over half of them commit the ultimate crime of allowing the baby up again once he has been put to bed.

This same indulgence towards the year-old child is shown again in the mothers' answers to the question 'What do you do if he wakes during the night?' Forty-three per cent of the total sample give the child active comfort in the sense of changing his nappy, talking to him, rocking him, and either staying with him until he settles or taking him into the parents' bed. In addition to this, 55 per cent of the University sample and 33 per cent of the Health Visitor sample say that they would give the child either a bottle or his dummy to suck. Twenty-three per cent tell the health visitors that, having given the child a minimal amount of attention (i.e. changing his nappy and tucking him up), they would let him cry himself off again; only 6 per cent report this 'firm' behaviour to the University interviewer. Thirty-three per cent of the University sample specify taking the baby into their own bed for comfort; 21 per cent mention this widely disapproved practice to the health visitors. Like bringing the baby down in the evening, taking him into bed is an action fraught with guilt; for most of the mothers who do it, it is a last resort, and those who refrain regard it, in common with almost every authority, as the quickest and surest means of 'spoiling' the child.

Toolsetter's wife:

'I'd try to get her to sleep first in her own crib, by stroking her head and talking to her, but if that really doesn't work, take her out and walk up and down with her. And if that doesn't work, I find that nearly always they'll go to sleep in your bed; but I don't like to do that, because even children are crafty young devils, and they don't want to go back again.'

Salesman's wife:

'Just once when we were on holiday – we were in a hotel – I mean we had other people to consider, you see; and we got to the stage – we did the worst thing we could – but we never made a habit of it – we took her in with us. We had to.'

The general picture of bedtime at twelve months, then, seems to show a very widespread preference for indulgence rather than discipline. Whether the child faces a sudden tightening up of the rules at a later age, or when he is displaced as the privileged youngest, we cannot predict from this survey. Certainly most of these mothers, in this area of upbringing at least, appear to be ignoring the advice they are given to start early in the firm handling of routine habits. In the next chapter, we shall examine in some detail their attitudes to the more general discipline of the one-year-old.

CHAPTER FOUR

THE ROOTS OF SOCIALIZATION

What the mothers told us about how they dealt with bed-time and wakefulness gave us some indication of their attitude towards their babies' crying, and led naturally into a more general discussion of how they felt about crying and rebellion in situations other than bedtime. Since crying is the child's main means of expressing protest at this age, the feelings and responses which it evokes in the mother are of considerable interest, for they will be closely related to the behaviour she adopts on questions of discipline and socialization. We were therefore concerned to find out something of the mother's own assessment of the significance of her child's crying, and the quickness of her response to it; to investigate the incidence and the circumstances of that more emphatic form of protest, the temper tantrum, and the results it produced in the mother; and to inquire into the existence, at this stage in socialization, of sanctions other than generalized disapproval: the forms of punishment, and the moral attitudes with which punishment was associated.

In Nottingham, the baby who cries a good deal is usually referred to as a 'mardy baby'; but this dialect word which everybody understands carries rather subtle variations of meaning, depending on the referent. Used of a very young baby, it merely indicates that the child cries rather a lot, and implies no moral overtones; but of the older child, from a year onward, it almost always denotes a 'cry-baby', a child who habitually whines and cries for little cause, or simply as a means of attracting sympathy and attention, or to get his own way. Thus the adjective 'mardy' seems to be directly derived from the verb 'to mar', or spoil, and a mardy baby is a spoilt baby;[1] indeed, the word is occasionally used as a verb, the exact equivalent of pamper or spoil: 'I don't mardy them, you know, I don't mardy them up a lot. I mean, I love[2] them and that, but I don't make them *mardy*, if you know what I mean'. Most mothers seem to feel that there is a danger of spoiling the child, either by fussing over him too much or by indiscriminately 'giving in' to his attention demands; but many also believe that some children are constitutionally difficult, and are therefore especially demanding from birth. A few mothers believe that playing with the child and generally making much of him may be overdone, and result in a spoilt child.

'She's a bit distempered, her great-uncle spoils her, you see. He's been off work a few weeks, and he's always picking her up and playing with her. He tells me I'm always nagging at her. But she's got to be checked. I think she's a bit spoilt really.'

While most of these mothers appear to agree that spoiling is possible at twelve months, their opinions vary very widely as to how much attention is permissible and where to draw the line. Some are extremely permissive at this age, respond easily and quickly to the child's demands, allow any behaviour short of that which will bring him into physical danger and, where danger threatens, divert rather than forbid. Others seem constantly aware of the child as a kind of moral predator, waiting to take advantage of any relaxation of principle; they bring up their children, even at this tender age, on what we came to think of as the 'give them an inch and they'll take an ell' philosophy. Others again are in theory restrictive, but in practice permissive: conscious of

1. 'Mardy' may also be used of the older school child, especially of the 'tell-tale-tit' type of child; one frequently hears derisive cries of 'mardy-baby!' being shouted after a retreating child during street play. It may even be used of an adult; cf. its use concerning a woman crying out in labour, p. 158.

2. 'Love' is probably used here in the very common sense of 'cuddle'. It is used in the same sense in the statement by Mrs West on p. 86; cf. an adult's direction to a child to 'love dolly!'

the risks which they believe they run of spoiling the child, they yet give in much or most of the time for the sake of peace; one receives the impression of great inconsistency in the child's treatment, as the mother continually makes and breaks new resolutions not to spoil him.

These three general types of behaviour are of course spread out along the permissive-restrictive continuum, so that one pattern shades imperceptibly into another, and one cannot rigidly categorize mothers, nor give percentages for each type. Nevertheless, it is very easy to discern the three points of view – permissive, restrictive and inconsistent – having their effect in the behaviour shown by mothers in individual areas of the child's upbringing: crying, tantrums, punishment and so on: and in this chapter we will try to show the different ways in which they find expression.

Leaving the baby to cry

Against the background of what we had already learned of the mother's attitude towards crying at bedtime, we asked: 'Do you think it does a child of this age any harm to be left to cry?' The main purpose of this question was to provoke discussion, and in this aim it was usually successful: few mothers answered with a simple 'yes' or 'no'. The question was followed by a check: 'How long would you leave him if you thought there was nothing wrong with him?' This we found was very necessary; many times we were told 'No, it doesn't do any harm at all,' followed by 'Well, I wouldn't leave him more than a couple of minutes myself.' Thus the question 'does it do any harm?', while useful for prompting discussion, was not successful in itself obtaining an accurate measure of the mother's attitude or practical permissiveness; and we often felt that the answer 'No, it does them no harm, but . . . ' was a form of lip service paid to the prevailing medical advice. We also found it important for the interviewer to obtain a definite statement of the maximum time the mother would leave the crying child; the vague answer 'Oh, I wouldn't leave him for long' might be completed '– not more than five minutes', or, by another mother, 'not more than an hour'. The form of the question '. . . if you thought there was nothing wrong with him' is perhaps worth mentioning: it was intended to give the hard-hearted mother an opportunity to tell the truth without feeling that she sounded unkind, and the soft-hearted mother the chance to say that if the baby was crying then she *would* think there was something wrong with him. We received plenty of both types of answer.

While we did not, unfortunately, deliberately investigate the point, several mothers stressed that there would be a difference in their attitude towards the crying of the one-year-old and of the tiny baby; but the conclusions they arrived at were contradictory.

'Do you think it does a child of this age any harm to be left to cry?'
Iron-works labourer's wife:

'Not at this age, I'd say. If he cried a lot younger I'd see to him, but not at this age – if he did cry, I'd leave him. Well, for a certain length of time anyway – he could carry on for an hour, maybe. Of course, it's partly the *way* he's crying, isn't it, and if he cries really hard you would go to him sooner, wouldn't you?'

Baker's wife:

'Now . . . well, in a way, yes. When they're babies they can cry for crying's sake. When it's a year, they *feel* more – they're beginning to know. There must be something wrong if they cry.'

Foreman's wife:

'No – I don't – not once they get to this age – I don't think it does them a bit of harm at this age, because I think if they *know*, like, that you're going to pick 'em up, they do it all the more; they do, yes. I'd leave her quarter of an hour, anyway. If she cried longer than that I should pick her up, and if she stopped put her back again – you see – because there's nothing really wrong with her, because a baby *knows*, like, you know.'

Lorry-driver's wife:

'I think it does do some harm at this age, because they're fractious at this age – you know – if I ever get cross with her, you know, and say "I can't pick you up, like, just now, I'm too busy just now", she comes round you in such a pitiful way, you've got to in the end. Now she's older, you see, I know she doesn't cry for nothing. I used to leave her half an hour when she was tiny.'

Minister's wife:

'I don't like to leave them to cry. I don't suppose it does harm them, but I don't think it's a nice thing to do. I wouldn't do it to mine, just leave them to cry – no I wouldn't. I think a baby of *any* age will only cry for some reason. I think there must be something the matter, there *is* a reason. I don't think babies cry for fun.'

Some also distinguished between different sorts of cry; sobbing was particularly mentioned as a type of cry that few mothers would resist, although one or two did say they had attempted to ignore even this. The 'mardy cry' and the 'temper cry' were especially singled out by some as demands which it was safe, and indeed sensible, to ignore.

Brick labourer's wife:

'Well, I don't leave her long to cry, because I can't stand to hear her cry; if she cries, you know, really broken-hearted, I go up, I don't like it, I think it does do her some harm, there's really something wrong with her. I let her cry if I think she's just mardy, like, I'd let her cry a good while until she got fed up herself, about quarter of an hour; I'd leave her till she got tired of it, and if she didn't do she'd get a smacked bum.'

Chauffeur's wife:

'I don't like to hear him cry – not unnecessarily, like. If it seems a mardy cry, I might let him cry a few minutes, but not for long.'

Furniture dealer's wife:

'For too long, yes, it might do him some harm; I think –

certainly if I knew there was no reason for it, you know, if it was just probably a temper or something, I would leave him until he really *wouldn't* quieten, you know; but very often I've found that if he does cry it's either that he's dirtied his nappy or he's too wet, or something like that, and usually that does the trick; but I certainly wouldn't leave him for an awfully long time, you know. The longest I ever left him was about three-quarters of an hour, I think, and I knew then that there was nothing wrong with him, he'd been playing in here and we'd had visitors and he just didn't want to go back, you see. But I just left him, and eventually he did cry himself to sleep. But I think it was more a temper cry than anything, you know.'

It was sometimes pointed out that you couldn't always be sure that the cry was 'only temper'.

Toolsetter's wife:

'I don't think there's any harm as long as they don't cry for too long. I mean, I couldn't stand a child crying for too long, but they get crafty, you see. Perhaps if they're being temperamental I'll take no notice; but . . . I mean . . . well, a little while back we found that she was crying, and took no notice, and it went on for about a quarter of an hour, and she was absolutely screaming; and I said to my husband, "Will you fetch her down, there must be something wrong"; and when he went up she was standing up and she couldn't get down, and she was tired out . . . and as soon as he laid her down she went right off.'

Having specified that the question referred to the twelve-months child, and discounting if necessary both sobbing and mere whining, there were still very wide differences of opinion. In the permissive group, a common response was that babies, especially at this age, do not cry for nothing. These mothers thought that crying, and unhappiness generally, should be avoided as much as possible, for the sake of the child's mental and physical well-being; the underlying attitude (not by any means universal among mothers) was that a crying child was an unhappy child; the possibility of naughtiness in connexion with crying hardly arose; and, therefore, unhappiness had no moral value and was naturally to be prevented as far as possible. Particularly constructive in her approach, and articulate about her ideas, was Mrs West, the thirty-eight-year-old mother of three children and wife of a craftsman just setting up his own business. Although she expected her little boy to 'get over' his own temper crying, she seemed to take far more trouble than most mothers to avoid tempers in the first place, and they occurred very rarely.

'Yes, I think it does do them some harm, if they're unhappy. If he's not happy – if he's got a pain or any kind of trouble – then he *shouldn't* cry, he should be coaxed and loved. After all, it's not fair to just bung somebody in a room and shut the door on them and let them cry till they're unhappy – that's not right at all. And you find in the long run, if you coax them and love them, that they don't cry so long with their unhappiness as if you just pushed them away, that's making them *more* unhappy. But tantrums, yes, just let them cry them out, because they must learn to get over tempers; but not unhappiness cries I shouldn't – never . . . If he's on the floor, and he goes into things, into the books, and you want him to come out – it's no good just pulling him out and making him cry; you find something that attracts his attention over the other side of the room, which *brings* him out without causing tantrums. Because if you start them on tantrums – I know a good example of it, of a child who's been made to leave things alone while his mother got on with the work – he must always keep out of the way, the work must be done, it's the first thing; with the result that he's been pushed around while the housework's been done, and now he's full of tantrums; because nobody *loved* him out of a situation, he was *bullied* out of the situation. Yet they thought they was being kind to him, but I don't. You shouldn't *make* them do things that way.'

'You don't know what damage you're really doing to a child's mind when you leave them to cry on their own,' said the father whom we quoted in the last chapter; and his feeling was echoed by many other parents, some of whom specified the damage, mental or physical, which they believed might be done to the child.

'Do you think it does a child of this age any harm to be left to cry?'

Labourer's wife:

'I don't like to. I don't believe in it. Even my husband don't believe in it. It's not right. They don't feel secure.'

Depot manager's wife:

'I think so – they cry and they get worse as they go along. She perspires – her hair gets quite wet, and I don't like to see her like that.'

Bottling manager's wife:

'Well, I do; I think it causes a lot of bed-wetting. My sister leaves hers to cry, and they all wet their beds.'

Labourer's wife:

'Well, I don't know anything, but me mam says to me, don't let 'em cry too long, because they say – if it's a boy – it can give him rupture, don't know how true it is.'

Cabinet-maker's wife:

'Yes – because at this age they're beginning to be aware of people, and they'd be bewildered if you just left them.'

Miner's wife:

'You could leave them quarter of an hour – then they want a bit of love. You have to let them know you're there. It frightens them if they think you're not there. I don't believe in frightening children.'

Chemical worker's wife:

'It upsets their nerves. I've seen children tremble and shake after crying a lot.'

(This baby is brought downstairs during the night, every

night, and played with for two and a half hours, rather than let him cry.)

Cycle-packer's wife:

'I've never left a child to cry. I can't do it. I can't do things if a child's crying – I couldn't get on with my work if Anne was grizzling. I think they get thoroughly disturbed. There must be some reason why they cry.'

The more restrictive, 'give them an inch' mothers were convinced that children must sometimes be left to cry as a matter of principle. In their view, all children tended to be both wilful and cunning – 'crafty' was the usual adjective – and at twelve months these traits were already well developed and needed to be dealt with firmly; the child had to learn 'who was master', and was not too young to understand that he couldn't always have his own way. He must not be allowed to become addicted to indulgence, and any temporary relaxation of rules might bring about such an addiction: we were often told how upsets in family routine, such as holiday periods, had forced the parents to pick up the crying baby 'for the sake of other people', with deleterious results to his moral fibre. After such a set-back, we were told, it was extremely difficult to make up the lost ground in the baby's training. For this group of mothers, then, crying was an inevitable part of the child's upbringing.

Sales clerk's wife:

'I did want to go up to him, but at the same time it can become a regular habit, and it might go on for months. And of course you can't always let them rule the roost like that, even though they are so tiny. They've got a certain amount of will of their own, and I think they do learn even if you are inclined to think it seems hard-hearted at the time.'

(Do you think it does a child of this age any harm to be left to cry?)

'No. They are getting opinionated, they're self-willed, they find they can do things. I'd leave him twenty minutes, anyhow; a baby soon forgets at that age, he hasn't got any memory, or very little memory, and they soon forget, especially if there's something else to interest them.'

Joiner's wife:

'No, I think it does them good sometimes. If you pick them up, they seem to want it *every* night, don't they? They get used to it, and they play on you.'

Departmental manager's wife:

'They get to know if you give in, they start expecting it. You can't just leave your housework to attend to a baby's whims. If I was busy or we were having our lunch, well he'd just have to wait. I'm a hard sort of mother, you'll find that out.'

Haulier's wife:

'At the time now – at this age – they're trying to see who's master. I'd leave him an hour or so – then I'd begin to think there *was* something wrong.'

Builder's wife:

(Do you think it does a child of this age any harm to be left to cry?)

'No, not really, not for a short time, you can spoil them.'

(How long would you leave her to cry if you thought there was nothing wrong with her?)

'Knowing Linda, about an hour, because she's so crafty, you know.'

B.R. fireman's wife:

'Not just for a little while. I wouldn't leave him for a long while; just for a little while, to see whether he's just trying to get attention. Most often it's not real tears, because when I walk into the bedroom he starts to laugh.'

Caretaker's wife:

'You find with children when they get to about one, you know, they get very crafty, and if they know that you're going to keep running up and down they do it all the more, and then they stop and they laugh at you.'

These last two quotations, and that of the foreman's wife on p. 83, illustrate the attitude of the restrictive mother to a common enough situation. Baby cries; mother, sooner or later, picks him up; baby stops crying. To this, the restrictive mother typically reacts: he stopped crying as soon as I picked him up – so there was nothing wrong with him at all, he was just having me on. The result is that the baby is put back again to cry it out, sometimes with a smack to drive home the lesson. The permissive mother's interpretation of the same situation is totally different. She will report it thus: he stopped crying as soon as I picked him up – so it must have been that that he needed. The result in this case is that the baby is held and cuddled, and is given the comfort that he has been demanding. Again and again we have encountered these two contrasting interpretations, both stemming from the same action on the part of the baby, and they seem to typify the basic attitudes of the two groups: the restrictive mother's suspicion of the baby as a small enemy in a continual battle of wits, the permissive mother's matter-of-fact assumption that the child's immediate happiness is her chief aim. We might perhaps go further, and say that the permissive mother looks upon crying, not as a cunning attempt to obtain indulgence, but rather as a simple act of communication, which naturally requires a response. Two more examples will suffice. Mrs Brown, the twenty-nine-year-old departmental manager's wife who called herself 'a hard sort of mother', had always left the baby to cry on principle; but he had recently 'got into bad habits' on holiday, when the family had been staying in a hotel and had had to pick him up to avoid disturbance. He was at the time of the interview under regular sleeping drugs in order to break him of the expectation of being picked up when he cried.

'We were worried it might rupture him, he cried so hard, and for two hours sometimes, just screaming; but the doctor said, "Rubbish, it can't do him any harm, just let him cry it out"; so I'm going by what he says. If there's something wrong with the child, you don't mind getting up to him, do you? – tummy-ache, or something like that. But him – well, you should see the change – *he can be screaming his head off for an hour, and then you pick him up and it's all sunshine. There's nothing wrong at all. That makes me cross.'*

Mrs Matthew, the twenty-two-year-old wife of a long-distance lorry-driver, made no claim to be a competent manager of children; with an uncooperative husband and two extremely active toddlers, she admitted that she was often at her wits' end. She had met us at the door with 'I don't know what good it'll be asking *me* questions. Honestly, if they do anything wrong I just shout at them!' All through the interview, however, she showed a warm sympathy with her children, talking of her three-and-a-half-year-old daughter particularly as of an equal.

'You don't know if they're frightened when they cry. I did let him cry once – I didn't know he was, I was in the other room, and when I came out I could hear him and *he was screaming himself blue; and as soon as he saw me he stopped, he was all right, so I thought he must have been frightened because he'd been left on his own.* It's a terrible thing to be frightened. I'm frightened of the dark, and so is Michelle [three and a half], and I wouldn't like Julian to get like that, so I don't let him cry. No, I think that's cruel.'

(How long would you leave him to cry if you thought there was nothing wrong with him?)

'To tell you the truth, the minute I heard him crying I'd be up there with him.'

There was a substantial group of mothers who thought that, although crying might not harm the baby, it would certainly harm *them*. Many of these mothers had been told by well-meaning outsiders that they ought to allow the child to cry and that they were 'making a rod for their own back'; some had attempted to follow this advice, but had been too soft-hearted to keep it up, so that the child had been subjected to very inconsistent treatment; others had consistently followed their hearts rather than what they felt to be their better judgment.

Cycle-assembler's wife:

'I'd let him cry half an hour maybe. You can't stand too much of it, can you – that's the point.'

Printer's cutter's wife:

'I just don't like to hear her you know – because I mean, the way she cries now – I didn't mind when she was younger, I let her cry a bit; but now, I mean, she really breaks your heart you know, if she is crying.'

Furniture dealer's wife:

'I can't bear to hear him – I don't suppose it does any harm really.'

Laboratory technician's wife:

'Well, yes, I think it does do them some harm, I proved that with Robin [older sibling] when *he* was a year old. You know what it is, they tell you to let them cry, oh, I got really fed up with it, all my neighbours were always on at me, leave him to cry, leave him to cry, they said; so one night I did; and he cried for an hour, and when I finally went up to him he was in hysterics, and after that he wouldn't go near his crib, he really took against it, he seemed frightened of it, and we had him in our bed every night for three months.'

Cook's wife:

(Do you think it does a child of this age any harm to be left to cry?)

'Well, no, I don't, definitely not; it's just if you can stand it. I can't. I'm one of those who can't stand to hear a kiddy cry. I mean, sometimes with *him* [older sibling] I've shut myself in the kitchen, you know – I've gone in there so I can't hear him, and then I kept going to the stairs to see if he was still on. You know, I just can't stand it, not for long. But with her I've stood it a bit more, because of course it's *use*, you see.'

Miner's wife:

'Oh no, no harm at all; I'd leave her indefinitely till she gave up.'

(Do you think you'd pick her up after an hour?)

'Well, yes, because it'd be getting on my nerves by then.'
(Would you be picking her up because it was harming her or because it was getting on your nerves?)
'Oh, because it was getting on my nerves!' [laughed].

Other mothers could stand the noise of crying themselves, but had to consider the neighbours, other children or fellow-tenants; it was these considerations which prevented them following a firm line with a lusty one-year-old.

'It's a bit loud at this age, isn't it!'

'I don't like to leave her – I think it annoys the neighbours to hear a baby cry.'

'The only reason I do bring her down is in case she wakes the others – if she was the only one, I'd just let her cry, if I knew there was nothing the matter with her. I'd leave her a good couple of hours, I should say, then if she *didn't* stop I'd gather really there *was* something the matter.'

'She shouts so – folks'd think I'm killing her!'

'I don't think it's worth it to let them cry at this age, they just about blow the roof off.'

Finally, there was a small group who believed that crying was positively beneficial to the child, and one mother who propounded the theory that the child enjoyed it, an argument which we seemed to have heard before in relation to fox-hunting.

(Do you think it does a child of this age any harm to be left to cry?)
Depot manager's wife:
'No – I think it does them good to have a cry now and again. I think it exercises all the lungs and that for them. Because if you let them cry, it gives them a deep voice and that. I think it does them good to cry.'

Labourer's wife:
'No. Makes them sleep better, a good cry does.'

Lorry-driver's wife:

'They say it makes them a bit more strength, but I don't like to hear them cry.'

Salesman's wife:

'I don't like to hear her crying – not because it worries *her* so much, she seems to enjoy it once she starts – but because it worries *me* more. But I mean *she* thinks it's lovely, just opening her mouth and letting it come out, you see. And sometimes there are days when you *don't* know why they're crying; and think it *must* be because they just *like* it.'

Our general impression was, then, that the majority of mothers were aware of some kind of conflict over the problem of crying. They were frequently torn between the desire to be firm on principle and a natural inclination to be kind to the child. In consequence, some of them felt guilty whatever they did. A few of them were to some extent forced by pressure of circumstances to behave in a particular way, despite personal feelings and theories. For a variety of reasons, few mothers found it possible to adopt a whole-hearted policy of being firm, and they could seldom remain unresponsive to prolonged crying in the one-year-old. Only 33 per cent said that they would leave a child of this age longer than fifteen minutes, even if there were nothing obviously wrong, and less than 8 per cent would leave him for more than half an hour.

Because a large number of mothers mentioned the theory that crying is 'all right for girls' but 'might give a boy a rupture', we looked for a possible difference in the treatment of girls and of boys. We found none. Evidently, while the belief has wide currency, particularly among working-class mothers, it is not acted upon.

It was clear that many mothers were on the defensive against any implied suggestion that they might be spoiling their children. In replying to the health visitors, 16 per cent admitted that they would leave the baby only for a very short while (five minutes or less) before going to him; but when the questioner was the University interviewer the proportion in this category rose significantly to 31 per cent. Whenever the mothers reported receiving professional advice from doctors or nurses, it was in fact invariably in the direction of urging them not to 'give in' to the child. They were often told that in the long run it was kinder to the child to be hard-hearted than to give way; yet most of these mothers found the advice either impractical or incompatible with their attitudes and principles, and, in consequence, they either felt guilty or resented the source. It will be noticed, in the quotations that follow, that the assertion that 'crying does a child no harm' seems to have been presented with an authoritarian certainty which is hardly a good advertisement for the scientific humility of the medical profession.

(Do you think it does a child of this age any harm to be left to cry?)
'No, I don't think so. They leave them to cry in hospital. They leave them to cry for hours in hospital. Two hours I've seen babies cry there when I was there, he was a tiny baby then. They don't take a bit of notice. And it can't do them any harm, they must know, mustn't they?'

'Doctor told me to leave him; and if he cried, let him; if I put him to bed and he wouldn't go to sleep, to let him cry – to leave him an hour, and if he still cried to go up and slap him and leave him another hour; but I couldn't – not to let him cry like that.'

' . . . We were worried it might rupture him, he cried so hard, and for two hours sometimes, just screaming; but the doctor said, "Rubbish, it can't do him any harm, just let him cry it out"; so I'm going by what he says.'

' "Let her cry," he said, "she'll get over it".'

'Well, I've been to the clinic – they say, "Leave her, mother, let her cry; it won't do her any harm, it'll do her the world of good – strengthen the lungs." "Well", I used to say to them, "it's all right for you"; and they said, "Put her in a room on her own, turn the wireless up, do anything so you won't hear her".'

95

' . . . So I told the clinic about it, and they told me to just leave her, to let her cry it out. Well, that's what I do do, you see.'

'Of course, the clinic say it does them no harm . . . When she was born, she cried on and off for a whole day. I was worried, but the midwife said, "Put her in the bathroom and shut the door so you can't hear her, it won't hurt her". But I didn't.'

Temper tantrums

By their first birthday, most babies have achieved a fair degree of mobility. They are also reaching out to explore the world around them in other ways. They try to pick up many different objects and to manipulate them. They handle things and put them in their mouths; they drop things; they push things that get in their way, and knock them over. They pull open cupboards and drawers, and empty out the contents. They spill liquids and packeted goods, and they bang things that make a noise. They are finding out about their world; and they are beginning to make their mark upon it.

Although all these manifold experiences of roughness and smoothness, softness and hardness, fragility, heaviness, stickiness, plasticity and so on are probably indispensable to the development of understanding in the child, few households are so organized that he is free to explore without restraint. Most mothers inevitably find that the child of this age needs continual supervision, both to prevent his harming himself and to avoid damage to precious possessions. In short, from the mother's point of view mobility often spells mischief. But children of twelve months have also developed a certain degree of social awareness. When their most interesting and absorbing activities are rudely interrupted, it is perhaps not surprising that, sooner or later, they begin to recognize the agent of this interference, and to show their resentment in a rather obvious manner.

We asked the mothers: 'Does he ever have temper tantrums?'; and 70 per cent of them reported that they had already had to deal with such behaviour. For most of these children such outbursts were only occasional, but 14 per cent of all children were said to have temper tantrums quite frequently, some of them several times in one day. In follow-up questions we asked, firstly, what situations seemed to produce tantrums, and, secondly, how the mothers dealt with them. Various circumstances were described, in greater or less detail, as being provocative of tantrums; but by far the most common was that the child wanted something that he couldn't have, either because it was out of reach, or because, having reached it, it was quickly taken from him again. In a substantial number of cases, other children were mentioned as a major cause of tantrums: either they had taken something from the baby or the baby wanted some plaything of theirs which they refused to relinquish; and occasionally deliberate teasing by elder siblings was reported. Many mothers answered the question rather more generally by saying that tantrums were likely to occur whenever the child found that he couldn't have his own way: examples given were being offered the wrong food, or not enough of a favourite food, not being given attention, being left in a cot or pram and being told 'no'.

'It's just because she can't have her own way. She's got no other way of expressing herself, so she just dances with rage or bangs her head or something.'

Some children reacted with temper tantrums to physical restriction, such as that involved in dressing or nappy-changing, or being fastened into pram or high-chair; some were apparently outraged by being smacked.

'Ooh yes – when I'm strapping him in his pram and he don't want to go in; well, I just hold him down, you know, and strap him in and take no notice.'

'I've noticed one thing, that if I've tapped[1] Janice, she

1. 'Tap' is a Nottingham word for 'smack'; it does not imply gentleness in the correction, as it would in the south. For instance, a mother might say 'I give him a good smart tap across the legs'; or she might shout at a ten-year-old 'I'll gi' yer a tap in a minute!'

don't like it, and she'll scream all the more and she'll go on for an hour; whereas if I didn't lose my temper in the first place, she won't cry half as long. So I don't know how you take it from there? She don't like people to take things off her, y'know, if she's settled down. And sometimes she gets in spasms, she'll just let one scream out, y'know. I might say to her, that's naughty, y'know, and just give her a tap on the hand, like that, and of course that just does it, and she gets really naughty – she cries and cries and cries; and I could pick her up and I could nurse her and it wouldn't make a ha'porth of difference – just because of that one small tap.'

Occasionally, as in our next quotation, the child was reported as being frustrated by his own physical inability to do something which he was in fact allowed to do – to fit a lid on a box, for instance, or to manoeuvre himself past an obstruction; but it was clear that, in the majority of cases, the child was aware of some *person* with whom he was in conflict; and certainly most mothers saw such situations as a battle, sometimes carried on in physical terms, between the child's will and their own.

'Oh yes, he gets nasty. If he's playing with any toys and he gets them fast anywhere and he can't get at them, it starts him off. And if you move them, he cries because you've touched it. Or if he can't get out to play in the yard, that makes him mad ... When he does start, he gets his fists and goes stiff, and you can't do anything with him. Just have to leave him – let him get over it.'

'I've started now – I'm learning – to take no notice of her ... If she can't get just what she wants, she throws herself down and lays on the floor, but I think they learn that they can't have just exactly what they want. I started by thinking, well, she's just a tiny baby, you've got to give in to her; but they're not so small really, they know what they can get away with.'

'Well, if she's sitting on your knee and she's trying to get a hold of your hair and pull it, and if you say naughty girl, then she starts: and she tries to claw your face off, and then if you don't let her she makes herself go stiff and holds her breath; and when she does that I just turn her over and smack her backside three times, nice sharp smacks, and she's all right then.'

What do most mothers do when faced with a screaming, stiffening child? Their behaviour under these circumstances was evenly divided between three different courses of action. In the first of these, the mother's main concern was to reduce the frustration by trying to distract the child or by picking him up and 'loving him out of it'. Of mothers reporting tantrums, 33 per cent chose this method of dealing with them.

Machine operator's wife:

'I talk to him a bit, or give him something to occupy his mind.'

Lorry-driver's wife:

'I pick her up and walk about with her till she gets over it.'

Caretaker's wife:

'I pick him up and love him; I think that's the best thing to do. I don't think smacking does any good at all.'

Thirty-six per cent adopted a policy of deliberately ignoring any show of temper on the part of the child; nothing was done to mitigate the frustration.

Labourer's wife:

'I just let her get over it. I don't believe in pampering them up altogether – at that age they just begin to know, and if you start pampering them up they never stop.'

Butcher's wife:

'I watch him out of the corner of my eye to see that he is all right, but I don't let him think that I'm bothered.'

The remaining 31 per cent punished the child for having temper tantrums. Although such punishment was not usually physically very severe, its main intention seemed to be to show that the mother definitely disapproved not only of the behaviour which she had interrupted but also of the child's reaction to being thwarted.

Painter's wife:

'If she gets in a temper I give her a slap till she gets going properly.'

Cabinet-maker's wife:

'I give him a smart tap on his legs. He has a little cry and that's it. He gets over it. Then he realizes he mustn't do it again – until next time!'

Salesman's wife:

'I smack his bottom, quite gently. He's old enough now to understand. If you start with them this age, it's easier for them later on.'

Bricklayer's wife:

'Smack him on his backside, I do. Screams without a tear in his eye. I believe in it, I do. Because they can play you up so they get to *know* they're playing you up.'

Of these punishing mothers, a few used a combination of smacking and comforting, in either order.

Labourer's wife:

'Oh yes, he does it ever such a lot, just screams and screams – usually when he's having to wait for his dinner. I give him his dummy; and then if he doesn't stop I smack his bum sometimes.'

Postman's wife:

'Well, I smack her hand or her leg once, for temper. Usually it works, and then perhaps I'll talk to her nicely and that; I'll put something on her dummy, and that usually does it, does the trick.'

Many of them followed up physical punishment by ignoring the child's reaction to that.

Petrol manager's wife:

'If she's woken up; or if she's getting teased by all these

kiddies; that starts her off. Easily every day she has them. I slap her hand and put her in the pram and let her have it out.'

Salesman's wife:

'She holds her breath with it. I just say "you naughty girl", and I smack her legs and I leave her.'

To sum up, then: approximately half of the mothers reported either that their child did not have temper tantrums or that, when he did, their efforts were mainly directed towards helping him positively by distracting him and by 'loving' him. The other half regarded tantrums as a form of naughtiness which they were doing their best to train out of the child, either by deliberately ignoring him in the hope of teaching him that tantrums do not pay off, or by physical punishment. In so far as these last two methods were adopted as a matter of deliberate policy, they were usually justified by these mothers as necessary disciplinary measures forming an essential part of the child's morality training.

Punishment at twelve months

When a mother consciously sets out to 'punish' her year-old child, either as retribution or as a deterrent for the future, the punishment almost invariably takes the form of smacking. In asking 'How do you punish him when he's been naughty?',[1] we deliberately left the question open-ended in order to allow for the other forms of punitive behaviour – deprivation of sweet foods, warnings that 'Mummy won't love you any more' and so on – which are common in the disciplining of older pre-school children. The limits of the one-year-old's understanding, however, seemed, both in theory and in practice, to preclude these alternatives. The single exception to this was one mother who used a studied ignoring of the child as punishment. We have seen that ignoring plays a large part in the way mothers cope with temper tantrums, and no doubt from the child's point of view its effect is in fact punitive; at the moment, however, we are

1. For a discussion of the form of this question, see p. 267.

discussing more deliberate attempts at training by retribution, and in the context of tantrums these mothers were not conscious of imposing punishment on the child when they adopted the method of ignoring him: rather, from their point of view, they were merely making it clear that 'unreasonable' demands would not be attended to, and this intimation *happened* to be unpalatable to the child. The difference in attitude of the one exceptional mother is obvious:

'I ignore her; I just go out of the room and don't speak to her. None of my children can bear me to ignore them, and it always works. Smacking never works with my children.'

In thinking about their behaviour when faced with situations of 'naughtiness', many mothers realized that their main reaction was some expression of anger, or at least of disapproval and perhaps of warning, in their tone of voice. Again, this was not considered to be tantamount to punishment, but was simply reported as what happened in the absence of, or as a prelude to, real punishment.

Tobacco worker's wife:
'Oh, I don't know what I do; just shout a bit, I suppose.'

Machine operator's wife:
'I just say "You naughty girl, Jeanie", and I snap, like, at her.'

Twist-hand's wife:
'Well, I just say "naughty girl", you know, "baba!"[1] Oh no, I don't smack her.'

Miner's wife:
'I don't very often smack her – I shout at her – if she gets on my nerves – or if she wants to go outside all the time and you've got her cleaned up.'

By and large, then, non-corporal punishment of the one-year-old does not exist for this group of mothers in any con-

1. 'Baba!' is another Nottingham word, an interjection used in disapprobation or as a warning when the child is in mischief or about to be so. We continually heard it used in admonition to babies touching the tape recorder.

scious sense; and, in the discussion that follows, punishment simply means smacking.

As might be expected, the mothers' attitudes towards morality training came out particularly clearly in relation to their feelings about punishing the child. The question 'How do you punish him when he's been naughty?' was intended to be provocative. In fact it was particularly successful, not only in finding out exactly what punishment, if any, mothers considered appropriate for one-year-olds, but also because they frequently went on to explain and to justify their whole attitude towards smacking in general.

The first distinction that can be made here is between those parents who accepted the question at its face value, and were quite happy to discuss the punishment of babies, and those who strongly objected to the whole idea of punishment at this age. Sixty-two per cent of mothers did accept the idea of punishment, in that they practised it with their own children.

Salesman's wife:

'Oh, I sometimes smack his hand if he's too bad, not hard, just enough to make him realize he shouldn't do things, you know ... if he pulls the tablecloth off, or something like that. And sometimes if he gets mad he'll bang his head and smack himself, and I've smacked him for that as well. I'm frightened of him doing any harm to himself.'

Butcher's wife:

'If he's, say, touching the fireguard, I'll smack his hand; banging the table, I'll smack him; trying to do something – you know – trying to be destructive; and I think if I'm a bit off myself, you know, and he's crying all the while, I do tend to give him a little smack then, I think everybody does though.'

Labourer's wife:

'If she can't get at something quick enough, she'll go off in a temper, you see, and then she gets a smack, I do smack her on her backside, and it stops her at it, you see.'

(This child is also smacked for crying persistently and for wetting or dirtying her knickers.)

The remaining 38 per cent clearly objected to the very suggestion that one might punish children of this age, and showed a marked disapproval of the way in which the question was put. Sometimes, indeed, they were so vehement in their rejection of the interviewer's implied acceptance of punishment that it was difficult not to be forced into a real sense of shame.

(How do you punish him when he's been naughty?)
Labourer's wife:
(There was a shocked silence for a minute.)
'Oh, we don't do that. We just pick them up, don't we, and love them. Ooh, I wouldn't think of smacking them ... ooh! I'll give *her* [sibling aged four] a smack, because she does go too far, but she's older, but I mean – little'uns, like that! Not babies in arms, no!'

Railwayman's wife:
'I never punish mine at all, duck; a strict word is as good as any smack of any description. I had a lot myself when I was young: I know what the belt is, I know what the stick is, I know any instrument you could name; and I swore I'd never touch me kids.'

Doctor's wife:
'Well, I don't, she's too young. You can't smack them. Everything's a challenge at this age, I should be concerned if she *wasn't* investigating.'

Minister's wife:
'Children of one *aren't* naughty. But people *can't* say they're naughty. If a child cries at night, that's not *naughty*.'

Tailor's presser's wife:
(She looked shocked.)
'Well, he's not old enough, is he? Well I think it'd be ridiculous. He's too young to know what you mean by

naughty. He just wouldn't understand a smack. No, I'd never do that, I think it's dreadful when they're just babies.'

Of course, when a mother accepts the idea of punishing a year-old child, this does not necessarily mean that she is prepared to inflict a great deal of pain. Many so-called punishments were in fact little more than tokens of maternal displeasure. By lightly smacking the child, the mother merely intended to communicate with him at a non-verbal level, and to draw his attention to the fact that he had incurred her disapproval. The token nature of such checks is also indicated by the fact that some mothers reported that their babies often thought this was a kind of game. Most mothers were also aware that, to begin with at least, such treatment was of little use as a deterrent. The whole procedure generally seemed to be justified as an attempt at evaluating the child's behaviour morally from a very early age, in the hope that in the long run there would be some kind of cumulative effect. This attitude might be summed up by saying that, after all, the child must learn 'the difference between right and wrong' in the end, and that it is better to begin moral training early to be on the safe side.

Sales clerk's wife:

'He's going through a faddy stage at the moment. I must admit that I'm inclined to lose my temper sometimes – I suppose it's only natural. He must be taught that food is not to be played with, it's there to be eaten, and he's got to get on with it, even though he *is* only a year old.'

(What happens when you lose your temper?)

'I usually smack his hand.'

(Does it help?)

'No, it doesn't – I try not to do it very often. He'll spit his food out – not actually spit it out, but he'll drool it all down his chin, and I'll smack his hand for it – not very hard, you can't go hurting babies all that much; and if he persists in doing it I smack his hand again, and he gradually stops. But of course if he's feeling really cussed nothing'll stop

him. He's very self-willed, as I think a lot of babies are . . .
He's got to learn; though I don't think it makes a great deal
of impression at the moment, it is preventing him, and he'll
gradually learn to stop and think, "Now I mustn't touch
that, I might get smacked for it, my mummy'll be cross at
me, I mustn't do it"; and gradually, I think – it'll probably
take dozens of times to do it – but it'll gradually make an
impression.'

Draughtsman's wife:
'First of all I say No; if she goes on, after two or three
times I smack her, and after that I smack her every time she
does it till she stops.'

Printer's cutter's wife:
'Well, she's got a dirty habit of spitting her dinner out,
you know, and I've tapped her; and I've really got in a row
about that from my mother; but I can't bear dirty habits at
the table, I mean I don't care how old she is. She knows that
she's doing wrong; because, before she's done it again, she's
looked at me, you know – and then turned her head and did
it – and I tapped her again. Well, she doesn't do it now, so
they *can* learn.'

The attitude of a few parents, however, seemed to suggest
that they felt real anxiety that their children, even at this
early age, might get out of control unless severely checked.
For them, punishment was definitely not a game with the
child, nor did it appear that the child was given any chance
of thus interpreting it. When they gave a smack, it was in
earnest and it was meant to hurt. It was intended to cause
sufficient physical pain to deter the child; it was also claimed
to be effective.

Departmental manager's wife:
'I smack him across his legs pretty hard and sharp.
They've just got to learn there are certain things they can't
touch. And he gets very lazy over eating up his Farex and
things like that. I slap him and then he gets on with it.'

(This child also has his face slapped for holding his breath in tantrum.)[1]

A number of mothers admitted that there were certain situations in which they became somewhat more emotionally involved with the child than perhaps they would have wished, and, in consequence, sometimes administered a more-than-token slap. There are, for instance, times at which the child's blundering and persistent explorations precipitate a crisis which can try the patience of the most perfect mother beyond breaking-point. Often these situations will be of the 'last straw' variety, when a child, after continually getting into minor mischief all morning, drops and breaks a precious vase, or knocks the clean washing into the mud, or is found tearing strips from the new wallpaper, or empties his dinner all over his mother's dress. In circumstances such as this, one cannot but sympathize with the mother, even if she loses her temper momentarily and smacks the child quite hard; in retrospect, however, most of the mothers who mentioned that they had smacked on such occasions seemed conscious that punishment was rarely effective under these conditions, and could justify it only on the grounds that it helped to relieve their own feelings.

Electrical engineer's wife:

'It usually ends up in me slapping her bottom; it doesn't often happen. There's nothing special I do it for.'

(What had happened the last time you smacked her?)

'Oh – I'd been washing, and then I was washing the floor and she'd been paddling around, and she finally took the wet dishcloth out of the bucket of water and whirled it round. So I smacked her. Smacking makes her cry, but she'd do the same thing again if I didn't take the water away.'

1. The reader may have noticed that three of the 'smacking' mothers quoted in this chapter refer to spitting or refusing food. These quotations are chosen as being representative of typical attitudes to misbehaviour in general; the naughtiness specified is a matter of chance. In fact, while the throwing of food is often punished, refusal by spitting or slowness over eating is not, and these three mothers are atypical in this respect.

Locomotive fireman's wife:

'I don't smack much. At a year you can't sort of teach them that they're being punished. I have done once or twice when I've got annoyed – more for my own satisfaction than for Alan's sake.'

Mrs Bamford, eleven of whose fourteen children were of school age and under, and who also day-minded her grand-child, could well be excused for losing her temper occasion-ally.

'I'm not so strict as me mum was – I mean in them days they was really strict towards you, you used to get a good hiding for the least thing, but I mean – say these – sometimes they'll get all round you and you'll p'raps hit 'em or some-thing – you get mad – I haven't got the patience with 'em, somehow – you know, I can stand so far; but mind you, I wouldn't mark 'em or anything like that.'

Even at this age, some mothers also reported that they were apt to become emotionally involved in a battle of wills with the child. This usually occurred when the mother had given him repeated warnings not to do something and had been persistently ignored. After a while, the mother would begin to interpret the child's persistence as deliberate de-fiance, and the issue was then seen as a far more serious one. Mischief is one thing, they felt, but wilful disobedience is another. Punishment is then justified on the grounds that the child just cannot be allowed to get away with such behaviour, even if he is only a baby; as one father put it, he's got to learn who is the master. It is probably safe to say that, sooner or later, every parent, at least in our culture, gets driven into the vicious circle of a battle of wills with his child. Deliberate disobedience, defiance, ignoring of requests – call it what you will – seems to go to the roots of the parents' self-esteem, to touch them on the raw. On the other hand, the behaviour of very young babies is not usually interpreted quite in this way, so that it is a question of how old a child has to be before he merits punishment for this particular offence. Most of these mothers seem to feel that twelve months is really too young for the child fully to understand this situation: consequently they believe that, when they are goaded into such a battle, punishment serves mainly to relieve their own feelings as the inevitable loser, and does little to help the child. A minority, however, seem to believe that even small babies are possessed of a cunning in obtaining their own ends similar to, if not identifiable with, original sin, so that punishment of some kind is then thought to be justifiable from a very early age indeed.

It should be noted here that a few babies appear to vindicate their parents' appraisal of them as equal participants in the mother–child battle, and defend themselves with some spirit against physical chastisement.

'I smack her bum. She just turns round and gives you one back.'

'Well, actually I've smacked her hands – it makes no difference, she just glares at you and does it some more.'

'I smack his legs [for many things, including screaming, stiffening on the potty, genital play, throwing things, destructive behaviour]. But even when you smack him sometimes, he doesn't take any notice of you, he just does it again. And if you smack him he turns round and smacks you back.'

We found, too, that children seem to react very diversely to the preliminary expression of maternal disapproval. Some children, it appears, 'never need smacking' simply because they become sufficiently distressed at the sight of their mother's frown; others ignore all her warnings and 'defy' her to the point at which she finally loses her temper and smacks harder than she meant to. In either case, incidentally, the mother will tend to feel a little guilty afterwards. What causes children to behave in such strikingly different ways, we do not know. Possibly, when a mother who is almost always kind and comforting suddenly changes her behaviour and becomes stern, the child finds the whole situation bewilderingly unexpected and therefore becomes frightened. There does not seem to be any need for him to have experienced physical hurt as an accompaniment of disapproval; neither of the following babies had ever been smacked.

'I don't think you really do punish them, not at this age – if you speak a bit sharp, her lip drops, and you feel you want to pick her up and love her.'

'All you've got to do is to say a harsh word to her and she'll cry, and that's all I do – yes, she sobs her socks off!'

Compare these with the next baby, who is smacked for many offences, and whose behaviour under disapproval is obviously the result of a very thorough understanding of the situation, rather than of bewilderment: she does not waste time in showing distress, she takes practical avoiding action.

'Well, I smack her for temper; and then if she puts things in her mouth I smack her; or if she slops with her food. If I see her doing anything I don't want her to do, then I smack her; I don't think it hurts her, not just a smack. She knows when I'm going to smack her anyway, I just raise my hand, and she clears at the run.'

This baby and others who see their mother continually shouting and slapping at themselves and their siblings seem to become so accustomed to such behaviour as part of the normal home atmosphere that the harsh word and the token tap come to have little meaning for them; and it appears to be these children who develop the habit of ignoring their mother's disapproval, and so come to be considered 'defiant'. It is, however, difficult to rule out completely the possibility of individual constitutional differences in obstinacy or wilfulness which might equally well account for this: particularly as the permissive mother, besides creating a climate for her child which makes 'defiance' pointless, does not in any case recognize such a concept within the framework of the behaviour of so young a child. In the absence of any objective interpretation of these children's attitudes towards their mothers, it does not seem profitable to speculate further on this point.

The crimes of the one-year-old

We asked the mothers who did admit to using punishment to give us examples of the sorts of naughtiness they had in mind. Inevitably, of course, some of the answers they gave were of a rather general nature, such as 'getting into mischief' or 'persistent disobedience'; but a large number of more specific activities were also mentioned, and these we were able to classify under a number of separate headings.[1] We have already discussed temper tantrums, and these turned out to provide the greatest number of punishment-provoking situations; under this head, the mothers included screaming, wild kicking, and other behaviour associated with paroxysms of rage in the child, such as stiffening the body, breath-holding and head-banging. Punishment was also often given for personal attacks on the mother: biting, clawing, hair-pulling and face-smacking were especially frequent. Behaviour which in general expressed rage and aggression accounted for more than a quarter of all the offences which were cited as punishable by smacking.

The next most frequent category of punishable naughtiness (17 per cent) was that of generally destructive or disruptive behaviour. This included pulling things off the table, emptying drawers, shelves and cupboards, tearing or defacing wallpaper, throwing things, and touching or knocking over fragile or precious objects. It soon became obvious that certain glass-fronted pieces of furniture such as china cabinets and television sets were special focuses of anxiety in many households. But perhaps the most important single geographical area in which the child's activities were likely to be punished was the fireplace and hearth. In most houses, the fireplace seems to exert a magnetic influence upon the one-year-old; when the fire is alight, it is obviously a possible source of danger, particularly where there is no guard or where the guard is not secured; and even when the fire is not

1. This analysis is based upon the random sample only.

burning there is coal to be eaten and dirt to be smeared, and the delight of banging the fire-irons or using the poker to wreak more general destruction. Sixteen per cent of punished offences involved the fireplace and its equipment.

Another source of trouble was the exploration of various domestic appliances, especially of electrical gadgets. Switches, wall plugs and trailing flexes were frequently mentioned, and, in particular, radio and television control knobs seem to hold a peculiar fascination for the one-year-old; playing with television knobs alone accounted for half of the naughtiness in this category. Fortunately for domestic harmony, some manufacturers are now siting television control panels on the top of the instrument, where they are conveniently out of sight and reach of the toddler; but, at the time the survey was made, few sets were so designed. In the kitchen, the cooker is clearly a major source of danger, and therefore of punishment, but some mothers also spoke of conflict when an experimentally inclined baby discovered the tap of the wash boiler or attempted to test for durability the enamel of washing machine or refrigerator: labour-saving affluence brings with it the anxieties of ownership. About 13 per cent of all offences were connected with household appliances or electrical fittings.

About 7 per cent of the instances of naughtiness referred to mealtime behaviour; almost exclusively, it was the throwing of food that was punished. Spitting and standing up in the high-chair were occasionally mentioned. It should also be remembered that tantrums sometimes occur as a result of the child's impatience in the general feeding situation.

Finally, 7 per cent of the offences for which babies were smacked were accounted for by genital play, and a few mothers used punishment as part of toilet training; these subjects will be discussed more fully in the next chapter.

It will be seen that the behaviour for which a one-year-old is punished is of two sorts: sometimes he will be smacked for something which simply displeases his mother, but often punishment is given in an attempt to teach him to keep out of dangerous situations, and has as its aim his physical protection. There was a small group of mothers who did not believe in smacking children of this age for ordinary naughtiness, but who did think punishment was necessary in order to teach the child to keep away from things that might harm him. Eleven per cent of the mothers who used smacking at all, then, smacked for dangerous behaviour only.

Pursuing the concept of the generally permissive mother as opposed to the generally restrictive one, we decided to compare the individual mother's willingness to punish her child with her willingness to leave him to cry. For this purpose, we correlated smacking for general naughtiness, excluding smacking for danger alone, with leaving the baby to cry without attention for maximum periods ranging from seventeen minutes to two hours. Twenty-four per cent of all mothers were highly restrictive in that they did both of these things. Further analysis showed that 44 per cent of the 'smacking' mothers would also leave the child to cry alone for more than seventeen minutes,[1] while only 34 per cent of the non-smacking mothers would do this. This difference is statistically significant.

In this chapter, our analysis of the mothers' responsiveness to crying, their handling of temper tantrums and their use of smacking has shown that attempts at moral evaluation and character training begin very early in the upbringing of many of these children. Of course, at this age, a moral attitude on the part of the parents is not very effective in securing 'good' behaviour, but at the same time the children are not entirely oblivious to the pressures that are being exerted upon them. Even a one-year-old can show quite unmistakable opposition and non-cooperation, and may repay aggression with aggression or behave as if his feelings have been deeply hurt. The child's intellectual comprehension may be limited, but he is already capable of a fairly

1. The lower limit of seventeen minutes was chosen because, in the category below this, mothers commonly replied 'fifteen or sixteen minutes'. In practice, however, the lower limit is much more likely to be half an hour.

sophisticated emotional responsiveness towards changes in his mother's moods. From the mother's point of view, the child's persistent 'defiance' is capable of arousing strong feelings of indignation and anger. There is thus a two-way interaction, an interplay of emotions between the mother and her child. However, mothers differ considerably in the ways in which they interpret episodes of tension between themselves and their babies. At one extreme, the 'restrictive' mothers argue that some unhappiness is inevitable if the child's character is to be moulded in an acceptable fashion. The child cannot be allowed to get away with disobedience; give him an inch and he'll take an ell. 'Checks' must therefore be rigorously applied, mainly in the form of minor pain, which is thought to be the best way of 'making him understand'. Some of these mothers seem firmly to believe the old dictum that this hurts them more than it hurts the child; none the less, it is supposed to do him good in the end. The 'permissive' mothers, in contrast, tend to blame their own lack of patience when things go wrong. It is not the child's fault because he is, after all, not old enough to understand what 'naughty' means: nor is he capable of learning this concept through being punished, which would only bewilder him. Thus the permissive mother 'loves him out of a situation' because he is too young to understand a smack; the restrictive one smacks him because he is too young to understand anything else. At both these extremes, the mothers tend to justify their behaviour on grounds of principle; but it should be noted that very few mothers reject corporal punishment in general as a legitimate means of child upbringing: the principle seems to be purely a matter of age. An intermediate group are the mothers who do not seem to know which of these attitudes is correct for children at a year, or else are torn between toughness in theory and tenderness in practice; these therefore are likely to be rather inconsistent in their handling of discipline problems.

CHAPTER FIVE

HABIT MAKING AND
HABIT BREAKING

Habit making

According to many writers, particularly those of the psycho-analytic persuasion, toilet training is one of the most important and fundamental experiences for the child, and one which can have far-reaching repercussions upon his whole personality and future character development. To control the excretion of bodily waste until it can be deposited in what is considered by adults to be the 'proper' place – that is, away from the immediate eating and living quarters – seems certainly to be an accomplishment which infants universally are expected to acquire at some time during the first five years or so, whether the lesson is early and traumatic as it is for the Tanala child of Madagascar, slapped for wetting its mother at six months, or whether, as among the Siriono of South America, its inculcation is very gradual and gentle, and full independence in toileting not expected before the age of six.[1] Every child must, sooner or later, willingly or un-willingly, come to terms with sphincter control; for most children, it will be the mother in particular who provides the motivation for learning. And, whether or not we believe character to be deeply affected by the atmosphere in which this learning takes place, in our own culture at least toilet training is likely to be an important focus of emotional inter-action between the mother and her child during his early years. Frequently, it appears to involve intense anxiety and tension on both sides. The mother's own deep feelings and inhibitions seem quickly to become aroused by this situation,

1. See J. W. M. Whiting and I. L. Child, *Child Training and Personality* (Yale University Press, 1953).

particularly those connected with attitudes of shame towards the naked body and of disgust towards its excrements. The child in his turn may react to his mother's tension by developing fears or aversions surrounding either the excretory act itself or the potty or lavatory to which his mother seems to attach so much emotional value; or he may learn that in his performance or non-performance he has a potent weapon against his mother which he can use at will to secure her praise, her discomfiture or at least her attention. Either reaction on the part of the child is seen by the mother as an obstinate refusal to cooperate, which in its turn tends to increase her own emotional involvement and, through her, often that of the whole family.

Even the most superficial observation indicates that in our culture considerable emphasis is placed upon the desirability of early completion of toilet training. Higher standards of living no doubt contribute towards this; for the advent of wipable floor surfaces and plastic pants is matched by the widespread acquisition of stainable carpets and a commercially-induced intolerance of basic human smells, as well as by a more universal expectation of leisure. Few mothers can, however, yet afford to use either disposable napkins or the (rarely available) nappy-washing service; and the prospect of being relieved of a chore which even a modern washing-machine[1] does not entirely eliminate plainly provides high motivation for many mothers to try to get the child out of nappies as quickly as possible. In addition, the child who wets and soils indiscriminately is a social liability, the precipitator of awkward situations between the mother and her friends or less understanding relatives. Thus mothers are naturally inclined to feel some pride in a child whose training has been completed early; conversely, the child who is still incontinent when other children of his age are already trained may be a continual source of embarrassment and shame to his mother, who, even if she started out with a dis-

1. Forty-eight per cent of the mothers we interviewed possessed powered washing-machines, but almost none of these were of the fully automatic variety. Drying often presents a greater problem still.

passionate attitude towards the problem, may have such feelings forced upon her by the disapproval of others.

While the mothers themselves tend to place a high value on early training, the baby books are in some disagreement as to whether this is either desirable or possible, and, if it is possible, as to how it can be achieved. In general, advice seems to vary according to the date of the book, the trend in time being towards late introduction of the pot; but even those who recommend an early start hold out little hope of the child becoming fully trained before he is a year old. Thus some authorities advocate an unvarying routine almost from birth, in order to establish simple habit training; but it is readily admitted that, to begin with, the infant may only be making a reflex response to the touch of the pot against his buttocks. The reason given for this early start is that the mother may quite often manage to 'catch it' in this way, and that this at least saves some nappy washing at the time, even if the child does go through a period of having 'accidents' later on; there is furthermore the point that early training habituates the child to the use of the pot, so that he will not later object to it and so that training may well proceed smoothly right through to the time when he will perform the act voluntarily as a matter of course. The alternative point of view is that early attempts at training are in any case rarely successful, and that, faced with repeated failure, the mother is likely to feel some frustration, become emotionally involved, and put undue pressure on the child. In such circumstances, it is suggested that the child will almost certainly rebel against the whole procedure during the second half of the first year, and that it will then be far more difficult to coax him back into good habits later on; for these reasons, the advice given is to delay all attempts at training until the first half of the second year, when the child can not only understand what is required of him but can even begin to express his own needs verbally. Although these two views are in opposition over practical recommendations, it can easily be seen that there is a good measure of agreement as to the general attitude which mothers should adopt towards toilet training: neither advocates that strong pressure should be brought to bear upon the child at any time, and there is no question of punishing him for failure. It is also usually stressed that few children are reliably toilet trained before the end of the second year; and the anxious mother is assured that all normal children will come to be clean and dry in their own good time, provided that they are not fussed too much.

In the light of these considerations, how do mothers behave in practice? Our impression was that, although in general they were aware that it was useless to hope for too much too soon, they were none the less influenced by the subtle prestige attached to early and successful toilet training. This led to a curious process of double-think whereby a great many mothers, while paying lip-service to the official attitude that, for most babies, twelve months was too young to expect control, themselves gambled fairly heavily in time and patience on the chance that their own babies were different. From one point of view, they had little to lose by starting training early: if they were in fact quickly successful, they would be able to claim credit both for having a precocious child and for being patently efficient in this difficult sphere of child management; if they failed, they could fall back on the professionally authorized belief that 'all children are different', and that early success with any particular child is largely a matter of luck.

This conflict between the mothers' hopeful behaviour and their less optimistic expectations is shown in the figures we obtained. Less than 20 per cent of all mothers were expecting their children to be dry during the day before the age of eighteen months, and 40 per cent did not expect to finish with daytime nappies until after the child was two years old. The estimates of the age at which they would expect him to be able to control his bowel movements were very similar. Despite these prognoses, which might be called either pessimistic or reality-adjusted, the great majority of mothers – 83 per cent – had in fact started toilet training before the baby reached twelve months, and this figure includes 63 per cent who started before eight months. More than 20 per cent had been regularly holding the child on the pot since before he was two months old, most of these mothers having started as soon as they got up after their confinement. Only 17 per cent had not yet started training at the time of the interview.

It appears, too, that some mothers were a little over-sensitive to possible criticism of their babies' toilet habits, even at a year. In replying to health visitors, 29 per cent reported that their children were already successfully trained. In the University interviewer's sample, this proportion fell significantly to 10 per cent, and we suspect that even this estimate may be biased on the optimistic side of the truth. Apart from distortion due to mothers' tendency to boast of their children's abilities, it would be unwise to regard reports of 'successful' training at twelve months as final, since it is known that later relapses frequently occur. In passing, it should be noted that our evidence here conflicts rather emphatically with that produced by Douglas and Blomfield,[1] who estimated that as many as 47 per cent of all children are fully toilet trained before their first birthday. It must be borne in mind, however, that their evidence was obtained by retrospective questioning when the child in question was six years old; leaving aside the difficulty of remembering any 'milestone' dates for a particular child where the family includes more than one, the unreliability of such evidence is increased by the fact that the completion of toilet training does not occur on a definite day, like a baby's first step, but may be spread over a period of anything up to a year or more, during which time the child is fairly trustworthy but still has 'accidents'. Furthermore, the milestones of children's development, and especially this one, are notoriously apt to be remembered with advantages. It would seem that the only way of approaching accuracy in this sort of information is to ask the mother within the year in which the development in question has taken place; and even this method

1. J. W. B. Douglas and J. M. Blomfield, *Children under Five* (Allen and Unwin, 1958).

is still subject, as we can see, to the distortion of parental pride.

We have mentioned that the experts often warn mothers that if toilet training is begun early the child may develop an aversion to the potty at a year or so, either because he has come to associate it with the restriction of his own mobility and tenseness in his mother, or simply as an expression of his growing independence. We did indeed find many examples of this: and the modern baby books' deprecation of early training, for the reason that relapse may cause harmful anxiety and irritability in the mother, was vindicated by the manner in which our respondents often spoke of their reactions to this problem. Our factual questions on toilet training were followed by a more general attitude-probing question: 'Are you taking trouble to get him trained at the moment?'; and on the basis of the whole series of her responses in this section the mother was rated as 'very concerned', 'mildly concerned' or 'unconcerned' about this aspect of child care. Only 6 per cent of the mothers could in fact be rated as 'very concerned'; but in many of these cases it was obvious that an initial anxiety was being exacerbated by the mother's continual experience of frustration of her efforts after an early and successful start to training. A typical example was Mrs Lander, a driver's wife, who had attempted potty-training from birth, and whose little boy's increasing demands for independence, at mealtimes and when being dressed as well as over toileting, were plainly a worry to her.

'Yes, it's a lot of trouble. I'm a bit worried about it really. That is where he really is a problem. After all, he must know what his potty's for by now – and yet I've sat here with him for half an hour sometimes, and then he'll go and fill his pants. That really makes me mad. Well, I suppose he'll come to it eventually, but I do worry about it – yes.'

The next three babies are also examples of training started in the first month being followed by relapse and consequent disappointment and irritation, although these mothers were among the 28 per cent rated as only moderately concerned.

The situation in which the baby dirtied his nappy after a prolonged session on the potty was frequently quoted, and seemed to be the chief source of real anger in the mother, probably because it seemed usually to be seen as an act of deliberate malice on the part of the child: smacking was often the result of such provocation.

Cook's wife:

'She used a potty from when she was three weeks, and I hardly ever had a dirty nappy off her. Now – I can hold her on the pot for half an hour – no! The minute I put a nappy on – that's it! And yet, right till she was eleven months I hardly had a dirty nappy . . . I don't think she dislikes it – it's just something that's all of a sudden – you know – come over her.'

(Are you taking trouble to get her trained at the moment?)

'I can't say I'm going out of my way, you know, I'm just doing what I've been doing ever since I had her, you know, I put her on three times a day; and then I tell her she's a naughty girl and tap her bottom when she fills her nappy; but otherwise I'm not trying to force her or anything.'

Salesman's wife:

'This last month I've had a terrible tata with her over that potty. She instantly sees the potty and that's it. She refuses. She won't have anything to do with it. It's rather a touchy subject at the moment. But we keep trying.'

Tobacco worker's wife:

'Well, when the twins were tiny, they were ever so good; but just lately I can't get them to do anything for me at all. They don't like sitting on the potty, either of them. I started soon as I came home; and I really got them ever so clean; but as they got older . . . they're very obstinate now. Some days you can just put them down with a clean nappy and then they start. In fact, I gave John a tap for that yesterday. Because I'd been holding him out ages – and in the finish I put his nappy on, and blow me if he didn't go and fill his pants as soon as I put him down, next minute. I gave him a little tap for that – because I feel as if they understand, don't you think so, a year old? I think they know, because they know what they're supposed to do now.'

The baby's refusal to use his potty does indeed seem to rile his mother as nothing else can; the next two mothers quoted are both extremely easy-going in every other respect, but this potty business just gets under their skin. The first shows how even a very permissive mother may feel impelled, despite experience of failure, to persist in her attempts at early training; the second has been luckier, but is aware of her potential reaction to failure.

Machine operator's wife:
   'I made the same mistake over Stephanie, they told me that start a child off early, they usually do finish up where they won't use the potty. Well, I found that with Stephanie, and I've also found that with Adrian.'

Steel erector's wife:
   'I started him off when he was three weeks old, as soon as I got him back from the hospital [John was premature], and I could count the number of dirty nappies I've had on one hand. At one time I used to sit him on every half an hour, and in the week-end when his dad was home he'd help too, and I wouldn't have a wet nappy. I think a baby should be clean as soon as he can ask you – I think it would make me mad if he could walk and talk and wouldn't do it.'

Here is another highly permissive mother; she has not yet started training, but even she knows herself to be not immune from the over-concern which so often attends frustration of effort. She illustrates the way in which toilet training may become a worry for the whole family.

Minister's wife:
   'I don't worry, but . . . if eighteen months loomed up, you know, and I was nowhere near tackling the problem, I would think, Oh dear, I must spend *all day* over this, I mean I think I would, I should spend the whole day; with nylon panties

on, and, er – the toilet always in our conversation, you know, so that we'd all talk about toilets and nothing else all day [laughed]. By the time they're eighteen months I think I ought to tackle it and see some results.'

The mother's belief that the baby 'must know by now, you know' was often given as a reason both for intensive training at this age and for being angry with him when he wetted his nappy. The next two mothers, both rated as 'very concerned', claimed to have successfully completed toilet training, and their little girls were exceptional in providing some evidence of this: they were both wearing dry cotton knickers which stayed dry throughout the interview. The third mother below, the miner's wife, was rated 'unconcerned' and illustrates the danger of reading too much into the more vaguely hopeful statements on toilet training: this baby's nappy was removed upon his waking from a nap at the beginning of the interview, and he remained bare-bottomed during the next fifty minutes, his mother showing no concern at having her skirt wetted three times during that period.

Labourer's wife:

'I smack her now for wetting and that, I just give her a tap, because she knows, she's told me, you see, and I do smack her for doing that now, you see, because she's told me odd times when she does want to do it, and she knows when she's done it, you see, she'll come and tell me after she's done it; well, I just give her a little tap so she knows it's wrong, and then next time she'll mostly tell me. But she doesn't wear nappies any more, she's out of them. It *is* a bit of trouble. I mean, I don't like to keep smacking her for it, but . . . when she does it, I tell her "It's a baba" you see, I tell her she's wee-wee'd, like, so that she'll tell me "wee-wee", you see; I don't just smack her and make her think it's for nothing, like, I say "Look, you've wee-wee'd, it's naughty!"'

Shop-keeper's wife:

(Are you taking trouble to get her trained at the moment?)

'Oh yes, I do – I did with the others – I spent hours, but I found it was worth it in the end. A lot of my friends say Oh, that's too young, it's silly, and they'll do it in their own good time, but I don't believe in that – I think the few hours you spend is well worth it in the end. I have a lot of patience, you've got to.'

Miner's wife:

'I try my best to make him go on the pot and that – to be clean, you know – I mean, 'cause he's a forward baby; if he wasn't, I don't think I'd bother so much, I'd just let him have the nappy on.'

Smacking as a method of training is rarely mentioned by the baby books, which seem to assume that the mother will not smack in this situation; they merely warn that even the mild expression of disapproval is dangerous in connexion with excretory function, since the child may come to think that it is what he does, not where he does it, which displeases his mother. As we have seen, however, many mothers find that the strong emotions provoked by 'dirty habits' do occasionally lead to smacking; a few, too, seem to smack without emotion as a natural part of any training programme. The following mothers use smacking as a matter of course for showing their disapproval in many different situations.

Van-driver's wife:

'Well, I put him on the pot three times a day, and then if he gets off it I smack his bottom, that's all I do.'

Steeplejack's wife:

[Dirty nappy] 'I should hit her for that after eighteen months. If you don't drum it into them early, they never learn.'

Window-cleaner's wife:

'If he's been on the potty and not done anything and then he goes and wets his nappy, I smack his bottom and shout at him "You're a naughty boy!" I think if they're not out of nappies by the time they're two they should go and see the doctor, there must be something wrong with them. I don't believe in them not being clean by two, I think it's dirty.'

Just occasionally, a mother expressed the very strong physical disgust aroused in her by handling dirty nappies, which must obviously have played a large part in her attitude towards toilet training. Both the mothers that follow had been using the potty from the first week of the baby's life.

Lorry-driver's wife:
'Well, I hope we'll have it done with soon, or we shall have to buy some more nappies. Well, you know sometimes it's all messy, and you just think to yourself, Well, I just can't tackle that, you know, and you just chuck it on the fire. I've done that with nearly half of the nappies, you know, when I haven't been able to catch it.'

Labourer's wife:
'I've never had a dirty nappy since he was a fortnight old. I couldn't wash dirty nappies, they turn me up.' [Of a neighbour's untrained four-year-old]: 'I know what I'd do with him – I'd put him in a cold bath, first dirty nappy he had – he'd never do it again!' [spoken with a frightening vindictiveness].

Finally, let some of the mothers who, at this stage in the child's development, were still 'unconcerned' about toilet training, speak for the 66 per cent of mothers who make up the majority.

Cattle-factor's wife:
'It'll come to him a bit later on. The more you persist, the more they seem to be awkward.'

Tailor's presser's wife:
'They stop when they're ready. I don't think you can put a limit to it.'

Lorry-driver's wife:
'I haven't much time for training, I'm afraid. I just leave it to nature and let nature take its course. I won't start her till

she's eighteen months, anyway – when there's no fear of her toppling off it.'

Chauffeur's wife:
'Well, I'm not purging him at the moment! I'll give him a while longer. If you worry them too early, they seem to get a bit over-conscious of it, I think.'

Labourer's wife:
'He hasn't got a potty. I thought of getting one when I can afford it.'

Lorry-driver's wife:
'Oh, they're three or four really before they start to be dry, aren't they?'

Cycle-packer's wife:
'They'll get interested in what they're doing and then they'll have an accident. Well, I've known *women* to wait for the last minute, I know *I* do, I say "I'll just do the potatoes" or "I'll just hang out the washing", and then I'm standing . . . like this . . . and if a grown woman can do it, I don't see why you should thrash a child for it.'

Habit breaking

In toilet training, the mother is trying to teach the child to control his natural functions so that he will only empty his bladder or bowels at an appropriate time and in an acceptable place. However, the whole pattern of her behaviour in this situation – the emotive flavour of the words she uses, her facial expression, the degree of emphasis shown in her voice and movements, the distaste she may betray in her cleaning-up of the child and his clothes – all these will have the effect of impressing upon him certain more subtle cultural conventions. For instance, the child in our society must eventually learn that the act of excretion is essentially a private matter, that the subject is not a suitable one for general conversation, that the genitals are especially private parts of the body, that certain activities **and** postures are considered impolite, and so on. Thus, in addition to learning the control of urination

126

and defecation, the child is also expected to acquire a conventional sense of modesty and propriety in the whole way in which he behaves, talks and even feels about these matters. In our culture, very little of this training in 'natural modesty' is really explicit. The child is expected somehow to come to sense what is 'not nice' without actually receiving any positive instruction. In practice, this does not mean that no pressure is put upon the child to conform, but that the strong pressures which are exerted tend to be of an indirect kind. Although certain forms of behaviour are only referred to obliquely, if at all, the child is left in no doubt of the mother's feelings and attitudes regarding them; undesirable activities are checked in a special tone of voice, and by covert gestures and whispered admonitions if company is present.

All this, of course, takes time; and modesty training, even of the most direct kind, is not likely to be very effective with a one-year-old child. Once again, however, the way in which the mother behaves towards her baby, even at this age, can be a guide to her more general feelings about the importance or otherwise of physical modesty in older children; we therefore asked the mothers what body play they had observed in their babies, and whether they had attempted to restrict this behaviour in any way. We were, of course, chiefly interested in whether or not mothers felt it necessary to place restrictions upon genital play at this age; but, in anticipation of some constraint in their replies, the direct question was embedded in the more general topic of what anybody might regard as 'harmless' body play, thus: 'Does he play with his body much? for instance, does he scratch his face or pull his hair? or scratch his ears? or pull his eyelashes? Does he play with his private parts at all? Does he ever bang his head on purpose?'

Despite this attempt at an innocuous approach to the subject of genital play, it was clear that the question did sometimes cause a certain amount of embarrassment; when the mothers were finally asked whether the child played with his private parts, some of them replied with a rather hurried and definite 'oh no', as if they were perhaps more concerned to dismiss the topic than to discuss it further. This impression is reinforced by the fact that mothers were less willing to admit the existence of genital play in their children when the interviewer was a health visitor: in the Health Visitor sample, only 19 per cent admitted that such behaviour occurred, whereas in the University sample this proportion rose to 36 per cent. Again, of the 19 per cent reported by the health visitors, just over half were rated as permissive, while, of the 36 per cent from the University sample, less than one third were so rated; this perhaps suggests that those mothers who actively discourage genital play are less likely to admit its occurrence in the first place.

The quotations that follow illustrate various more or less restrictive or permissive attitudes towards this behaviour. In the first place, we have those mothers who smack their children for genital play; it will be remembered that this situation accounts for 7 per cent of the misdeeds which are followed by physical punishment.

Lorry-driver's wife:
(This baby does not wear nappies, owing to a history of severe nappy rash.)
'It's so difficult, you see, with him not wearing nappies. I smack his hand for it, I don't like him doing it, oh no – it makes me mad for some reason.'

Textile worker's wife:
'Yes – as soon as you come to change his nappy, he's there if you don't watch him. I smack him and tell him to stop it, it's naughty.'

Labourer's wife:
'He's only just started that. I have to smack him, because he pulls hisself, you know. I mean you never know, do you? But that's all – he's not a bad kiddy at all really.'

Roundsman's wife:
'Well – yes – he did that for the first time last week. I tapped his fingers for it. I don't think you can start too early

with that – you've really got to deal with it immediately, I think.'

Electro-plater's wife:

'I've just got him out of it. I tapped him. Now every time he puts his hand down he'll just look at me.'

Many mothers restricted the child's genital play simply by removing his hand or distracting him; a few were at pains not to show their disapproval explicitly, for fear of strengthening the habit by increasing the child's self-awareness.

Labourer's wife:

'Well, bath time and when I'm changing his nappy, he'll pull his little mike. I take his hand away, because this lad [sibling aged four] used to be terrible at it – he was near rupturing himself I think.'

Driver's wife:

'I take his hand away and say "That's a rude boy, Paul." It's because of Madeline, really [sibling aged ten], she's really disgusted with him. My husband says don't stop him, it not harm him, but Madeline thinks it's *very* rude, so I do stop him.'

Scrap-collector's wife:

'Well, he doesn't have the chance. He always has a nappy and woolly pants on. That's where I think some people are neglectful. They leave their nappies off, and then, well, of course they play with it.'

Labourer's wife:

'He plays with his – down here – you know. His father checks him for it, he speaks to him, like. I tell him he mustn't do that, it's naughty. I don't think it's good for little boys. He's getting really foxy – he looks to see if you're looking first.'

Railwayman's wife:

'Well, I give 'em toys to play with and it keeps their minds occupied.' (Her other children were listening.)

Eight-year-old sibling:
  'He plays wi' mine!'
Twelve-year-old sibling:
  'Yes, but we stop 'im!'

Butcher's wife:
  'Well, I did try to stop him at first, and then I thought to myself, Well, he's going to think "Oh, I'm doing something big", so I just leave it. When I go to my mum's, she's always saying "Oh, he'll hurt himself, he'll hurt himself"; but I think to myself, well, if he did hurt himself a little, he won't do it again, but if I keep telling him not to do it he might think "Oh, I'm doing something big, I'll carry on doing it"; so I only, if he's got, say, a feeder on, I just put it over the potty when he's on, so he can't find it.'

Some mothers thought this behaviour natural in the child, but still could not bring themselves to ignore it, or else thought that they would soon have to restrict it.

Company director's wife:
  'It's natural for a little boy. I just put on his nappy as quickly as I can.'

Clerk's wife:
  'Well, I do take her hand away, I must admit, but of course it's just innocent; but I don't like to see it.'

Bricklayer's wife:
  'I stop him as much as I can, but it doesn't bother me, you know. All boys do it, don't they? I just take his hand away. He laughs at me.'

Shop manager's wife:
  'Of course, being a boy – the other place – he does, if he gets the chance, he just sits and scratches it – and pulls it – he does. Well – at the moment I don't mind; if he carries on doing it when he doesn't wear a nappy, then I should try and keep it covered up as much as possible, and then they don't bother. But boys – well, they just seem inclined to do that quite a lot, I don't know why.'

Lastly, the attitudes of the wholly permissive group of mothers; it must be remembered, however, that the feelings they express here are specifically concerned with the baby of twelve months, and may not remain so permissive as the child grows older. The first mother quoted was halfway through Spock's *Baby and Child Care*.

Sales clerk's wife:

'It's a natural thing, for a boy at any rate, to masturbate a little, though you shouldn't allow them to do it a lot, I don't believe, but it is natural to a certain extent, I think – well, they're finding out about their own bodies, and if you're going to stop them they'll think there's something – not quite nice, perhaps. And, er – I don't know the psychological effect!' [laughed].

Cabinet-maker's wife:

'He does when I take his napkin off, he has a scratch, and he will play with his penis, yes. I don't stop him.'

Lorry-driver's wife:

'He just has a feel, you know, when I'm changing his nappy; they like to know what they've got, don't they?'

Lorry-driver's wife:

'I think it's natural for a kid to want to.'

Departmental manager's wife:

'All parts of their body are alike to them at this age.'

The reader will probably have noticed that the great majority of these quotations – all except two, in fact – refer to boys rather than girls. This probably simply reflects the fact that genital play is more noticeable in boys than in girls, whether or not it actually occurs more frequently. It would certainly be true to say that the mothers were more on the look out for its occurrence in small boys, leaving aside the question of whether they disapproved of it; and it is, of course, quite likely that the sight of genital play in a boy, especially if it is accompanied by erection, arouses far more immediate emotion in the mother than would the less obvious sexual stimulation of the small girl. It is clear that this type of sudden and disturbing emotion may well lead to immediate, and possibly violent, restriction of the child's behaviour, for reasons which may not be plain to the mother herself; we felt that Mrs Matthew's revealing comment, 'I smack his hand for it, I don't like him doing it, oh no – it just makes me mad for some reason', would have rung true for many of the mothers who preferred not to discuss the subject.

A certain difference in attitude between social classes may also be apparent; this point will be discussed in a later chapter.[1]

In view of the differences between the two samples, and of the fact that we are here only dealing with a minority of the total sample, it is hardly possible to draw any overall statistical conclusions about the incidence of genital play in one-year-olds, still less as to the restrictive or permissive attitudes adopted by their mothers. At an impressionistic level, however, we suspect that the cultural pressures are such that very few mothers would go to the extent of ignoring masturbation altogether, once their children had passed the toddler stage.

1. See pages 200–3.

CHAPTER SIX

FATHER'S PLACE IS IN THE HOME

Obviously the care of infants is a predominantly female occupation, and in most normal families the mother is necessarily the central figure in the child's early life. However,
there is a great deal of evidence to suggest that the traditional
pattern of family life is changing. Marriage today is ideally
envisaged as a partnership in which husband and wife share
each other's interests and worries, and face all major deci-
sions jointly. 'Tackle it together!' is the theme of today's
women's magazines and advertising copywriters, and the
suggestion is taken to apply equally to planning a holiday,
modernizing the kitchen or buying a new car. Marketing
surveys agree in recognizing the wife as primary spender of
the family income, and the makers of 'do-it-yourself' equipment acknowledge that not only will she decide when the
living-room needs to be redecorated, but she is likely to carry
out the actual work herself. Conversely, the old joke about
henpecked husbands doing the washing-up is now funny
only to the late middle-aged; to most younger husbands,
washing up is no longer a sign of henpeckery, but something
to be taken for granted. Thus the emancipation of women in
one generation has been followed by the domestication of
husbands in the next; and, in the home, many of the traditional distinctions between what used to be considered
women's work and men's work are wearing rather thin.[1]

This emphasis on partnership is, of course, equally

1. In illustration, we may quote our own five-year-old, who, exasper-
ated by the yearly preoccupation of both his parents with examination
papers, muttered at his mother, 'Marking exam papers isn't women's
work'. 'What is women's work, then?' 'Oh, painting ceilings and all
that sort of thing!'

apparent in the care of the children. Articles addressed to mothers-to-be almost invariably include a section on the importance of remembering that fathers are parents too, and often it is stressed that they must be encouraged to do things for the new baby so that they do not feel excluded and become jealous. Against such a background, it seemed natural for us to inquire into the extent to which fathers actually do participate in the care of one-year-olds. The procedure we adopted was to ask the mothers whether the fathers took an active part in doing things for the children: specifically, we asked whether the father would give the baby his food, change his nappy, give him a bath, get him to sleep, attend to him in the night, take him out without the mother, and play with him. The answers to these questions also had to be qualified according to whether he undertook each activity often, sometimes, or not at all. In investigating the frequency of the father's participation, we asked supplementary questions as necessary to find out whether, for instance, the father would change the child's nappy *as a matter of course* if he found it to be wet or if the mother happened to be doing something else (classified as 'often'), or whether he would do this only if he was specifically asked to or if the mother was out of the house or otherwise unavailable (classified as 'sometimes'); or, to take another example, whether he habitually gave the baby his bedtime bottle or would normally get on with feeding the baby if his food was prepared and the mother was still serving the rest of the family, or whether he would only feed the baby in a minor emergency. Often, of course, no supplementary questions were needed, the mother spontaneously giving us a detailed reply: 'Oh no, he never does that, he draws the line at that'; 'Yes, he will sometimes do that if I'm very rushed or if we're in a hurry to get out'; 'Oh yes, he'll give him his bath *every* night, he wouldn't miss bathtime for anything, it's the only time he really sees him.' Some fathers, because of the hours they work, do have much less opportunity than others to help with the baby – we found many who never saw their children except on Sundays – and this factor was often pointed out by the mothers, sometimes apparently in extenuation of their husband's failure to help. We tried to eliminate this possible bias by rating participation, not on an absolute basis of actual time spent by the father in caring for the children, but on the basis of the likelihood of his helping when he *was* at home, however infrequent this might be.

Another difficulty which arose in trying to assess the extent of the father's participation was that, where there was more than one small child in the family, it often happened that the parents shared the jobs to be done by a convenient division of labour. Thus very frequently, when both parents were present, the mother attended to the baby while the father took complete responsibility for the older children; in many households, for example, the father's arrival home from work in the evening coincides with a period of major domestic upheaval, during which all the children have to be fed, bathed, and settled down for the night, and few fathers are absolved from all duties at this time. Caring for other small children in this sort of way was taken into account in rating the father for his participation; taking the older boys out fishing was not.

Not unexpectedly, we found that some of the activities of child care were more popular than others with the fathers (see Table 5). Whereas 80 per cent were prepared to get the baby to sleep, for instance, only 57 per cent ever changed a nappy, and still fewer (39 per cent) ever gave him his bath. On the other hand, so seldom was a father said to be unwilling to play with the child, at least sometimes, that a report of this kind by the mother usually amounted to a complaint against her husband and seemed to suggest some tension in their relationship. Bathing and nappy changing are regarded as special skills; many women whose husbands were otherwise participant said that father would be 'afraid to bath him – he'd be frightened of dropping him', or, of nappy changing, 'that's a thing he can't do – he's all fingers and thumbs, it'd just drop off again'. One had the impression that the wives took some pleasure in this masculine clumsiness. Husbands often seemed to be disgusted by the job of nappy changing, and 'drew the line' here for this reason. One husband was said to be deterred by modesty:

Clerk's wife:

'He used to do anything for Nigel – well, he still does – he always bathed him. But Denise – well, I think really it's because she's a girl, he doesn't quite like ... I think he thinks it's not quite right, and he's the same about changing her nappy – a bit embarrassed, you see.'

The fact that half the fathers never go to the baby if it cries during the night is not entirely a matter of willingness or unwillingness on their part; it must be remembered that 60 per cent of one-year-olds sleep in their parents' room, and the cot will usually be on the mother's side of the bed, so that, for pure convenience, it will be the mother who reaches out to the baby. In addition, men doing heavy manual work during the day do not easily wake at night (although their wives tend to be somewhat sceptical of this useful disability); and an additional number are on regular night shift, so that for them the situation does not arise.

Feeding the baby meant either helping him with spoon and solid food or giving him the bottle; we did not include the habit of offering titbits from the father's plate. Getting the baby to sleep often involves feeding also, of course, since so many babies are nursed to sleep with the bottle. The total of 68 per cent who, at least sometimes, take the baby out without the mother is perhaps surprising in view of the traditional reluctance of the Englishman to be seen pushing a pram; and this percentage does not include fathers who 'wouldn't mind doing it, but we always go out as a family'. Many fathers took all the young children out of the mother's way on a Saturday or Sunday morning, while she cleared up; and a large number, especially those living on new housing estates, regularly took the baby without its mother on a visit to the paternal grandmother in the older part of the city. One father, who lived on the new council estate outside the city, cycled the seven miles to his mother's terrace house every Saturday afternoon with the baby sitting on the cross-bar.

Taking the various factors into account, for the purposes of our analysis we formed an overall impression for each father, so that each could be classified as 'highly participant', 'moderately participant' or 'non-participant'. Since 99 per cent of fathers were said to play with their babies, this activity was excluded from the analysis. In general terms, the meaning of these categories is as follows. A highly participant father is usually described as one who will 'do anything for the children'. At least three of the specific activities

TABLE 5

*Proportions of fathers undertaking various
activities in the care of one-year-olds*

	Feed him	Change nappy	Play with him	Bath him	Get to sleep	Attend in the night	Take out alone
	%	%	%	%	%	%	%
Often	34	20	83	15	31	18	29
Sometimes	44	37	16	24	49	32	39
Never	22	43	1	61	20	50	32

will be checked 'often', and the rest he will undertake 'sometimes'. Often the mother will add other child-rearing duties which he regularly shares, such as nappy washing, toilet training, getting the baby dressed in the morning and 'carrying him about everywhere'. Often, too, there will be at least one activity which is always carried out by the father if he is there: feeding, getting to sleep and attending to the child in the night are most usually chosen by the father as his regular job. Mr Holt, a baker's roundsman, always does all three for his little boy:

'He helps with everything, and that includes the housework. On Saturday mornings I do the bedrooms and he does the washing, and then I come and mop up the kitchen. We go through the house together.'

Mrs Frame has had arguments with her husband, a tailor's presser, about who should do something for their baby, who is slightly handicapped. She would like to do everything herself, but Mr Frame insists on sharing. He regularly washes Simon's nappies and reads and sings to him at bedtime. Mrs Piercy has three young children as well as the baby; when she was pregnant her husband, a crane repairer, twice took complete charge of them for the week-end while she went to the seaside with a friend; she says: 'If I hadn't got him, I don't know what I should do. Oh, he's a big help, he'll do anything, any mortal thing'. And Mr Ross, a cattle factor, was paid this tribute by his wife:

'Oh, he'll do anything for either of them – he always has – bath, change, feed, wash for them. They're all their Daddy. There's a scream when he goes and a howl when he comes back in case he's going again. We always have a tantrum when Daddy goes. Oh, they delight in their Daddy.'

A moderately participant father is one who in general is prepared to help with the children *if he is asked* or in an emergency, but who doesn't do a great deal as a matter of course. Most of the items will be checked 'sometimes', and there will usually be at least one job that he 'draws the line at'. To individual questions the mother will often answer 'he would do' or 'he does if I'm not here'. Sometimes the father makes a principle of doing certain jobs only if the mother is quite unavailable, and in general he tends to pick and choose as to what he will do and what he won't.

House-painter's wife:
'No, he'll not change a nappy if he can help it. If I'm out he will. But if I ask him, he won't. It isn't his place to change a nappy. He'll give her a bottle though, and fuss her up a bit.'

The non-participant father thinks that dealing with young children is definitely not a man's job. Items will nearly all be checked 'never', with perhaps one or two marked 'sometimes'. Specific questions will be answered with 'no, he's never done that', 'he did that once', or 'he'd probably do that if I was ill': that is to say, the circumstances have to be rather exceptional before the husband will put himself out. Often the mother will explain 'He's not really very fussy[1] about babies, he likes them better when they're older'; or 'I've never asked him to – that's my job.' Mrs Matthew, a lorry-driver's wife, admitted to finding life a continual battle with two high-spirited under-threes to cope with; her husband did not expect, and was not expected, to do anything at all in the house – not even to brush his own shoes.

'He never does anything for either of them – except he might perhaps give Julian a bottle if I was getting his supper ready. That's all he'd do.'

(Would he give Julian his dinner – feed him with a spoon?)

'Oh no – he'd say that was my job – I don't think he'd know how to, anyway.'

(Mr Matthew spends all his time at home lying on the sofa with the paper; his wife does not grumble at this, but thinks it fair and right.)

'He does just look after them on Saturday afternoon – that's when I do my shopping. Well – look after them – he just lies on the sofa and turns away from them, and I think he hopes they won't notice him – anyway, he lets them do whatever they like, just lets them get on with it. I *suppose* he'd stop them falling in the fire. Oh – you should have seen it when I got in last week! They'd got a packet of cornflakes and a packet of sugar out of the cupboard, and they'd emptied them out here all over the mat, and they were digging in it. And he just lay there!'

Using this three-way classification, we found that only about one in five (21 per cent) of all fathers could be rated as non-participant. The largest group, 52 per cent, fell into the 'highly participant' category, and the remainder, 27 per cent, took a moderate share in the care of their babies.

The willingness of so many fathers to participate actively in looking after such young children is, we believe, a very

1. See glossary of Nottingham usage, Appendix 3.

distinctive feature of modern family life in England.[1] Thirty years ago, the number of fathers rateable as highly participant by our rather exacting standards would probably have been negligible, particularly in this age range of children. A man used to be thought of as highly participant in his children's upbringing simply on the strength of playing with them often and perhaps reading to them or telling them stories; as we have seen, this is now so universal as to have become useless as a criterion.

No doubt this change has been prompted in the first instance by necessity. In middle-class families, it is probably due in large measure to the almost complete disappearance of domestic servants. Only 2 per cent of the total sample employed domestic labour at all; they were all the wives of white collar or professional men, so that the proportion of this social group paying for help in the house is 9 per cent. Half of these mothers had paid help for six hours a week or less. Among the wives of professional and higher white-collar workers in particular, however, there seems to be a continual hankering after the kind of domestic help which their own mothers expected and obtained as a matter of course; and, since the husbands, too, remember the days of cheap labour which their own mothers enjoyed, they may feel that they have a certain duty to provide for their wives by their own efforts the assistance which they can no longer buy.

Civil Service clerk's wife:

'Times have changed very much. I think my mother had a much easier time than what I've ever had. Well, mother had help, and I have no help – no domestic help, I have to do everything myself. My mother had a nurse to bring us up, things were very different – my mother did get out. We had a big house, I go there once a year. I find if you have help you have more time to amuse the children; I mean, in the morn-

1. E. Nesbit predicted this change when (in 1906) she described her vision of the London of the future: 'Men, as well as women, seemed to be in charge of the babies and were playing with them' (*The Story of the Amulet*).

ing I've got a *lot* of work to put in, and I want to be taking the children out instead. When I go up to Scotland, I do, I take the children to the seaside, and I mean the work's done when I come back, it's a great help, wonderful. My mother has a woman that comes in, and she does the washing and everything like that about three or four times a week, and it's a great help, and you're getting more pleasure out of your children.'

Among working-class families, a rather different factor seems to be of importance in the growth of the father's participation in infant care: the current trend towards the isolation of the immediate family unit from the wider circle of the extended family and the close-knit neighbourhood unit. The main reason for this trend is probably that it is in most cities extremely difficult to find accommodation of the standard nowadays expected within the areas in which the young mothers themselves have their roots. Having a number of small children is one of the chief qualifications for being allotted a house on one of the new council estates, which means that newly built neighbourhoods may consist almost entirely of young families; under such circumstances, wives can no longer expect the help from older women relatives living close by, upon which their mothers were able to call. Where so many of the children are small, entertainment outside the home is more or less confined to visiting between friends, and one might expect a good deal of this to happen in a community consisting largely of a single age group; in fact, however, many young mothers complain of the difficulty of making friends on the new housing estates. It is easier to be on dropping-in terms at a number of homes if sisters, aunts and cousins all live in the same cluster of streets; perhaps, too, affluence has brought with it a greater concern for appearances, an increase in house-pride, which is likely to have an inhibiting effect upon casual visiting between families. The mental isolation of these mothers is somewhat mitigated by television, but the fact that each house possesses its own complete home entertainment may also tend to throw the family in upon itself every evening, so that each small family unit learns to be entirely self-sufficient. The husband thus becomes the wife's sole and indispensable source of companionship, and he soon comes to share her own major preoccupations and interests – shopping, painting and decorating, doing the housework, and caring for the children.

You don't have kiddies to leave 'em

The term 'baby-sitter' has passed into the language, and therefore presumably reflects some demand for the function it describes. Certainly professional men's wives, at least, seem to set great store by going out regularly with their husbands in the evening; those who solve the problem of domestic help by receiving foreign girls in an 'au pair' capacity usually say that the main advantage of such an arrangement is, not the assistance they receive with the housework (these girls are officially expected to do no more than might be asked of the daughter of the house, and far more work could be done at the same expense by a daily cleaner), but the fact that a baby-sitter is constantly available. Sitters' services are frequently advertised in local newspapers and on newsagents' boards, and baby-sitting is widely recognized by teenagers and students as a means of earning money.

It therefore seemed worth while to investigate how far parents in general expected to leave their one-year-olds occasionally in the care of others, and how many of them were prepared to pay for this convenience. We asked the mothers: 'Do you and your husband ever manage to leave the baby so that you can both go out?' and followed this by asking what normally happened to the baby in such circumstances.

Over the total sample, and without reference to the provision made for the child's care, we found that 22 per cent of these parents were able to arrange an evening out together once a week or more often. Thirty-eight per cent occasionally left the children in the evening; and 40 per cent had been out together either once only or not at all since the one-year-old's birth. Between social classes there were considerable differences on the question of whether or not parents went out together at all, although class seemed to have little bearing on how often they went; these differences will be discussed in detail in a later chapter,[1] but we may note here that there was a very definite class trend, ranging consistently from the 25 per cent of professional workers who never left the baby with a sitter to 59 per cent in the unskilled labouring class.

We did not ask why those who stay at home do so, but we were often told spontaneously. The most obvious reason, which was not in fact given very frequently, is lack of opportunity: that there is no baby-sitter available. This most often seems to happen on the newer housing estates, where one might expect mothers to be able to organize baby-sitting on a *quid pro quo* basis; but here again there seems to exist a constraint in casual social relationships which prevents the easy give-and-take possible between relatives: so often we were told 'My neighbour has offered to come in, but I don't quite like to ask her really'. An explanation more frequently suggested was that the baby-sitters that were available were not satisfactory, for one reason or another; this applied mainly to paid sitters, and the most usual complaints were that the older ones were too expensive and the young ones irresponsible. Some middle-class wives referred to the difficulty of finding a regular paid baby-sitter, and preferred to stay in themselves rather than to use casual sitters unknown to the baby; others, with no relatives to call upon, had found that the baby objected to less familiar guardians, and were prepared to defer to this.

Departmental manager's wife:

'No, we never do – much to my disgust. The children won't put up with it, I'm afraid – they just cry. And then, between the two of them, I've never felt it's fair to burden anyone with them if they're going to cry all night.'

1. See pages 224-5.

The safety of the child was a major consideration, and many parents had renounced their free evenings because they felt baby-sitters were not to be trusted as a satisfactory substitute for their own care. This was carried to the point of moral principle in many working-class homes; most often it was the father who, according to his wife, had laid down the law on this point.

Twist-hand's wife:

'Oh no, we never go out – my husband would never go out – he wouldn't let anyone come in and let us both go out. I could go, as long as he was in. He's said, "Our turn will come when they grow up." He's that kind, you know, he's that way.'

House-painter's wife:

'Not unless I knew them properly. I've got to know the person and trust them. Because you've heard of one or two things, letting children look after babies, and they've gone out and . . . Well, my two are devils for coming down. That's what terrifies me; if that person what's watching them goes out – I mean, there's the fire – I mean, they've had it, haven't they? I mean, it would be your fault for leaving them. No, love, not unless it was *my* own family or his family, not with strangers.'

Cook's wife:

'Well, we don't actually, he doesn't believe in that – he says we should look after them now and we can go out when they're big enough to look after themselves.'

Machine operator's wife:

'We don't believe in it. We think if you have children you should take that responsibility and look after them yourself all the time.'

Warehouseman's wife:

'You don't have kiddies to leave 'em.'

It appeared to us that it was middle-class parents who tended to be concerned with the child's psychological well-being during their absence, while working-class parents thought mainly of his physical safety; since these remarks were made incidentally, and not in answer to a general question, we cannot substantiate this impression statistically. It may well be, however, that the middle-class parent, having chosen a baby-sitter, takes her conscientiousness for granted, so that it is only the child's tolerance of the arrangement which still needs to be discussed; whereas responsible working-class parents are conscious of the occasional case of neglect, sometimes with tragic physical results, *among their own neighbours*, and this is why they so often emphasize the possibility of accident if they themselves go out. A few working-class mothers did admit to inadequate arrangements for the care of the baby – the neighbour listening from the next house, the young sibling left in charge, or the baby left on his own in the expectation that he would not wake; and, since parents may be prosecuted for this practice, there were no doubt other such cases among our sample about which we were not told.

Railway worker's wife:

'Andrew [eight-year-old] usually stops in [with four other children aged twelve months to six years]; but I could get into trouble, you know, if They got to know, more or less; because they told us, like, you know, that you're not supposed to leave any child in under the age of fourteen; but you see, once they're in bed and they're fast asleep, they'd never wake up again, they're always very good once they go to sleep. Anyhow, there's a lady next door, she pops round, you know, to see if they're all right. When we first came here – we had an exchange from Clifton – and I had a grandmother that was dying in hospital, and of course I had a young boy from my mother's to come up and watch them, and somebody had the cruelty inspector on to me for it; and he came up and said it was cruel to leave them with this boy, like – I bet I wasn't gone two and a half hours, that's all, and she was dying, like, and I just wanted to see her. I know who it was told them, like – it was missus just up the terrace here.

I used to have someone to baby-sit for us, but she's left; so Andrew has to stop up and do it. Well, if he didn't we wouldn't get out at all, you see. And you want a break when you're sitting here looking at four walls same as I am – he goes to work at night-time, and I've got them all night and I've got them all day; and they do get on you a little bit, you know, especially with five of them.'

The greatest proportion of the stay-at-home parents, however, said that they had no desire to go out; usually they could have managed it if they had really wanted to, but they were content to sit by their own firesides. No doubt the lure of the television screen has a lot to do with this; probably, too, the fact that nowadays the majority of homes are indeed very comfortable and pleasant places in which to sit – particularly in the chilly but coal-producing Midlands, where the fire is always banked high. As one mother of eight children put it, 'I could go out – me daughter here's not courting yet – but I don't. Give me a good fire and me television, and I'm happy, love.'

Where the parents do leave the children in the evening, who in fact is responsible for them? In at least one in fifty of these homes, nobody: small children are left in bed, and if they wake they are entirely dependent upon somebody in the next house who may or may not hear their crying. Twenty-one per cent of the parents who ever go out are already living with relatives, usually the baby's grandparents, and leave the child with them, and 37 per cent call upon relatives living elsewhere to baby-sit for them: most of these parents, of course, live in the older parts of the city. Eighteen per cent leave the baby in the charge of older siblings, who are not necessarily old enough to be responsible: their ages range from eight years to adulthood. Sixteen per cent have friends or neighbours who come in (unpaid) to look after the baby; and, finally, 6 per cent of parents who ever leave the child (only 3 per cent of our total sample) employ a paid baby-sitter. Here again, the social class differences are considerable, as we shall see later; the number of unskilled workers paying for this service is negligible. Except in certain very restricted areas of the community where a satisfactory source of supply coincides with an above-average demand (among university wives, for example), the baby-sitting business does not appear to be booming.

Seventy-nine per cent of fathers taking a practical part in the care of their small babies; 52 per cent of parents never leaving them, during the first year at least: here is a picture of active and willing domesticity. The cinema owners and the brewers may well lament over their declining clientele: parents of young families are rejecting the evening-out habits of their courting days; both mother and father are becoming home-centred, finding their interests, their occupation and their entertainment within the family circle. At a time when he has more money in his pocket, and more leisure on which to spend it, than ever before, the head of the household chooses to sit at his own fireside, a baby on his knee and a feeding bottle in his hand: the modern father's place is in the home.

PART TWO

INFANT REARING AND
SOCIAL CLASS

CHAPTER SEVEN

THE CLASS FACTOR

It seems to be fashionable among some contemporary political commentators to suggest that Britain is rapidly becoming a classless society. Social scientists, on the other hand, are for the most part much more cautious in their appraisal of the situation, and approach this question only with many reservations. They point out that, while there has indeed been a shift towards greater equality in the way people live, the goods they possess and the standards to which they aspire, men and women in this country are still, in other ways, extremely conscious of social class differences; in other words, it is conceded only that, in present-day society, it is increasingly difficult to define social class in terms of the simple overt criteria which served well enough in the past. It is, for instance, far less easy to assign people to their appropriate social category on the basis of the clothes they wear when not at work or how lavishly their houses are equipped with durable consumer goods such as television receivers or washing machines. The milkman is almost as likely to have a car and to go on continental holidays as the bank clerk; his wife is more likely than the bank clerk's to push a fashionable perambulator. A successful plumber may spend his week-ends sailing, and the factory worker may have the latest hi-fi equipment installed in his council house; the length of a man's car is no longer a foolproof measure of the length of his bank balance. However, American experience seems to suggest that in an affluent society the abandoning of one material status symbol probably indicates only that it has already been replaced by others, often less conspicuous, but no less effective in maintaining social stratification. Where class distinctions have become blurred, the wish for social prestige impels people to create new, more artificial, more subtle barriers against which to gauge their upward progress. Indeed, it has been argued that, as affluence spreads through the lower strata of society, class boundaries tend to be drawn ever more rigidly.

All this, of course, poses problems in the identification and differentiation of the various socio-economic groups within the general population. From the practical point of view of the research worker, this is made especially difficult in that he frequently wishes to allocate a particular family to a definite social class on the basis of a single objective criterion such as income or residential district. In the present investigation we have attempted to use the father's occupation for this purpose, but it must be obvious that a simple procedure of this kind will be subject to error in the sense that some families will be classified in a way which is inconsistent with other known facts about the parents. Social class is notoriously difficult to define, largely because any really adequate definition must take into account the complex pattern of social values to which people adhere as well as the material achievements and expectations which determine their way of life. Indeed, if we knew enough about it, the way in which parents bring up their children might well provide a safer guide to social categorization than can the father's occupation alone.

The classification adopted

Our use of the father's occupation to determine social class was based upon the Registrar General's classification of occupations, modified somewhat to meet our own special requirements. For the purposes of our analysis, we combined the professional and managerial Classes I and II, and we divided Class III into two separate classes: Class III WC, consisting of the white-collar workers and including also skilled manual workers who were foremen in their trade, and Class III Man, consisting of skilled manual workers. The result was the five-point scale shown in Table 6.

A certain amount of discretion must inevitably be allowed in allocating families to particular class groups on a scheme of this kind. Occasionally, for instance, we thought it proper to use some information about the mother's occupation or former occupation in order to amend the father's classification upwards. Thus the family in which the father was a shop

TABLE 6

Classification by father's occupation

	Class	Description
'Middle Class'	I and II	*Professional and managerial:* Doctors, solicitors, clergymen, teachers, nurses, company directors, shopkeepers (own business), police officers, etc.
	III WC	*White collar:* Clerical workers, shop assistants, etc.; tradesmen in one-man business, foremen and supervisors in industry.
'Working Class'	III Man	*Skilled manual:* Skilled tradesmen in industry, drivers, etc.
	IV	*Semi-skilled:* Machine operators, bus conductors, window-cleaners, drivers' mates, porters, etc.
	V	*Unskilled:* Labourers, refuse collectors, cleaners in industry, messengers, etc.; persistently unemployed.

assistant but the mother had qualified as a teacher was classified in Class II; similarly, the man whose occupation was described as a driver but who in fact worked in his father's transport business was up-graded to Class III WC. Some occupations are so loosely defined that it is difficult to allocate them unambiguously to a single social class: the father who is said to be an 'engineer' may be a professional man with a university degree engaged on research or engineering design; or he may be a mechanic, a skilled tradesman but without any prospect of qualifying for professional status. Again, the 'representative', 'salesman' or 'traveller' is not easy to classify: he may be no more than a door-to-door salesman (Class III WC), or he may carry considerable authority in a large wholesale firm (Class II). In such cases as these, it is necessary to take additional factors into account; for instance, it is possible to use information about the kind of house the family lives in, or the extent to which the wife appears to be an educated or cultured person. Material possessions are, as we have indicated, not much help nowadays; we saw more tape-recorders, for instance, in working-class homes than in middle-class ones. Books, however, are useful as a pointer (though their absence means nothing); and a glance through the bookcase will often reveal, for instance, a pile of professional journals on which a fairly safe guess can be made as to the status of the owner.

The number of categories which is used in any attempt to specify social class is, of course, a purely arbitrary matter, and, whatever system is used, anomalies are bound to occur occasionally with borderline cases. The method of classification by occupation, while it is fairly simple to apply, can provide at best only a relatively crude indication of the true social class affiliation. For this reason, in assessing the results of the survey as they are affected by socio-economic levels, we have concentrated mainly on class differences which are comparatively clear-cut, and upon trends which remain consistent as one ascends the class scale.

The social class structure of our total random sample is shown in Table 7, and the last column provides the best available estimate of the relative sizes of the different classes

TABLE 7

Social classification of the random sample

Social class	H.V. sample	Univ. sample	Combined	%
I and II	53	18	71	14·2
III WC	49	16	65	13·0
III Man	184	70	254	50·8
IV	53	19	72	14·4
V	26	12	38	7·6
Totals	365	135	500	100

in the population from which this sample was drawn. Approximately half of all the fathers are skilled manual workers in Class III Man. The groups comprising Classes I and II, Class III WC and Class IV each account for 13 or 14 per cent, and the unskilled manual workers in Class V occupy the smallest group of all, accounting for less than 8 per cent of the total.

It was necessary initially to take a fairly large random sample of 500 cases, since this was the only reliable method of determining the class structure of the general population with

TABLE 8

Social classification of the stratified sample

Social class	H.V. sample	Univ. sample	Combined	%
I and II	47	19	66	31·6
III WC	42	15	57	27·3
III Man	4	5	9	4·3
IV	27	14	41	19·6
V	23	13	36	17·2
Totals	143	66	209	100

reasonable accuracy. Having done this, we decided to increase the numbers of cases in all the groups except Class III Man in order to provide sub-samples of a size more adequate for making comparisons between the social classes. In practice, we began by drawing a further large random sample of names; these were then sent to the appropriate health visitors, who were asked to give the father's occupation in as many cases as possible from their personal knowledge or from records kept in the district welfare clinics, and this information was checked for accuracy at the time of interview. In this way we were able to obtain our further sample stratified on the basis of socio-economic class. The composition of this sample (209 cases) is shown in Table 8. By comparison with the previous table, it will be seen that it was eventually possible approximately to double the total number of cases in Classes I and II, III WC, IV and V, without adding substantially to the already well-represented Class III Man.

The control of variables

One of the major problems which the social scientist has to face arises from the fact that he can hardly ever assume that the variables in which he is interested are strictly independent of one another. The complexity of his data is frequently such that everything is connected in some way with everything else; a consequence of this is that it is almost never possible to make simple unqualified statements about cause and effect. In observational field studies, in particular, the classical scientific procedure in which the investigator attempts to control all but one of the factors which might possibly affect the outcome of the situation has to be abandoned. Control can sometimes be achieved over some of the more obvious confounding factors by selecting matched cases for comparison; but there is generally a strict limit to the number of variables which it is possible to govern in this statistical fashion. In the attempt to investigate the effect of social class on infant-rearing practices, the possible influence of confounding variables must continually be kept in mind; and before any conclusions can be drawn it is necessary to discuss whether the groups which we have isolated according to the father's occupation may not also differ consistently in a number of other ways which might materially affect our results.

In the sample which we have used in the present study, for example, one of the variables most obviously bound up with social class is the age at which mothers give birth to the first child of their family. Table 9 shows the average age of these mothers at their first successful confinement (miscarriages are excluded since our information on this point may not be wholly accurate), compared with their socio-economic classification.[1] This table also illustrates the way in which family size varies with social class.

TABLE 9

Analysis by social class of mother's age at first confinement and size of family

Social class:	I and II	III WC	III Man	IV	V
	%	%	%	%	%
Average age of mothers at birth of first child	24·37	24·09	23·04	23·00	22·63
Average age of mothers at time of interview	28·96	29·05	28·27	29·63	28·56
Average no. of children in family at interview	2·13	2·09	2·59	2·70	3·43
Proportion of families with three or more children	27·7	27·1	39·5	44·2	63·5

It is clear that the average age at which the mothers gave birth to their first child decreases as we go down the social scale. The difference between classes is statistically significant, and the trend is quite consistent. There is, on average, more than a year's difference between the white-collar occupational group (Classes I and II and III WC), which we have called 'middle-class', and the wives of manual workers (Classes III Man, IV, and V), the 'working-class' group. Closely related to this finding is the fact that at the time of the interview there were also significant differences between the average sizes of families in the various classes: this is shown most clearly in the last line of the table. Thus in our sample as we move down the scale from professional to unskilled workers we are more likely to be dealing with mothers

1. It must be remembered that our sample excludes mothers whose *current* one-year-old was illegitimate; thus, for some of these mothers, the first birth may have been illegitimate whereas later ones were not.

who began childbearing earlier and who are also, on average, slightly more experienced in the sense that they have had more children.

These facts are presented at this point mainly as an example of one of the basic differences which may incidentally affect attitudes and methods in infant handling in the different groups which we are contrasting. In practice it would be extremely difficult to give an exhaustive list of all the many other factors of this sort. There are, for instance, a large number of environmental factors; standards of housing provide one example. Whether the children have adequate playing-space, whether the mother has a pleasant kitchen or merely a scullery-outhouse, the too close proximity of neighbours: any of these may well have an effect, not only upon the general irritability of the mother, but also upon particular aspects of child rearing such as whether the baby is left to cry ('Well – I don't like to leave her – I think it annoys the neighbours to hear a baby cry'), or whether he is kept in the living-room during the evening ('I think if I put him to bed he would go to sleep, but it's so noisy round here'); we even found the thin council-house walls affecting the mother's attitude to child-birth.

'Well – I think I would have enjoyed it, but – the trouble was, I didn't dare make a noise because our neighbour – his bed's just the other side of the wall from our bedroom – it worried me. If I'd have been mardy, I couldn't look him in the face again. I'd have had to move or something.'

Again, any woman who has an automatic washing-machine will testify to the dramatic effect this has upon her ability to show equanimity when her toddler continues to wet nappy after nappy; the mother who has to wash every one by hand, in water she has heated on top of the kitchen stove, is likely to be far more emotionally involved in toilet training. Obviously, too, class differences in income are likely to influence not only material standards of living but the parents' ability to relax with their children; as one of our informants explained:

'Our mam was stricter, we got a lot of shouting at. Well, she was worried all the time about money, where the next meal was coming from and that. And we'd be asking, like kids do, "Mam, can I have a penny for this and a penny for that" – Well, you're bound to get nasty if you haven't got it to give them. It gets on your nerves. Ours was a good mam, but it was the money you see.'

The difficulty is, however, that the sum total of all such differences is in part what we mean by social class; that is to say, they are so inextricably involved in the whole concept of class that any attempt to discount or to partial out these factors would distort the very picture of class differences which we are trying to investigate. On the other hand, it is very important when attempting to interpret these differences that such influences should not be underrated; indeed, they must constantly be borne in mind whenever we try to give an explanation of why mothers in different social classes adopt particular attitudes and behave in the way they do.

When class differences are under discussion, there is always the danger of making facile and sweeping generalizations. Each section of the community has its own prejudices about the other sections, and it is only too easy to interpret the behaviour of people in other class groups in terms of existing preconceptions which may themselves have their roots in the defence systems of one's own group. Members of one social class tend to conceptualize those of a different class in terms of a few well-defined stereotypes which may or may not be true, but which in any case take the place of real observation. In the field of child-rearing, for example, there is a stereotype of the upper-class mother, rather cold emotionally, providing material luxury for her children but depriving them of mothering by leaving them to the care of paid nannies while she spends her time at bridge-parties and committee meetings – 'not what you'd call a real family life', as one working-class informant said. On the other side, middle-class people seem to have two pictures of the working-class mother: the 'poor but honest' type, over-worked, her house shabby but well scrubbed, fond of her children in an undemonstrative way and ruling them with a rod of iron and the threat of father and the policeman; and the cheerful slut with the heart of gold, living in comfortable disorder and bringing up her children on a mixture of slaps and lollipops, fish-and-chips and love. Father is little in evidence in either of these pictures of working-class life, for he spends most of his leisure time at the pub on the corner. When we start looking at real families, however, we are forced to appreciate that truth is not quite so simple nor so well categorized as this. Sometimes the stereotype embodies only a half-truth; sometimes it is out of date; sometimes it was never true at all. Where a pattern can be discerned, we may be sure that it is not universal, even within the limits of a small social group; there are always the misfits and the independents. It is with this caveat that we attempt to analyse the interconnexion between two such complexities as child-rearing behaviour and social class.

CHAPTER EIGHT

CHILDBIRTH AND SOCIAL CLASS

We have seen that middle-class mothers tend to be somewhat older than working-class mothers when they have their first baby. At first sight the average age differences shown in Table 9 may not appear to be very large; when we come to interpret them, however, we find that their effect is maximized by certain strong cultural pressures which are brought to bear on young women in our society, and which in this connexion seem to be largely independent of social class.

The cultural expectations of our society are such that only a relatively short period of time – the four or five years following the attainment of full adult status at twenty-one – appears to be regarded with complete approval as being the 'normal' time for a young woman to start bearing children. The critical nature of this period may be understood when one reflects that a 'girl' of twenty will be considered by most people to be too young to want to be tied down by the cares of looking after a family, whereas a married woman of twenty-six or twenty-seven is thought to be leaving it rather late if she intends to have a family at all. In addition, the evidence indicates that a large proportion of marriages under the age of twenty are precipitated by the girl becoming pregnant;[1] while experience suggests that once a woman has reached twenty-six or so a strong motivating factor may be the fear of being left on the shelf. Although, statistically speaking, childbirth is easier and safer at eighteen than at twenty-eight, it is unlikely that this medical consideration affects a girl's choice in the matter; what may influence her

1. About a third for the country as a whole, and no doubt considerably more for Nottingham; see Registrar General, *Statistical Review of England and Wales for 1960*.

is the fact that, in terms of social expectation, the woman of twenty-two or twenty-three is considered to be ideally most ripe for the experience of motherhood. If she is forced to assume the role of mother at an earlier age, there is some anticipation of her regret, possibly even resentment, because she has had to relinquish the independence and freedom of late adolescence so soon. On the other hand, if she has not started having children by the time she is twenty-six she is expected to feel somewhat left out of things and even unfulfilled.

Against this background it is instructive to analyse our information about the age of the mother at her first confinement in a slightly different way. Table 10 shows the proportion of women who gave birth to their first child at the age of twenty-one or earlier, according to social class.

TABLE 10

Social class and the proportions of mothers aged twenty-one or less at the birth of their first child

	Social class				
	I and II	*III WC*	*III Man*	*IV*	*V*
Proportion of mothers 21 and less	24%	25%	40%	46%	53%

It can be seen from this table that working-class mothers as a group are much more likely than middle-class mothers to have conceived a child before the age of twenty-one. Assuming that we are correct in our analysis of cultural pressures, it can be argued that for the working-class mother the arrival of the first child involves a change of role for which she is frequently not adequately prepared. Even if she is already married, to become pregnant before the age of twenty-one is not generally regarded as an unmixed blessing, and the birth of subsequent children is the more likely to be welcomed with mild resignation; while a large number of the first

162

children in this group will be definitely unwanted, in so far as they were conceived before marriage. For the middle-class mother, by contrast, there is more likely to be a sense of fulfilment, either because motherhood has been achieved at the most desirable time or because it is better to become a mother somewhat late than not to be a mother at all. Thus the well-worn congratulatory phrase which was referred to earlier – ' . . . you wouldn't be without him *now*, dear, would you?' – expresses a sentiment which is not generally endorsed by middle-class mothers: indeed, with many of them one has the impression that they would be shocked by the mere suggestion that the arrival of children might not be contemplated with joyful anticipation.

Other factors tend to reinforce these basic differences in attitudes towards impending motherhood. Middle-class mothers, on the whole, will be better educated: this means that anxieties about the prospect of childbirth are less likely to be aggravated by ignorance and superstition. Moreover, middle-class mothers are better able to overcome any worries they may have by verbalizing them and asking for information. They find it easier to communicate socially with doctors, nurses and other educated persons with whom they come into contact and into whose care, as prospective mothers, they will normally pass. In the specific field of sex education, the middle-class girl may also have received a better preparation for marriage and parenthood. Even if their own parents are too embarrassed to give them adequate sex instruction, middle-class children generally have easier access to books and biology lessons; and not only are their requests for information less likely to be fobbed off with stereotyped evasions, but they have less opportunity to absorb those attitudes towards sex which are expressed in the conversational use of obscenity.

Class differences in education and outlook might be expected to affect not merely the mother's general attitude in contemplating childbirth, but whether she takes active steps to prepare herself for the experience. This expectation is borne out in the proportions of mothers in the different

163

social class groups who reported that they had undertaken relaxation exercises. With very few exceptions, the fact that a mother did relaxation exercises implies that she also attended the ante-natal classes which include talks and discussion on various aspects of mothercraft as well as giving information about the normal course of labour and the process of birth. Table 11 shows the proportions of middle-class and working-class mothers who reported that they did these exercises; the information for first births and later births is also presented separately.

TABLE 11

Proportions of mothers undertaking relaxation exercises according to social class

	Social class		
	I and II, III WC (middle-class)	III Man, IV, V (working-class)	All Classes
	%	%	%
All births	32	17	21
First births	52	36	41
Later births	19	9	11

All the class differences shown in this table are statistically significant, but in particular the difference for first births implies that middle-class mothers are more likely than working-class mothers to attend ante-natal classes; for later births the position is a little more complicated because some of these mothers will have been carrying out exercises learned when attending classes for their first babies, whereas others will have been attending classes for the first time in preparation for a later birth.

Class differences are again in evidence in connexion with the place of birth. We have already mentioned that mothers expecting their first babies have a much greater chance of qualifying for a maternity bed under the National Health Service; first births and later births must therefore be considered separately. Table 12 shows the proportions of home births for first and later babies according to social class.

TABLE 12

Proportions of births which took place at home, according to social class

| | | Social class | | | | | |
		I and II	III WC	III Man	IV	V	All Classes
Home births	First births	% 18	% 27	% 31	% 22	% 14	% 26
	Later births	59	78	75	72	83	74

The differences for first births are not large enough to be statistically significant. If there is a trend at all, it suggests that mothers at both ends of the social scale are less likely than others to have their first babies at home; in particular, the small percentage (14 per cent) in Class V can probably be accounted for by the relative youth and poverty of the parents, who are not so likely to have accommodation which would be considered suitable for a home confinement. For later births, Class I and II clearly has a smaller proportion of home confinements, and this time the difference is statistically significant. It can be accounted for almost entirely by the fact that a number of Class I and II parents made use of private nursing homes: in this class these account for 2 per cent of all first births and 16 per cent of all later births. The only other mothers who made use of this facility were a few in Class III WC (less than 3 per cent of later births). That the use of private nursing homes is restricted almost exclusively to mothers in Class I and II can obviously be explained on the grounds of cost. Further than that, however, there does seem to be a feeling among some middle-class parents that to have a baby at home is, at best, a necessary and makeshift expedient forced upon them by an abnormal shortage of hospital beds and maternity hospitals.[1] It may be a hangover from the days before the inception of the National Health Service that some middle-class husbands are still expected to provide that during childbirth their wives shall receive residential treatment away from home under specialized medical supervision; the tradition dies hard, even though nowadays only a minority of middle-class parents can afford the privilege of a bed in a private nursing home. At the same time, however, there is a growing body of middle-class mothers who have their babies at home for choice; this movement seems to have started as a revolt against the authoritarian attitudes still prevalent in many hospitals and nursing homes, but has gathered way as many mothers discovered in home confinement positive benefits beyond freedom from hospital restrictions, and, because they *were* middle class, ventilated these discoveries in the press.[2]

For working-class mothers, the position for later births is probably much as it was. Unless there is some special medical reason, a maternity bed in hospital is not to be expected unless the mother's living conditions are extremely unhygienic or considered by the local authority to be otherwise unsuitable.

In these circumstances, we were interested to see whether middle-class mothers were getting a disproportionate share of maternity beds within the health service. Considering the overall provision of maternity beds, and assuming that the medical need for them is not a function of social class, there was no real evidence for any effect of this kind in Nottingham. If, however, the one maternity hospital and the various maternity wards in general hospitals are considered separately, it can be seen that, whereas a higher proportion of

1. This shortage is particularly acute in Nottingham where the proportion of births in hospital is well below the national average of 64·5 per cent (see Cranbrook Report, Maternity Services Committee, H.M.S.O., 1959).

2. Gordon and Elias-Jones found that, of 336 mothers who had had at least one baby born in hospital and one at home, 80 per cent preferred home confinement and only 14 per cent preferred the hospital birth (*British Medical Journal*, 1960, Vol. 2, p. 51).

working-class mothers are admitted to the general hospitals, the maternity hospital definitely caters for a larger proportion of middle-class mothers. That this is not due simply to a higher proportion of first births in the middle-class sample can be clearly seen in Table 13, in which first and later births are again presented separately.

TABLE 13

Proportions of births in maternity hospital and in maternity wards of general hospitals, according to social class

| | | Social class | | | | | |
		I and II	III WC	III Man	IV	V	All Classes
First Births	Maternity hospital	% 49	% 33	% 25	% 28	% 14	% 30
	Hospital maternity wards	31	40	42	50	71	43
Later Births	Maternity hospital	6	3	3	2	0	3
	Hospital maternity wards	19	17	21	26	17	21

But, since the hospital at which the mother is confined depends in the first instance upon her letter of referral from her own doctor, it does seem that some unofficial discrimination is being exercised by the general practitioners in Nottingham to send more middle-class mothers to the maternity hospital; an additional factor may be that middle-class mothers both expect to have a choice of hospital and are articulate enough to see that their expectations are fulfilled. This does not, of course, imply that treatment at the maternity hospital is in fact superior to that in the wards of the general hospitals. There are, however, a very few 'amenity beds' available at the maternity hospital, which may make it more attractive to middle-class mothers; these provide extra privacy on payment of a fee, but do not give priority of any other sort, and may be used without payment in case of medical need. They do not account either for the preponderance of middle-class cases or for the consistent trend shown throughout the class scale. These findings confirm what might be expected, that the middle-class are better served by the Welfare State if only because they are better equipped to find out what is available and to make sure that it is available to themselves.

A similar situation exists with regard to the use of home helps after confinement. This service is provided by the Health Department on payment of an amount assessed according to income, plus one half of the state home confinement grant. Despite the subsidy, however, the use of home helps by working-class mothers is comparatively small: it varies from 11 per cent of Class I and II mothers, through 3 per cent of the skilled manual workers' wives, to only 1 per cent in Class V. It is thought by the authority that this is partly due to the cost of this service to the mother: in 1957, for instance, 136 of the 301 applications for home helps after confinement were cancelled, mainly for this reason.[1] That working-class mothers are not entirely unwilling to pay for help at this time is, however, shown by the fact that, of those who had been assisted by neighbours, a large proportion had in fact made some payment for this work. Exact figures cannot be given here, since in the earlier stages of the survey we did not follow up reports of neighbours' help with an inquiry as to payment: an omission which was probably due to the investigators' own middle-class assumptions! Middle-class mothers in practice probably have more need of the home help service than working-class mothers, simply because middle-class convention makes it far more difficult for them either to ask their neighbours for help or to offer payment for it.

We have described how, in order to assess their general

1. City of Nottingham, *Eighty-fifth Annual Report of the Health Services*, 1957.

attitudes in looking back on the experience of childbirth, we asked the mothers 'how they got on' in labour. Although there was poor agreement between the University and Health Visitor samples in the proportions rated as having a positive attitude, the results did indicate that middle-class mothers were significantly more likely to be positive towards birth in retrospect. It will be remembered that the use of relaxation exercises was found to be correlated with positive feelings, and we have seen in this chapter that the middle-class mothers are the more likely to avail themselves of this service as of others. As we have already pointed out, this conjunction of circumstances does not necessarily imply a direct causal relationship between relaxation exercises and happy childbirth; rather, it would seem that greater educationa opportunity engenders in middle-class children both a readiness to seek specialist technical information in the activities they undertake in adult life and a receptiveness to the basic attitudes underlying technique – in this case, the almost mandatory expectation of pleasure in childbirth prompted, obviously with beneficial effects, by Grantly Dick Read and his followers.

All the evidence suggests, then, that middle-class mothers tend to become pregnant in happier, or at least more socially acceptable, circumstances; that they enter the experience of motherhood with more 'enlightened' attitudes; and that they are likely to be more adequately prepared for the adjustments which the arrival of any new baby inevitably demands. Perhaps too much should not be made of this, especially in relation to the class differences in infant-rearing practices with which we are mainly concerned; our impression was that once the infants had arrived the great majority were treated with warmth and loving kindness, during babyhood at any rate, regardless of social class. However, the educational influence does need to be kept in mind; not so much because middle-class mothers know more, but because they seem to be more aware of the *existence* of different theories, more willing to consider different methods of doing things, more inclined to act on principle rather than out of expediency: in general, more self-conscious about the whole business of bringing up children. There is some evidence that this rather introspective approach to child rearing is gradually spreading down the social scale; and we shall pursue this point in our last chapter.

CHAPTER NINE

CLASS TRENDS IN INFANT FEEDING

Class differences in the methods of infant feeding are clear-cut and consistent. As we ascend the social scale, both the incidence and the duration of breast feeding show a definite increase. Thus in Nottingham professional families nearly twice as many babies are being breast fed at one month as in labourers' families; by the time the baby is three months old the gap has widened, so that the wives of professional men are more than three times as likely still to be breast feeding at this age; and at six months only 7 per cent of Class V babies are still being breast fed at all, compared with 20 per cent of the babies of Class I and II mothers. The class trend can clearly be seen in Table 14, which shows the proportions of mothers breast feeding at one month, three months and six months according to social class.

TABLE 14

Class differences in the proportions of mothers still breast feeding at different times after birth[1]

Still breast feeding at	I and II	III WC	III Man	IV	V
	%	%	%	%	%
1 month	60	50	50	51	34
3 months	39	34	24	22	12
6 months	20	12	11	11	7

1. Although there were differences between the Health Visitor and University samples, the class differences were consistent in both and the two samples have therefore been combined for the sake of simplicity in presentation. For statistical testing, however, the two samples were treated separately.

The fact that the decline in breast feeding is predominantly a working-class phenomenon may be thought surprising. We have already suggested that artificial feeding, as a widespread practice, only becomes possible when a society has reached an advanced stage in technological development. In particular, there must be a dependable supply of disease-free cow's milk, either fresh or suitably preserved, easily available at a reasonable price throughout the area. Once artificial feeding becomes feasible at all in a society, one might well expect that any trend towards this method would start at the upper end of the social class scale and spread gradually downwards, so that, at any given time, artificial feeding would be most popular among those women who enjoy the highest material standard of living.

This would seem a reasonable supposition from several points of view. Purely on economic grounds bottle feeding is something of a luxury, since its cost includes not only the price of the food itself[1] but also the provision of bottles and teats and their frequent replacement; nor is fuel a negligible item, for all milk and water must be boiled, and containers, too, must be sterilized – either by boiling, or by the use of a chemical sterilizant which will cost about 10d. a week. These are all necessities; the price can, of course, become considerably higher if one includes such refinements as the thermometers, funnels, bottle-muffs and electric warmers for night feeding which some mothers consider indispensable. Breast feeding, in contrast, need cost nothing at all, provided that the mother is already having a reasonable diet. Apart from the question of expense, middle-class mothers are more likely to have the basic equipment – extra saucepans, refrigerator, hot water on tap – which makes the preparation of feeds a less arduous business. Finally, it might well be supposed that middle-class women, being more conscious of a desire for emancipation from the purely domestic role, would tend to resort to artificial feeding almost as a

1. *Which?* (Consumers' Association Ltd), August 1961, estimates the cost of artificially feeding a 12-lb baby as ranging from $4\frac{1}{2}d$. (subsidized National Dried Milk) to 1s. $9\frac{3}{4}d$. per day: this covers milk only.

matter of principle; from a practical point of view alone, middle-class women are likely to have more of their interests and social contacts outside the home and family circle, and they might therefore be expected to be less willing than the working-class mother to allow themselves to be tied down by breast feeding.

Why, then, do we find a reversal of this expected trend? The answer seems to lie in the feelings and attitudes of mothers towards breast feeding, rather than in economic considerations. The wives of professional and other white-collar workers appear to be strongly influenced by the demands of 'duty' and 'principle'; and breast feeding, often referred to in books and magazines as 'baby's birthright', has the flavour of a moral obligation that they ignore only at the risk of painful guilt feelings. It is 'natural' to breast feed, therefore it must be right; it is of some significance here that while working-class people embrace what used to be the luxuries of civilization – the soft white bread, tinned fruit and so on – it is among the middle classes that we find a return *on principle* to the home-baked bread and unrefined foods which used to be the necessary economy measure of the low-income family. This sense of the synonymity of naturalness and goodness is reflected both in the baby books and in the advertisements for baby goods. 'Breast feeding is best feeding. In breast milk Nature has provided the best food for babies';[1] 'Such service to one's offspring is surely one of the most beautiful and wonderful of Nature's plans';[2] the baby 'should . . . not be taken from his mother's breast to be brought up on an alien milk never intended by Nature for him':[3] these quotations are fairly typical of the baby-book attitude, while the advertisers extol their 'natural feeding bottles' and 'natural laxatives', claim naturalness for half a

1. The Radio Doctor (Dr Charles Hill), *Bringing up your Child* (Phoenix House, 1950).
2. Mabel Liddiard, *The Mothercraft Manual* (12th edition, Churchill, 1954).
3. Dr John Gibbens, *The Care of Young Babies* (Churchill, 1955 edition).

dozen shapes of rubber teat, and recommend dried milk as 'the nearest to nature'. So middle-class mothers are firmly committed to breast feeding as a matter of principle; whether or not they find the experience enjoyable, few seem to doubt that breast feeding gives children the ideal start in life, and that bottle feeding, however well contrived the formula may be, is at best an inferior substitute. It may be that this attitude is partly the result of reading the baby books, a highly middle-class activity; but it might equally well be argued that the books themselves simply reflect the established middle-class attitudes of their middle-class authors. Be that as it may, the principle that one 'ought' to breast feed seems generally agreed, with the result that only a very 'good' reason for resorting to bottle feeding will prevent the duty-conscious middle-class mother from feeling guilty about what she regards as her defection; and this is again reflected in the baby books,[1] most of which are at some pains to assure the mother that, while breast feeding is indubitably best, she need not feel guilty if she really cannot manage it.[2]

In our sample one major reason for giving up breast feeding was the mother's reluctance to expose her breast, even within the family circle. Here again, our impression is that there is a marked class difference in attitude. The middle-class mothers whom we interviewed seemed to be much less prudish in this respect than were mothers from lower down the social scale. The reader may have noticed that the quotations which express this point of view (see pp. 37–8) are all from working-class mothers, and it is a fact that, while a

1. *The Good Housekeeping Baby Book*, for instance, says: 'If in spite of your taking all the steps outlined in the previous chapter, you find it is not possible for you to feed baby yourself, consult your doctor or the doctor at the Clinic before you put baby on the bottle. But please do not feel that you are a failure; set to work instead to make a success of bottle-feeding.' (12th edition, 1959.)

2. A comprehensive comparative study of the physical advantages of breast feeding and bottle feeding is reported in 'Breast Feeding and Artificial Feeding: the Norbotten Study.' Mellander, Vahlquist, Mellbin *et al.*; *Acta Paediatrica*, Vol. 48, 1959.

number of middle-class women said that they had disliked or had not enjoyed the process of breast feeding, not one suggested that a 'natural' activity like feeding a baby might cause them any embarrassment. Thus the mother who 'feels a bit conscious' about feeding before her husband and children, and even in front of the infant itself, seems to be voicing an attitude which is found only in working-class families, and which is probably only one aspect of that general prudishness about nudity which has been noticed by other observers.[1] Many middle-class parents have experienced the disapproving glances of delivery men and workmen at the sight in summer of young children playing naked in a secluded middle-class garden; it is possible that overcrowding and the lack of privacy in most working-class environments arouse deep fears that the incest taboos may too easily be violated. Whether or not this is so, the practical situation as it affects breast feeding is that the working-class mother often feels the need for a degree of privacy which because of her circumstances she is unable to obtain. A further consideration is that she realizes that by using a propped bottle she can save a great deal of time and, unlike the more psychology-conscious middle-class mother, she does not think of this as depriving her baby of emotional contact; in any case, psychological obligations to one's children (as opposed to material ones, of which they are very conscious) probably do not loom so large to working-class parents. Thus working-class mothers feel free to suit themselves in the matter of infant feeding; and often, as a result, they are completely out of sympathy with the advice pressed upon them by middle-class nurses and doctors who in general try to encourage breast feeding where it is at all possible. In consequence, for many of them, pretending that one intends to breast feed is just part of the ritual involved in having to have babies under predominantly middle-class supervision. That they meekly appear to comply only so long as they are under medical supervision is in line with a traditional

1. For example, Richard Hoggart in *The Uses of Literacy*, (Chatto and Windus, 1957, Penguin Books, 1958).

working-class attitude when faced with middle-class authority: direct opposition nearly always involves endless trouble, verbal acquiescence costs nothing and generally gets one out of the situation more quickly.

We can now see why it is that the class trend in breast feeding should be in the reverse direction from that expected on economic grounds alone. Probably the beginning of the move away from breast feeding was indeed to be found among middle-class mothers; but over the years since the end of food rationing a rising standard of living has made it feasible for any mother to choose her own method of feeding, and it has thus become possible to discern the operation of other class factors, all of which work in the opposite direction. The most important of these, as we have seen, are the reiteration by the books of a quasi-moral principle of breast feeding and its acceptance by the middle-class mothers who are almost alone in seeking guidance from this source, together with the working-class squeamishness which higher wages now make it possible to indulge.

It is interesting to find that precisely the same change of trend has been observed in the United States. For some years, in the late forties and early fifties, American class differences in infant-feeding habits were the subject of some controversy. While the evidence from some surveys[1] showed that working-class mothers were more likely to breast feed, other investigations[2] showed significant trends in the reverse direction. This dilemma was resolved, however, by a comparison of the different studies in historical sequence.[3] It then became clear that, while artificial feeding was in the

1. For instance, A. Davis and R. J. Havighurst, 'Social Class and Color Differences in Child Rearing'; *Am. Sociol. Rev.*, 1946, XI, 698–710. See also their *Father of the Man*, pp. 90–1 (Houghton Mifflin Company, Boston).

2. R. R. Sears, E. Maccoby and H. Levin, *Patterns of Child Rearing* (Row, Peterson and Co., 1957).

3. U. Bronfenbrenner, 'Socialisation and Social Class through Time and Space' in E. Maccoby, T. M. Newcomb and E. L. Hartley, *Readings in Social Psychology* (3rd edition, Henry Holt and Co., N.Y., 1958).

main pioneered by middle-class mothers before, during and immediately after the Second World War, the movement later spread quickly downward through the other social class groups, where it was adopted as a matter of convenience rather than on principle. At the same time other middle-class mothers were refusing 'on principle' to feed their babies artificially. This latter group and its ideas now dominate middle-class thinking to the extent that, although there has been an overall decline in breast feeding, middle-class mothers are a good deal more likely to breast feed than are mothers lower down the social scale. The main difference between the American experience and our own seems to be that medical opinion in this country has in general been far less willing to give public sanction to feeding by formula where the mother is physically capable of breast feeding.

Weaning

Unless the baby is fully breast fed, weaning occurs in two stages: the first when the breast is exchanged for the bottle, the second when the bottle is given up altogether. As we saw in Chapter Two, we have little information on the final stage of weaning, for the simple reason that at twelve months only 31 per cent of babies in Nottingham have reached it. What information we do have relates in the main to middle-class families, although even here only half of the babies had given up the bottle at the time of the interview; among the families of unskilled labourers, however, 85 per cent of the babies were continuing regular bottle feeds beyond the first birthday. Table 15 shows the proportions of babies, analysed by social class, who were completely weaned from both breast and bottle by the ages of six and of twelve months.

Although only a minority of mothers, whatever their social class, do feed their babies exclusively by the breast, the acceptance by middle-class mothers of the principle of breast feeding leads to the middle-class assumption that, if the bottle has to be used as a preliminary to total weaning, this is not really a matter of free choice: it is simply that the unfortunate mother either has become incapable of producing

177

sufficient milk or, for other strictly medical reasons, has been compelled to stop. Breast feeding remains the ideal at which to aim, and the traditionally recommended pattern of natural feeding – involving deliberate and complete weaning from breast to cup some time in the second half of the first year – is likely to be at least attempted by middle-class mothers. Thus, of babies weaned completely by six months (almost ten times as many from middle-class homes as from

TABLE 15

Proportions of babies whose weaning was completed (from breast or bottle) by six months and by twelve months, according to social class

| | Social class | | | | | |
	I and II	III WC	III Man	IV	V	All Classes
No bottle after 6 months	% 10	% 9	% 4	% 1	% 1	% 5
No bottle after 12 months	50	47	29	21	15	31

semi- and unskilled workers' homes), the majority were those whose mothers had breast fed exclusively for less than six months and had weaned then rather than start the child on bottle feeding. Possibly some of these mothers were influenced by the consideration that if they could boast that the baby had been entirely breast fed honour would be well and truly satisfied; whereas, if bottle feeding had been allowed at all, their duty would not so clearly have been seen to be done. Certainly, the statement 'I've never used a bottle' had more than a touch of pride in it.

Once a baby has become used to a bottle, it is probably true that weaning will take longer unless considerable pressure is to be put on the child. Most babies as they get older derive a great deal of pleasure and comfort from sucking their bottles, which they are now able to manipulate for themselves, and as they learn to communicate they will begin to demand the bottle specifically. This is a request which it is difficult for the mother to deny unless she is very determined, since, unlike a gradually failing supply of breast milk, this is something with which it is easily in her power to satisfy the child. Moreover, we have seen that the bottle of warm milk is very widely used as a soporific; and, since most parents place a high value on peaceful sleeping habits in their babies, this is a practice which, if it achieves its aim, the mother has little incentive to discontinue. Thus while breast feeding, if persisted in, will gradually be given up simply because there is no longer enough milk to make it worth while for the growing child, bottle feeding, once begun, tends to perpetuate itself, partly because of its convenience to the mother as a quick means of comfort for the baby and peace for her, partly because of the child's increased ability to make specific demands which are less trouble to comply with than to refuse. In the absence of a strong sense of moral duty with regard to weaning, then, the trend towards bottle feeding and away from breast feeding almost inevitably in practice involves prolonging the sucking period; and this is what is happening in most working-class homes and in about 50 per cent of middle-class homes. Middle-class mothers are, however, slower to accept the changes in weaning patterns associated with the more extensive use of the bottle, and even where they have succumbed, to the extent of weaning to bottle rather than to cup, they tend to attempt complete weaning earlier or at least to feel that the use of the bottle at a year is a rather shameful sign of their own weakness of will.

There remains this gap in our knowledge of the weaning process: at what age is the bottle finally given up by the 69 per cent of all babies who are still using it regularly at a year? This is extremely difficult to estimate,[1] since it is a practice which is frowned on by authority; on the evidence we have, and judging also from the apologetic tone of many middle-class mothers when admitting to the continued use of the

1. The sequel to this book, which deals with 4-year-olds, is still unable to provide a 100% age limit for bottle-sucking.

bottle, it is safe to assume that middle-class babies are actively discouraged in bottle feeding a good deal earlier than working-class ones. We often saw two- and three-year-olds in working-class homes drinking from a bottle; whether it was officially their own or whether they were borrowing the privilege of the younger sibling we did not ask, but the mother seldom made any comment. In many more homes, most mothers' apprehensiveness of neighbourly disapproval being what it is, the bottle habit must go underground, as it were, so that the toddler is in fact allowed to continue having the bedtime bottle, but only *because* it is given at bedtime alone, away from censorious eyes; if company is present, the bottle will be filled and presented somewhat surreptitiously by the guilty parent. Mothers who allow bottle-sucking well into the second or third year, or even later, are more likely to be working-class, then; but if they are middle-class they are more likely to hide their permissiveness, and to dissemble about it if asked retrospectively. 'If the whole truth were known about middle-class care of babies', write Davis and Havighurst in *Father of the Man*,[1] 'there would probably be many surprises on this score. For example, a good number of middle-class young women have told us that they let their children have a bottle, as a pacifier, for two years. But they concealed this fact, even from their friends, because they thought their friends would be shocked by this violation of "the book".' Several examples from our own personal experience confirm this, both in the behaviour of the mother and in her embarrassed attitude towards it.

Dummies

The use of the dummy also seems, among middle-class mothers, a matter for embarrassment. While working-class mothers took the question about dummies as a matter of course, even if they personally did not approve of them, middle-class women who had not made use of them were inclined to answer with some asperity, as if we really should have known better than to ask someone of their class such a

1. A. Davis and R. J. Havighurst, op. cit., p. 91.

thing; while those who *had* given the baby a dummy were at some pains to justify their action. The wife of a craftsman in his own business, asked whether she had tried to stop her child sucking the dummy, explained:

'Oh no – I deliberately gave it to him at six months; because he started to teethe, and he put everything in his mouth, and I thought you could wash that, you could keep it in his mouth, and it'd save him putting paper and things in.'

The following is only a part of the very lengthy apologia of a sales representative's wife:

'Yes, she has a dummy. But she doesn't have a dummy during the day, she only has it when she goes to bed; and I go up and look at her, you know, and it's not in her mouth, she'll hold it in her hand or just on her pillow. But she does, I'm not ashamed to say, because she just – she enjoys it. I mean, I know they're horrible things, but I mean, really, you think of yourself when you've got toothache . . . So she has a dummy, but we call it a nunny because it *sounds* better.'

In brief, working-class mothers tended to assume, quite correctly, that dummies were a normal part of the baby's equipment, even if individual mothers chose to opt out of the general pattern; middle-class mothers, on the other hand, inclined to the mistaken belief that if they used a dummy they were extremely atypical of their class, and an almost defiant attitude was often adopted by such mothers in anticipation of disapproval. The proportions of babies who had been given a dummy at all, and of those who were still using one at a year, are analysed in Table 16 in terms of social class. The fact that over 70 per cent of working-class babies have dummies will surprise nobody; what may be surprising to middle-class readers, even to those who use dummies for their own babies, is that well over 40 per cent of middle-class mothers reject what they themselves obviously think of as the accepted middle-class attitude against this practice.

Here again, we do not know at what age the dummy is normally given up. A number of mothers said that they had had some difficulty in breaking the habit with their other children: for some, this was a reason for discouraging the dummy with the latest baby. Many older siblings of two and three years were seen to be sucking or playing with dummies, and in the back streets of Nottingham the miniature cowboy, Stetson on head, six-shooter in hand and dummy in mouth, is no uncommon sight; the University interviewer did not see a single dummy being sucked by a middle-class baby,[1]

TABLE 16

Proportions of babies who had had a dummy at some time during the first year, and of those who still used one at twelve months: analysed by social class

	Social class					
	I and II	III WC	III Man	IV	V	All Classes
Dummy given at some time	% 39	% 53	% 71	% 75	% 74	% 65
Dummy still used at 12 months	26	38	55	57	46	48

and it seems probable that, like the pacifying bottle, the dummy in middle-class homes is kept firmly in its place as an adjunct to sleeping rather than a continual gob-stopper.

Conclusion

The general picture of children's sucking habits is, then, one of a rather high permissiveness. Especially when linked with our findings on the incidence of demand and near-demand feeding (75 per cent of the total sample), it seems that most

1. Some middle-class mothers who, if actually asked, would warmly advocate dummies, still are reluctant to buy them from the chemist round the corner, where they are known, and prefer the anonymity of the multiple store.

babies in Nottingham have plenty of opportunity to suck when they please and for as long as they please. When this general pattern is analysed into separate class groups, however, we find that the child's socio-economic level has a considerable effect upon the *kind* of sucking which his mother approves and allows. The middle-class baby has a much bigger chance of being breast fed, both during his first month and on into the second half of his first year; on the other hand, he is expected to give up the pleasures of sucking earlier than the working-class child, and is not nearly so likely to be offered any substitute in the form of a dummy: if he does have a dummy, its use will be carefully restricted. The working-class child, more often denied the close relationship of prolonged breast feeding, has as compensation a very long period of bottle feeding to look forward to, with the additional comfort of the dummy, both usually available at any time. The withdrawal of the breast seems to be accompanied by permissiveness in the use of artificial sucking media; and, just as middle-class mothers are slower to follow the general trend away from breast feeding, so they do not quickly accept the free and protracted use of substitutes. Nevertheless, the fact that middle-class mothers do use both dummies and the soporific bottle, to an extent that surprises those pioneers who fear to expose these practices to the expected disapproval of their middle-class friends, suggests that what we may call secondary oral permissiveness (as opposed to the primary permissiveness of breast feeding) is gaining ground throughout the social scale.

CHAPTER TEN

PATTERNS OF INDULGENCE

The problem of discipline, in the sense of the prevention of 'naughtiness' and the promotion of 'goodness', has hardly yet begun to assume any importance for the parents of the twelve-months-old baby; nevertheless, as we have seen, the infant's behaviour, even in the first few months, is frequently evaluated in moral terms. Thus, although babies are rarely described as bad or wicked, difficult babies who demand a lot of attention often seem to be regarded as little tyrants deliberately trying to get the upper hand in a struggle for power ('she's on the fiendish side', as one mother said), while easy, passive babies are held up as models of perfection and natural goodness.

Together with this assumption of good or bad intent in small babies goes the theory, sometimes explicitly stated, sometimes merely implied, that early and correct 'habit training' is of considerable importance as a foundation for later character building; and, conversely, that the wrong sort of training in infancy may permanently mar or spoil the child's character. Criticism of a parent's methods of upbringing frequently revolves round this central idea of the spoilt child; and this applies not only to neighbour's criticism of neighbour, or a woman's of her sister, but also to that inter-class criticism which is directed by the member of one social class against the stereotype of another. Thus the middle-class mother may have an idea of the 'spoilt' working-class child, continually indulged with sugared dummy, sticky sweets and chips; the working-class woman sees the 'spoilt' middle-class child getting away with wilfulness and 'temper' which a good unselfconscious slap would soon cure. And here at once it becomes apparent that the idea of spoiling may mean different things to different mothers. For some, its chief ingredient is material indulgence: the child is too often given the sweets, the rich food, the toys that he demands; for others, it is an indulgence of the child's self-esteem: he is allowed to be 'cheeky' or 'cocky', he 'answers back', he demands and receives his mother's attention – in short, he 'needs to be taken down a peg'. Some mothers are criticized for spoiling their children by letting them leave food on their plate, or eat cake before bread and butter, or choose their own bedtime; others, for sparing the rod and thus failing in their traditional parental duty. Spoiling may be taken by one to mean that the parents exercise all too little control and supervision over the child; by another, that they are over-protective of him and control him so closely that he expects everything to be done for him and is unable to develop his own spirit of independence.

It is clear that two separate factors are involved in the notion of spoiling: firstly, the *type of behaviour* which, unchecked, denotes a spoilt child; secondly, the *method of checking or correcting* which, if used, would presumably have prevented his becoming spoilt. We need to have these two issues in mind when we investigate class differences in the moral attitudes expressed by mothers in their handling of their children. On the first issue, are there reliable class differences in the kind of behaviour which is considered 'naughty'? That is to say, do parents in different social class groups attach importance to different aspects of child training? If they do, then it is probable that the notion of the spoilt child will vary from class to class as each group labels as 'spoiling' any failure to check the special forms of behaviour of which it disapproves; and it may even happen that behaviour considered 'spoilt', 'naughty' or 'rude' by one class may be valued by the members of another class for its 'independence', 'character' or 'grownup-ness'. On the second issue, do social classes differ in the means parents employ – the pressures they bring to bear, the punishments they use and the persistence with which sanctions are enforced – as they attempt to make the child conform to whatever standards they consider desirable?

This distinction can be illustrated from the findings which we discussed in the last chapter. There appear to be fairly clear class differences in parents' attitudes towards indulging a baby in his desire to suck, once this is no longer important as the primary means of taking nourishment. In comparison with working-class mothers, middle-class women often seem to have a deep-seated objection to the idea of allowing a child to continue with the infantile practice of sucking for mere pleasure during the second year of life. For some reason, the bottle is totally unacceptable as a mere drinking-vessel for the older toddler: it seems to have emotional over-tones for the middle-class woman which make her regard weaning to the cup as a matter of great importance, and failure to wean[1] as something to worry about. As the child nears his first birthday, the middle-class mother begins to feel that she really must make a special effort to separate him from his beloved bottle; and, if the dummy has been allowed at all, she will be setting limits to that 'bad habit' too: 'Once he's finished teething, I shall really have to do something about it'.

On the other hand, the *means* by which children, of any class, are discouraged from seeking oral gratification are not, in general, severe, especially when compared with the methods which have been advised in the past. Rarely, it seems, does the baby meet with an absolute refusal to his demands to continue sucking; the mother will hide the bottle or dummy in the hope that the child will forget about it, but she will not actually get rid of it. She may attempt to provide attractive alternatives – a special new drinking-cup perhaps, or playthings which she hopes the baby will find preferable to the dummy. There seems to be no question nowadays that the mother should insist on the child's giving up the bottle against his will: even where she is determined

1. By 'failure to wean' we imply here only that the child is still using a bottle for drinking purposes, not that he has failed to take solids.

to wean him, the process tends to be one of gentle discouragement, distraction and very gradual change, and the firmness that used to be so strongly advocated[1] has quite disappeared. This leniency in the method of weaning from bottle or dummy seems to apply in all occupational groups; the main difference between classes is simply that the middle-class mother starts the process earlier. We saw the working of this principle particularly clearly in the homes of those working-class mothers who were beginning to think of breaking the dummy habit (it will be remembered that middle-class dummies are kept well hidden from callers). Often the dummy would be pointed out to the interviewer, high on the mantelpiece where the baby could not see it, but ready for immediate use if necessary: 'I keep it up there so she'll not think about it, like. But I wouldn't stop her off it, not if she wanted it. If she cries for it, I'll give it her.' So the older toddler may be ridiculed, scolded, even smacked for still sucking a dummy; but it doesn't seem to occur to the mother simply to throw the dummy away and refuse to replace it: that would be cruel. Sometimes the mother will have 'managed without' a dummy for the latest baby, having experienced difficulty in breaking an earlier sibling of the

1. Compare this quotation from *The Mothercraft Manual* by Mabel Liddiard, 1928 edition: 'A right beginning at this time is half the battle. The mother who gives in because she has not time, or because she cannot bear to see the little one cry, is starting on the downhill path. The infant will soon realize that he is master, and can get his way in other things as well as feeding – the result being a spoilt child.

'As an example, a little girl of ten months of age who had been in the [Truby King] Home for four months was to go home in a fortnight. It was decided that she must be taught to take her food with a cup and spoon, and give up the bottle before going. She was a *very* determined little person, and for a whole week mealtimes were one struggle amidst fightings and tears; at the end of that time, she suddenly gave in. After that there was no trouble with her feeding; she took all that was given her with a spoon and drank from a cup. Surely one sharp short fight is better than weeks and sometimes months of giving in and beginning all over again.

'The importance of a firmness at this time cannot be over-emphasized; the mother or nurse must be strong enough to do what is best for the child's ultimate good.'

habit; here again, it is the long process of relatively lenient discouragement that she is consciously avoiding – a short, sharp break is simply not entertained as a possibility.

Builder's wife:

'How *can* you stop it? I don't know. I've been trying for three years to stop that one [sibling aged three and three-quarters], but he still does it. I've tried everything, I think – talking to him, tapping him, everything.'

Factory worker's wife:

'I left it off for four days, and oh she was grizzly! I wanted to leave it off completely, like, because I don't believe in her having it over a year. But I had to give it her back, because of course it helps her teeth and that.'

Electrician's wife:

'The other two had them, and they took such a time breaking off them we didn't give this one a dummy.'

Father:

'We got them to throw them away themselves, we didn't take them off them.'

Lorry-driver's wife:

'Jane still sucks it, and she's four, and I'm quite worried about her, I think she'll still have it when she's twenty-one!'

Returning, then, to our analysis of 'spoiling', in this area of upbringing we find agreement between social classes on the means by which training should proceed but some disagreement on what in fact constitutes the spoilt child. Both middle- and working-class mothers do their best to make weaning as easy and pleasant as possible; but the middle-class woman already begins to feel that she is spoiling her baby by allowing him the bottle beyond his first birthday. For the middle-class mother, then, the situation is anomalous: she has rather puritanical expectations of what the baby *should* be doing, but she is not prepared to back them up with a firm enforcement of discipline; in other words, she has rejected the strict, Truby King-inspired regime of her own mother's day, but still hankers after the well-behaved baby which, ideally speaking, was its product. The result is that she is apt to feel guilty and ashamed of behaviour which the working-class woman accepts as natural and reasonable.

The general trend against imposing one's will too forcibly upon the baby has interesting repercussions in the mothers' attitudes to thumb-sucking as opposed to dummy-sucking. Only a very small proportion of our sample ($8\frac{1}{2}$ per cent) sucked their thumbs at twelve months, probably because most of them had more satisfying alternatives; the great majority were middle-class babies. Where thumb-sucking did occur, however, it was accepted by middle-class mothers as a lesser evil,[1] in the small baby even a pretty sight, and at least a 'natural' comfort rather than an artificial one; mainly, however, because they had no choice, since thumb-sucking cannot be stopped except by rather forceful and unpleasant means which are no longer tolerated: one cannot put the thumb on the mantelpiece in the hope that the child will forget it!

Local government officer's wife:

'Well, I haven't tried to stop her because I don't see how I *can* stop her, other than putting anything on, and I did read that you shouldn't really do that.'

Probably no mother nowadays would follow the advice of the 1928 edition of *The Mothercraft Manual*, the chief exponent of Truby King methods in this country, which suggested:

Sometimes it is enough to put on cotton gloves; if not, the best plan is to make a splint of corrugated cardboard . . . ; this allows free movement of the arm from the shoulder joint but prevents the hand from getting to the mouth. These splints should be taken off twice daily and the arms exercised and rubbed.[2]

1. Despite what seems to be the general medical view that dummies, provided they are not sugar-dipped, do less harm to the teeth than thumb-sucking.

2. Mabel Liddiard, *The Mothercraft Manual* (6th edition, Churchill, 1928).

Bedtime and wakefulness

Mothers of different social classes also seem to diverge in their opinions of how far soothing the child to sleep is permissible before he is in danger of becoming spoilt. There seems to be a strong middle-class feeling that babies should learn early to go to sleep at a 'reasonable' hour without help and without making a fuss. Ideally, the baby is tucked up in his cot at the appropriate time, and left without distraction or social companionship to get on with the business of going to sleep. In line with their general tendency to discourage sucking at this age, middle-class mothers are much less likely than working-class mothers to allow their children the solace of a bottle or dummy with which to fall asleep. Table 17 shows the proportions of mothers in different social classes who give the bottle or dummy in bed at bedtime and if the child wakes in the night; these figures substantiate our previous findings on oral permissiveness and its relation to class.

TABLE 17

Proportions of children allowed a bottle or dummy in bed, according to social class

	I and II	III WC	III Man	IV	V	All Classes
	%	%	%	%	%	%
To go to sleep with[1]	23	36	47	52	51	43
If wakes during night[2]	24	36	40	47	42	39

1. This excludes children who had a bottle in their mothers' arms before being put into bed, many of whom did in fact fall asleep over this feed and were put to bed already asleep.

2. In this case the figures for the Health Visitor and University samples show a significant difference, since when talking to health visitors some mothers are reluctant to admit to such a 'spoiling' practice as giving a bottle during the night. Between-class differences are, however, in the same direction in both samples, and the combined statistical significance of the effect is quite clear.

The comfort of something more than a thumb to suck in bed is not the only form of soothing which working-class babies in Nottingham are more likely to receive than those of the middle class. When we exclude all the babies who appear in Table 17, we still find that working-class mothers are far less reluctant to give the child some sort of active help in getting to sleep – holding or rocking him, sitting with him, lying down beside him, and so on – while the middle-class mothers in our sample tried to avoid such methods and clearly thought it important that their children should become accustomed to going to sleep without assistance of any sort.[1]

TABLE 18

Early and late bedtimes of one-year-olds, analysed by social class

	I and II	III WC	III Man	IV	V	All Classes
Normal bedtime at or before 6.30 p.m.	%	%	%	%	%	%
	47	31	29	24	31	31
Normal bedtime at or after 8.0 p.m.						
	7	12	20	23	26	18

Middle-class mothers also expect their children to settle for the night somewhat earlier than do working-class mothers. This is shown by the times at which the children had in fact been put to bed on the evening preceding the interview: as before, those for whom bedtime was abnormal on that day have been excluded. Table 18 shows the proportions of babies in the different social classes whose normal bedtimes were before 6.30 p.m. or after 8.0 p.m. Here

1. It would be misleading to give composite figures for the Health Visitor and University groups here, as the difference between them is fairly large. As before, however, the trend is the same for both.

professional families differ significantly from the rest in the proportion of babies who are settled to sleep early; while the percentage of mothers allowing a relatively late bedtime increases fairly steadily as we descend the class scale, and the overall difference between classes is again significant.

That middle-class babies are much more likely to be put to sleep in a room alone is shown in Table 19.

TABLE 19

Children sleeping in a room alone, analysed by social class

I and II	III WC	III Man	IV	V	All Classes
54%	42%	20%	18%	3%	26%

These proportions could, of course, be attributed entirely to the fact that middle-class families enjoy standards of accommodation which make it possible to give the baby a room to himself, while working-class families are far less likely to be able to do so. Middle-class mothers do seem to show greater concern over this question, however, and we found indications that the availability of bedroom space was not the only consideration involved. The convenience of being able to reach out of bed to comfort the restless infant in the cot alongside has already been pointed out; where the dummy or bottle is used, the advantages of the baby sleeping in the parents' room are even greater, since teat can be popped in mouth at his first stirring and he may thus be soothed back to sleep before he is actually awake. The child in a separate room, on the other hand, will probably be fully awake before his parents hear him, and will be all the more difficult to get back to sleep. Thus, unless middle-class parents have special reasons for being prepared to endure the discomforts of getting up in the night – and it may, of course, be true that they do worry more than working-class parents about the psychological consequences of the baby witnessing the sexual act – the belief that a child of this age should have a room to himself implies an act of faith that if he has been properly trained in good sleeping habits (if he has not been spoilt, that is to say) he will not in fact demand attention at night. An act of faith: for, at this age at least, there are no consistent or significant differences between classes in the proportions of children who actually do wake during the night.

Despite the middle-class emphasis on 'good' sleeping habits, it would be wrong to assume that middle-class mothers are especially harsh in the way in which they deal with the problem of settling the baby at bedtime or of getting him back to sleep if he does wake. They are, of course, less likely than working-class mothers to use bottle or dummy during the night; nor are they so willing to take the baby into their own bed to comfort him. But the middle-class baby is not more often left to cry than the working-class child, nor for longer periods; again, expectations may be higher, but treatment of the baby is not in practice any more strict.

It seems probable that the middle-class insistence upon getting the children off to bed early is partly a reflection of other social habits associated with class. One important factor must be the 'high tea'. As we have seen, for many working-class families this will be the main meal of the day, the time when the whole family meets round the table; geared to the homecoming of the 'mester', it will probably take place at about 6.0 to 6.30 p.m. This means that what by middle-class mothers is thought of as the 'proper' bedtime for a baby or toddler falls right in the middle of the period needed for the preparation and consumption of high tea. Thus the baby must either be put to bed before his father comes home or wait until after tea; and the latter seems to be more usual, perhaps partly because 'her daddy likes to have that little time with her, it's the only chance he really gets of seeing her during the week'. The high tea habit is, of course, spreading rapidly, not only from the north of England to the south, but also from working to middle class;[1] but this would seem to be a change to which there is some resistance in middle-class families until the children are of school age: our own (non-statistical) observations are that a five o'clock tea for small children is the norm, particularly in families at the professional level. This is followed by father's return home and a short playtime, after which the children are packed off to bed and the parents are free to enjoy their evening meal together. For many middle-class mothers this is a time to be hotly defended against any incursion from the rest of the family: the evening is looked forward to throughout the day as a time for relaxation in the company of husband and perhaps other adults. People no longer dress for dinner, but middle-class women cherish the more formal pleasures of polite conversation about adult affairs in a more leisured and sophisticated atmosphere than is possible in the daytime clamour of children and chores.

Attitudes to eating

It would seem reasonable to expect that middle-class mothers, as compared with working-class mothers, would be more conscious of the nutritional values of different foodstuffs, and that they might therefore take greater care to ensure that their children should have an adequately varied diet. When our sample diets are broken down by social class, we do in fact find that the food of the babies in the professional class was more carefully planned than that of other babies, and that the diets of the children of unskilled workers were especially likely to be deficient in some way. It must be remembered that only the rather arbitrary standards 'adequate in protein' and 'adequate in vitamin C' were applied here; no account was taken of the general attractiveness or variety in the meals presented to the individual child, nor had we any means of judging how far any adequacy or inadequacy in a sample day's diet was likely to be maintained over several days. The class trend is shown

1. W. S. Crawford, Ltd, Market Research Division, *The Foods We Eat* (Cassell, 1958).

in Table 20; significant differences are found between Class I and II and the rest, and between Class V and the rest.

TABLE 20

Percentages of sample diets judged to be inadequate in protein or in vitamin C, analysed by social class

I and II	III WC	III Man	IV	V	All Classes
5%	10%	13%	13%	32%	14½%

We are inclined to think that these differences reflect a lack of understanding of food values, or perhaps a casual attitude towards a subject only imperfectly understood, rather than a real inability in Class V to afford a properly balanced diet. Poor homes there were, living on disability allowances or short-time wages; but there seemed to be no constant relationship between very low incomes and deficient diets. Many of the diets judged as inadequate were, like this one from Class V, relatively expensive.

Breakfast: Rice crispies, milk; boiled egg; bread and butter, jam; bottle of milk.

Dinner: Potatoes and butter; biscuits; about 3 oz. chocolate; bottle weak tea.

Tea: Egg, bacon, chips; bread and butter, jam; cake; bottle weak tea.

Bedtime: Bottle Ovaltine.

Between meals: Orange drink from milkman (negligible vitamin C); biscuits.

Total milk: about 1 pint.

No vitamin supplements. Deficient in vitamin C.

One might well expect that, since middle-class mothers are more careful to ensure a balanced diet, they would also more often be rated as showing some concern over their children's eating behaviour: that is, that they would take special trouble to see that the diet they had provided was in fact eaten, using strong persuasive methods if necessary. It will be remembered, however, that only a small minority of mothers could be rated even as 'mildly concerned' about getting the baby to eat; and, although we found a slight trend in the expected direction, the between-class differences were not significant, so that this hypothesis cannot be substantiated. Probably more concern is shown by mothers over the older child's eating habits, and at four or five one might find that class differences too were more clearly defined.

Toilet training

When we come to analyse class attitudes to toilet training as evidenced by the mothers' efforts to teach their babies the use of the potty, we find that Class V mothers again show a very marked divergence from the rest of the population. The first difference is that so many of them do *not* in fact make

TABLE 21

Proportions of mothers who at twelve months had not yet started toilet training; and, of babies whose training had started, proportions who had never yet used the potty for wetting: analysed by social class

	I and II	III WC	III Man	IV	V	All Classes
Training not yet started	% 12	% 16	% 17	% 13	% 32	% 17
Of those started, percentage never successful	36	38	46	42	79	46

any such effort at this stage; more unexpected is the finding that those who do attempt toilet training report such a very high comparative rate of failure. The figures in Table 21 show, in the first place, that the proportion of unskilled workers' wives who at the child's first birthday had not yet attempted potty training is significantly greater than the proportions in other social classes; and in the second place that, even when all these late-training mothers are excluded, the proportion in Class V whose babies had 'never used the potty for wetting' is almost double the proportions in other classes.

It appears, then, that as we move down the social scale, and especially as we approach the lower end, mothers tend to place less emphasis on the use of the potty and the control of urination. The trend is similar to that found in other forms of habit training, except in the very big difference between Class V and the rest, which is not very easy to interpret. Some mothers have a very casual attitude towards wetting, and allow the child to make puddles where he pleases and to spend much of the day bare-bottomed in order to save washing; but this seems to be an aspect of the individual mother's personality rather than of class; we have encountered it in every type of home, and in general it is atypical behaviour, rather disapproved of by the majority. In any case, working-class modesty seems to preclude such an explanation; in answer to our question on masturbation, it was working-class mothers in particular who emphasized the importance of keeping the child well covered below the waist.

Nor is it true that mothers in Class V all have the latest washing machines on hire purchase, and can therefore afford to be casual over toilet training. The middle-class belief that the majority of working-class mothers are more lavishly equipped than themselves with television sets and washing machines has been disproved before; our own figures for the possession of washing machines are shown in Table 22. Of course, the fact that a mother is casual in her attitude to toilet training does not necessarily mean that she has immense quantities of nappies to wash; we did not inquire into the number of times any given child's nappy was changed, but observation suggests that many children spend much of their time encased in sodden nappies inside the universal plastic pants.

197

Equally difficult to understand is the very noticeable failure of Class V mothers to persuade their infants to use the potty. The criterion here is a very low one: simply that the baby occasionally uses or has used the potty for wetting. If this is largely a matter of luck at this age, why are so many Class V mothers unlucky? If there is an element of skill or patience involved, of course, it may be that Class V mothers are less persistent in their attempts to train the child; on the evidence of those few mothers whose children were more or less trained by twelve months, a good deal of time and

TABLE 22

Social class and ownership of washing machines

	I and II	III WC	III Man	IV	V	All Classes
Mothers with washing machines	72%	61%	45%	51%	26%	48%

attention must be given to the job, and perhaps Class V mothers, with less sense of urgency about the whole business of toilet training, are unwilling to make the necessary effort at this stage. One other explanation, or partial explanation, is possible: that Class V mothers, because of their casual attitude towards toilet training, are less concerned to make a good impression and are therefore more willing to admit any failure to achieve results: while other classes, for whom the affair has greater significance, find failure unpalatable and so give more optimistic answers.

In bowel training, as distinct from training for dryness, no class differences can be shown for success or failure. For obvious aesthetic reasons, 'getting him clean' tends to be taken somewhat more seriously even by the most casual mothers; and from a practical point of view it is probably easier to 'catch' a bowel motion, since the child usually gives some involuntary warning – grunting, flushing or some other individual symptom or symptoms which soon become familiar to his mother. In Nottingham, however, we found a widespread working-class habit of holding the child out over newspaper for this purpose; and it may be that where this is done bowel training tends to become divorced from general training in the use of the pot.

Where toilet training has already been started, some mothers back up regular potty sessions with a smack for non-performance or, especially, for performance in the wrong place; as we have seen, the child is particularly likely to get smacked if he annoys the mother by wetting or soiling his nappy immediately after a fruitless interlude on the pot. There seem to be class differences in the use of smacking in this situation. We did not ask the direct question 'do you smack him for wetting his nappy?' and we have no statistical evidence on this point; but it was clear that spontaneous mention of smacking for this sort of 'naughtiness' was far more likely to be made by the working-class mother. Middle-class mothers, even those who approved of smacking in general, almost never mentioned it in connexion with potty training. One had the impression that the middle-class mother who, tried beyond her endurance, did smack for wetting in the wrong place would be ashamed of her action; whereas a fair number of working-class mothers used this method as a matter of course.

Cook's wife:

'I can't say I'm going out of my way, you know, I'm just doing what I've been doing ever since I had her, you know, I put her on three times a day; and then I tell her she's a naughty girl and tap her bottom when she fills her nappy; but otherwise I'm not trying to force her or anything.'

Labourer's wife:

'I just give her a little tap so she knows it's wrong, and then next time she'll mostly tell me. . . . I don't just smack her and make her think it's for nothing, like, I say "Look, you've wee-wee'd, it's naughty!"'

Van-driver's wife:

'Well, I put him on the pot three times a day, and then if he gets off it I smack his bottom, that's all I do.'

Steeplejack's wife:

'I should hit her for that [dirty nappy] after eighteen months.'

Miner's wife:

'I think a child shouldn't wet his bed after he's three; if he does, he should get smacked for it. That one's three this month, and she wets her bed *every* night. Well, we're only waiting for the twenty-seventh; after that she'll get smacked every time she does it, same as him [four-year-old].'

These last two quotations are representative of a few mothers, again working-class, who said that they would start smacking at some particular stage in the future if they had not been successful by that time; although no middle-class mothers spontaneously suggested that they would do this, we cannot of course predict what would happen in any household, of whatever class, if a child persisted in wetting or soiling in the daytime beyond the age of three or four. Probably, indeed, few individual mothers could accurately predict their behaviour in such a situation until they had encountered it; this does seem to be an area of mother–child relationships in which emotion is easily aroused and the mother finds herself acting in a manner that she would deplore in anyone else. All we can say here, then, is that some working-class mothers take smacking for granted as a method of toilet training, an attitude which is extremely rare among middle-class women when dealing with a year-old baby.

Attitudes to genital play

While mothers in every class showed some embarrassment in talking about masturbation, we found very clear class differences in whether the child was checked when he tried to 'play with himself'. The picture here is somewhat confused by the fact that we do not know how many of the mothers who denied genital play in their children were in fact doing so because they preferred not to discuss the subject. However, the reported incidence of masturbation did not show any consistent class differences; this means that, if some mothers do hide this behaviour out of embarrassment, the proportion doing so is fairly constant throughout the population, since we may presumably assume that the actual incidence of attempted masturbation does not vary from class to class, in babies at any rate. But, whatever doubts one may have as to the frankness of some mothers about what the baby does, the class trend in the mothers' behaviour in response to masturbation is very marked indeed. Nearly all Class V mothers try to stop the child touching or playing with his genitals at this age; only a quarter of professional men's wives do so, and it is interesting to notice that there is a considerable difference between their attitude and that of the wives of other white-collar workers.

TABLE 23

Of mothers who report genital play in their children, proportions who attempt to prevent its occurrence; analysed by social class

	I and II	III WC	III Man	IV	V
Mother checks genital play	25%	50%	57%	69%	93%

We can suggest two factors which contribute to this trend. One is the working-class sense of modesty which we have mentioned before: in breast feeding, in toilet training, in the father's care of his small daughter, this squeamishness about the exposure of the body appears as an exclusively working-class feeling; it is only in the actual handling of the genitals that a few middle-class mothers begin to impose sanctions at this age, and even here they are in a minority for their class. The second factor is probably the influence of the baby books. Genital play is a subject on which the books seem to be united in advising that it is natural behaviour for a small child and that nothing need be done about it; the older child may be distracted and 'care must be taken to fill their lives with interest and to give them plenty of affection (but) the habit itself should be ignored'.[1] That standard manuals of baby care should take this line is of course a comparatively recent development, in terms of generations of children: a comparison of two editions of *The Mothercraft Manual* illustrates the shift in advice. The quotation above appears in the 1954 edition, and ends: 'Parents need no longer look upon it as a vice'; the 1928 edition, while advising distraction rather than scolding for the older child, for fear that he should learn to do it secretly, is very definite that preventive measures should be taken where the baby is concerned:

... The great thing is to recognize the condition early ... Untiring zeal on the part of the mother or nurse is the only cure; it may be necessary to put the legs in splints before putting the child to bed. He must never be left in such a position that he can carry on the habit, he must be made to forget it; this sometimes takes three months, or longer in the worst cases. ... This habit, if left unchecked, may develop into a serious vice. The child's moral nature becomes perverted; one such child has been known to upset a whole school. The important thing is to detect the habit in infancy, when it is much easier to stop than in later years.

If we are correct in believing that the correlation between class trends in the use of reference books and in the toleration of genital play is a causal one, then one would expect that historically we should find the same sort of cross-over in class attitudes as we found in attitudes towards breast feeding: this would be shown in the middle-class mother's conscientious restriction of masturbation in the twenties and thirties, followed by an equally conscientious permissiveness in the fifties and sixties, while the working-class mother would have been relatively unaffected by book advice in

1. Mabel Liddiard, *The Mothercraft Manual* (12th edition, Churchill, 1954).

either period. Having no information on class differences in the treatment of babies' genital play in the nineteen-twenties, we can only speculate.

Even within the group of mothers, of any class, who do try to stop the baby playing with his genitals, class differences are found in the methods used to achieve this. It will be remembered that masturbation accounted for 7 per cent of the offences reported as being punishable by smacking: not a single mother in Class I and II, however, said that she would do more than simply 'take his hand away' or 'put his nappy on quickly'. Thus, even where a professional-class mother both smacks and checks genital play, she does not do the two things in conjunction; a few of the wives of other white-collar workers do smack in this situation, and in Class V more than a third of the mothers who try to stop masturbation do so by smacking the child's hands. The numbers involved in these comparisons are small, of course, since only a minority of mothers reported this behaviour in the first place.

The concept of 'spoiling' is probably not relevant to the behaviour of either mother or child in relation to toileting and genital play. While women may talk of their friends' children with disapproval because of their 'dirty habits', they do not usually use the word 'spoilt' in this connexion. The child who continues in nappies for two or three years or more shows a lack of control which offends fastidiousness but which it is assumed that he will sooner or later correct: whereas spoiling involves the possibility of a permanent marring of the personality. At a year, at any rate, 'there's plenty of time yet' for the child to learn the use of the potty, and even masturbation is 'just innocent', even if the mother 'doesn't like to see it'. A very different matter, to most mothers, is the child's control of anger: tantrums are generally taken to be a sign of the spoilt child, and the angry child meets with his mother's disapproval from a very early age. Here again, there are significant class differences, as we shall see in the next chapter.

CHAPTER ELEVEN

AGGRESSION AND COUNTER-AGGRESSION

By the time it reaches its first birthday, as we have seen, the Nottingham baby is more likely than not to have experienced being smacked by its mother. Sometimes the smack will be no more than a token expression of the mother's disapproval; sometimes it will be, very definitely, painful, and the baby will be left in no doubt of its mother's intention. Whether they do it 'quite gently' or 'pretty hard and sharp', however, the 62 per cent who smack have as their common aim the formation in the baby's mind of the concept of 'naughty'.

We found it useful in an earlier chapter to distinguish between two main sorts of 'naughtiness': that which involved or was likely to involve the child in physical danger (touching electric points or fireguard, for instance), and other miscellaneous forms of misbehaviour, from tearing wallpaper to twiddling the television knobs. This distinction was made because it had a practical significance for the mothers themselves: 11 per cent of those who smacked (7 per cent of the total sample) did so only in dangerous situations, and checked other kinds of naughtiness by milder methods.

In Table 24, these two groups are analysed by social class. It will be seen that punishment for 'danger only' shows no clear class trend: every class has its group of mothers who, while they do not really believe in smacking so young a child, find it a necessary, or at least expedient, method of warning him against dangerous behaviour. When it comes to the other offences of childhood, however, the wives of professional men are comparatively reluctant to smack at this age.

An interview dealing with the upbringing of the one-year-old is perhaps not the best setting for an investigation of

204

attitudes towards physical punishment: feelings about smacking children in general become confounded with feelings about smacking babies in particular. Our concern was with the latter; the schedule was not designed to discover how mothers regarded physical punishment in principle. From spontaneous remarks made by a large number of mothers, however, it would appear that the baby who is still unsmacked at a year has little reason to expect that this lenience will continue past the toddler age. Many mothers

TABLE 24

Class differences in the use of smacking at one year

	I and II	III WC	III Man	IV	V	All Classes
	%	%	%	%	%	%
No smacking	56	38	32	42	35	38
Smacking for danger only	5	9	8	4	7	7
Smacking for other offences also	39	53	60	54	58	55

who were visibly shocked at the thought of punishing a one-year-old in any way voluntarily suggested (and often demonstrated) that they would have no hesitation in chastising the three- or four-year-old: it was smacking 'babies in arms', not smacking itself, that was called in question. From the small group of mothers who did declare themselves to be against smacking in general, it is impossible to draw any conclusions as to class differences; it is probable that the same class trend would persist in dealing with older children, but this is not clear from the data we have. Whether a mother deprecated physical punishment as such (and it must be remembered that the question was not in fact asked) seemed to depend more upon her particular personality than upon her social class; she was likely to have shown her individuality from the beginning of the interview in a general tendency to talk at length, to think before speaking, and to offer both examples of her behaviour in certain situations and the principles upon which that behaviour was based. Her methods seemed to be characterized by a conscious decision-taking, a keeping in mind of thought-out intentions, often accompanied by a certain amount of self-criticism when she failed to reach the standards which she had set herself. The following quotations are all from mothers of this general type; the first belongs to Class IV, the second to Class III (Manual), and the third to Class I.

'We don't smack them. If you raise your voice to them, that's enough. I mean, a child's got to have trust in his parents, I mean at this age especially, there's no need to lift your hand to them at all. Like Stephanie [sibling aged three and a half], I can tell her to do something very quietly, and she'll know I'm being cross with her.'

'I don't believe in continual hitting. I think word of mouth should be enough for them.'

'I *don't* [punish her]. There's no such thing as "naughty".'

One incidental class difference which should perhaps be mentioned is the acceptance by working-class mothers of the *possibility* of really violent punishment. While middle-class mothers may distinguish between 'a little smack on the hand' and 'a good sharp slap', this seems for them to exhaust the range of physical punishment, at least for pre-school children; only once was a cane mentioned by a middle-class mother (as having been considered, by her husband alone, for a four-year-old boy). Working-class mothers, on the other hand, often referred to the use, or threat, of strap or stick or belt, and to 'good hidings', in the punishment of older but still pre-school children. Often, too, we were told of what the parents *didn't* do to the children: 'mind you, I wouldn't mark 'em, or anything like that'; the inference being, presumably, that 'marking' a child is not uncommon in the mother's experience.

Labourer's wife:

'I'm very strict in a way, you know – I can't get it out of

206

them, not really. I smack them a good deal, not hard; and I do try to make them do what I tell them – pay attention to what I say. That fellow now [sibling aged four] – you tell him a thing one minute, and he goes back and does it again another minute; and I try to get it into his head that he must do as I say, and make him pay attention to his father, you know. [Example during interview when siblings, aged four and two, wriggled behind glass-fronted cabinet, making it sway dangerously]: Come *out*, Mike, when I tell you! Aren't those bold children? You'll know that stick you're going to get when that lady's gone!'

(The children took no notice at all, and probably didn't get the stick, as they went out shopping immediately after the interview.)

Fitter's mate's wife:

'I'm really soft with kiddies, I am. I *am*, I'm really soft. I hate to see a kiddy get a good hiding, you know, or anything like that.'

Cycle-assembler's wife:

'I don't know, everybody says I'm too strict, because I'm always giving mine good hidings. I mean, the least little thing. They're falling out in the yard, and it always seems to be my two that are the two main culprits. And it's my two that get more good hidings. Other people don't bother . . . [Of four-year-old]: This is the one that has the tempers. You can't do anything with him. His Dad hits him to mark him sometimes but it doesn't do any good.'

This distinction between ordinary smacking and really severe corporal punishment, while it is unlikely to have confused our findings on the one-year-old, might well give rise to misunderstanding if the discipline of older children was under discussion. One foundry worker's wife, for instance, told us firmly: 'I don't hit any of them'; it was only in further conversation that this turned out to mean that she didn't use the strap or the stick; on her own admission, she was an energetic swiper.

Temper tantrums

How far tantrums are a necessary part of the young child's behaviour and how far they are avoidable is a matter for speculation; what seems certain is that at twelve months many children are already displaying these outbursts of rage. Some indication that they can be avoided may be given by the fact that class differences do appear in the numbers of children having 'frequent' tantrums; on the other hand, there may be other factors influencing the class trend, which is shown in Table 25. Significant differences are found between all white-collar workers and the rest, and between unskilled workers and the rest.

TABLE 25

Temper tantrums and social class

	I and II	III WC	III Man	IV	V	All Classes
Tantrums reported as 'frequent'	9%	8%	14%	15%	23%	14%

Temper tantrums in the small child seem to be his reaction to a frustrating situation which he is unable to deal with otherwise. Sometimes the source of frustration will be his own lack of skill in manipulating his material environment; more often, frustration will have been imposed upon him by some person, usually his mother. In this situation of social frustration, typically there is a clash of wills between mother and baby; either she wants him to do what he doesn't want to do – have his nappy changed, for instance – or she prevents him in doing what he does want to do.

Inevitably, in the normal everyday life of a baby there will be many opportunities for frustration, and therefore for temper tantrums. Children cannot be allowed to tear wallpaper or books, to fling cups off the table or to climb into the fire. Some mothers, in addition, cannot tolerate the noise of clanging fire-irons or the mess that a baby can get into when he tries to mop the kitchen floor or take a hand in his feeding. In general, a mother has three alternatives when a situation of this sort arises: she can give in to the baby's wish (but this may be dangerous or inexpedient); she can insist on her own course of action, possibly giving the child a smack for good measure, and risk a tantrum; or she can, while insisting that the child conforms to her will on the point at issue, so distract him by special cuddling or by drawing his attention to other attractive occupations that his frustration is reduced and a tantrum averted. In the words of Mrs West (quoted in full on p. 86), the child is *loved* out of the situation rather than being *bullied* out of the situation. Loving and distracting, however, take time and effort, and it is easier to slap a child and then let him have his tantrum out; to judge from what they say, many mothers do in fact use slapping as a short-cut method of temporarily relaxing a child's grip or his resistant body.

'He goes stiff – I tap his fingers sometimes, just to loosen him, like – he goes stiff when you're dressing him, and he's so big I can't manage him when he's like that.'

In this we may find some clue to the reason for the very small number of professional-class children who have frequent tantrums at this age. This group of mothers, as we have seen, is also more inclined to manage the baby without recourse to smacking; and it may well be that non-smacking is a good indication at this age of the mother who is prepared to reject short-cut methods in favour of treatment which demands more patience on her part, but which proportionally reduces the child's tension and therefore his need for anger and aggression. The class differences in reported incidence of tantrums cannot be entirely explained on this basis, however. We still have to account for the fact that Class III white-collar mothers, although smacking almost as often as manual workers' wives, are also rare to report frequent tantrums; in addition, there is the sudden increase in tantrums in Class V children.

Since we can presumably discount between-class constitutional differences in the children themselves[1] (and there is no reason to suppose that the more intelligent child, for instance, is any less prone to tantrums at this age), we are left with two possibilities: firstly that, aside from smacking, there may be other class differences in treatment which affect the incidence of tantrums; and, secondly, that there may be certain class factors which influence the accuracy of the mother's report. Probably both of these are involved.

Smacking is not the only short-cut method in discipline. The mother who first leaves out of account her child's wishes and then is able to ignore his furious reaction is, in the short term, saving time. A good many mothers do seem to ignore and indulge in a rather haphazard manner: a typical pattern of mother–child interaction is shown when the baby firstly is frustrated without mitigation, then has a temper tantrum, then is slapped for the tantrum, then is given a sweet or a dummy to help him get over the slap. Completely *ad hoc* methods of this sort seem to be relatively common only among Class V families, however; skilled workers' wives tend to be a little more consistent, and white-collar wives to deplore such treatment, and, whether they are strict or lenient, to show a greater consciousness of the total sequential pattern of their actions. This *taking thought* about the methods they use, typical of white-collar wives, is probably as important as any other factor in reducing the frequency of temper tantrums. An additional impression, which we shall mention again in the next chapter, is that Class V babies are more likely to be teased and exploited for the parents' amusement than are other babies; in Nottingham as in Bali,[2] this sort of treatment is likely to be productive of temper tantrums.

One other environmental factor which should be mentioned in this connexion is the extent to which the father is

1. One cannot, of course, ignore constitutional differences as a general factor in proneness to temper tantrums.

2. See Gregory Bateson and Margaret Mead, *Balinese Character: a Photographic Analysis* (New York Academy of Sciences, 1942).

personally concerned in the care of his children. From the table on p. 226, it will be seen that the most participant fathers are those of Class III white collar, whose children are the lowest in temper tantrums, and that the least participant are the unskilled labourers, whose children show the greatest frequency of tantrums. One is tempted to conclude from this that the increased total amount of attention which a child receives when his father shares in his care must help to prevent tantrums occurring. This supposition does not, however, survive analysis; correlation of tantrums and failure in the father to help with the child shows no significant result: indeed, so far as any trend exists at all, it is in the reverse direction.

There remains the possibility that the mothers' reports of temper tantrums may not be strictly comparable between classes. The mother's own attitude towards angry behaviour may affect not only whether or not she is willing to admit that her child has frequent tantrums but also whether she labels such behaviour as 'temper tantrum' in the first place. It may be, for instance, that a mother who sympathizes with her child's need to display aggression as a stage in his development – typically a middle-class mother – may not think of this as 'temper', a word which for many has connotations of unreasonable wilfulness; the mother further down the social scale, who seems more often to think of her child as a small adversary, may be far more ready to talk of his temper in a critical or even half-admiring way. Similarly, the mother's report may be affected by the degree to which she values conformity at this age; the Class III white-collar mother, for instance, may feel that she is being let down by a child who shows rage, and may thus minimize the extent to which this happens.

Obviously a peaceable child is more pleasant to deal with than an angry one; and tantrums, while they may be tolerated as a developmental phase, are seldom approved of. The child who continues to have frequent tantrums is either 'spoilt' or well on the road to becoming so: 'she's a bit distempered, her uncle spoils her, you see'. Twelve months is, of course, rather early for tantrums to be presenting a real problem; nevertheless, as we have seen, they already account for more than a quarter of babies' punishable offences. Preferences in the methods of dealing with tantrums once they have occurred are fairly equally divided between ignoring, punishing, and cuddling or distracting; there are no significant class differences to be found here. It is interesting that professional-class mothers, who smack less in general, smack almost as much as others when confronted with an enraged baby; although they are more skilful at taking avoiding action, aggression finally provokes aggression. Once again, perhaps, this leads us back to the concept of 'spoiling'. Though the characteristics of the 'ideal' spoilt child (if one may use such a term) may vary from class to class, the fear lest one's child should appear spoilt seems almost universal; and as the child grows older the temper tantrum is the plainest and most shaming symptom of all.

CHAPTER TWELVE

MOTHERS, FATHERS AND SOCIAL CLASS

Many of the class differences which we have found in the way children are handled can only be interpreted in terms of more general differences in the styles of life associated with the various occupational groups. To an extent, of course, this is true of all areas of child upbringing, and indeed of behaviour in general: we tend to live surrounded by members of our own social class, so that pressures are exerted upon us to conform in our behaviour to the norms of that class; class differences thus become defined and are perpetuated. Depending both upon the type of neighbourhood in which we dwell and upon the kind of activity involved, we retain certain degrees of choice in what we do and the attitudes we express. In some streets of a town it will be easy, in others difficult, for a mother to pop a dummy in her baby's mouth or to slap or shout at her four-year-old in public; on the other hand, whether she leaves her new-born baby to cry for half an hour at a time is far more a matter of her own personal choice. There are some areas of behaviour, however, in which the class differences that are shown are very clearly linked with the whole manner of living of the occupational group, and this in its turn may be largely determined by the conditions of work which are considered normal for that group. Adequacy of pay, degree of physical exhaustion entailed, regularity of work, stability of income and working-place – all these are likely to show significant variation between classes, and to have some influence upon, for instance, what women expect of a 'normal' marriage relationship, whether they are satisfied or dissatisfied with their maternal role, what standards of living they aspire to, how they prefer to spend their leisure time (and whether they expect to have any), and so on.

It is clear that what the father does for the children, and what he is expected to do, must be considered in this broader context. His job is likely to affect not only the amount of time he spends with his family but also the extent to which he is prepared to help in the baby's care; indeed, the whole pattern of family living is determined by the father's hours of work. This is especially obvious in certain occupations: miners and factory employees often work in alternating shifts; commercial travellers, long distance lorry-drivers and steeplejacks may spend several days at a time away from home; electricians, railwaymen and doctors may be constantly on call; teachers, shop-keepers and young professional men often work late in the evening preparing lessons, doing accounts, or working for qualifying examinations. Thus some men have finished with work once they get home, some bring it home with them and are therefore only semi-available to their families for much of the time, and some, like small shop-keepers and writers, live with their work and are in and out of the living quarters all day, as their children are in and out of the working-place.

Of particular importance in its impact on family life and routine is shift working, since it makes a good deal of difference to the amount of time the father spends at home while his children are actually up and about the house. Among working-class fathers in Nottingham, shift working is very common indeed. Some factories work three shifts: a morning shift from, normally, 6.0 a.m. to 2.0 p.m., an afternoon shift from 2.0 p.m. to 10.0 p.m., and a night shift from 10.0 p.m. to 6.0 a.m. Workers may take one shift and stick to it, so that the father is 'on nights' or 'on afternoons'; or they may alternate between shifts, working a week of nights and a week of days, for instance, or mornings and afternoons only, or sometimes all three shifts in rotation. Unfortunately, our information on the extent of shift working in our sample is not at all complete. Questions about the exact hours worked by the father were not included in the interview schedule, and the importance of this information only became clear to us as the work proceeded and we found so many afternoon interviews being shared by a father who bounced the baby on his lap, changed a nappy if necessary, and couldn't refrain from interrupting his wife.

The only question we did ask about hours of work was whether the father's occupation caused him to be away from home at nights. Table 26 shows the proportions, according to social class, of fathers who were frequently or regularly away during the night. Significant differences are found between Class I and II and all the rest, and between Class V and the rest of the working-class group.

TABLE 26

*Proportions of fathers spending an average
of two or more nights a week away from home*

I and II	III WC	III Man	IV	V	All Classes
6%	15%	20%	20%	12%	17%

Our original reason for including this question was that we supposed that having the father away from home at night would be disruptive of family life and especially of the father's participant role. There is, however, an important distinction to be made here between those fathers who normally or regularly work night shifts and those whose work takes them away for forty-eight hours or more at a time. Night-shift working, and to some extent morning and afternoon shift work also, may mean that the father in fact becomes much more intimately involved in domestic life and the care of the baby than if he were doing an ordinary eight-till-five job. The reason is that, whatever hours a man works, he will on average spend only a third of his time at work and a third asleep. For a man not on shift work, the remaining third of his life – the time he takes for eating and leisure – largely consists of the evening hours

215

when the children are likely to be in bed and most of the daily chores have been done. Workers of these hours often only see their children for half an hour or so at bedtime during the week. The shift worker's life is quite different. If he is 'on nights', he will probably sleep from about 7.0 a.m. until about 2.0 p.m., have his dinner and then be free until the late evening; if he is on a day shift, either his mornings or his afternoons and evenings will be free. Either way, he is awake and at leisure for some hours during his wife's working day. Furthermore, there is little incentive for a man to go out to seek amusement on his own at a time when most other people are occupied in more serious pursuits.[1] He is thus likely to spend his time around the house or garden where, since his wife is herself busy, he will probably be expected at least to give an eye to the baby or to look after the small children while she does her shopping; if he wants a breath of fresh air, the park or recreation ground is as good a destination as any, and the children need an airing too. Often he will busy himself doing odd jobs of painting or joinery around the house, while his wife works beside him and the children play round their feet. In general, he is likely to become more highly domesticated than the eight-till-five worker.

By contrast, the man whose job demands his absence from home for two days or more at a time is forced to make new social contacts to help him to occupy his leisure hours; and, even though he may restrict himself entirely to members of his own sex for this purpose, his feeling of participation in family and domestic life is bound to suffer somewhat. Wife and children have to adjust to becoming a self-sufficient group, exclusive of the father, for a relatively large proportion of the time, and daily routines must be established which do not include the father, and which may through habit continue to exclude him even on the days when he is at home. From the point of view of social class, however, this latter

1. The exception in Nottingham is fishing, a regional pastime which accounts for many hours of leisure time; but this, too, can become a family outing, especially in the school holidays.

216

group is not of great interest. The total involved is only about 4 per cent, and the occupations which take the fathers away from home fairly regularly account for roughly the same proportion of men in each social group; examples from each class are engineering consultants, commercial travellers, steel erectors, drivers' mates and contractors' labourers.

Night-shift work, on the other hand, is almost exclusively restricted to manual workers. A few foremen and supervisors may be required, although where possible night work seems to be left to charge hands; office workers were very rarely involved at the time of the survey, although the problems of running large electronic computers economically were beginning to make this a possibility (and a headache for personnel managers). Some professional men have to be on call, but the number who can expect regularly to spend two or more nights a week on duty is very limited indeed.[1] In practice, this means that, for most professional and other white-collar workers, being at home during 'normal' working hours is a strange and rather uncomfortable experience, often associated with illness and convalescence; holidays are the only exceptions to this, and they are restricted to certain times in the year and often involve going right away from home. White-collar workers, because of their terms of employment, are also less likely to be 'resting' at home between jobs (a situation which appears common enough in Nottingham among such skilled workers as bricklayers and painters, as well as among casual labourers); they also have less experience generally of being on strike, short time or unemployment benefit.

Working-class far more than middle-class fathers thus take being at home during the day as a matter of course; and, even if this is not their own personal routine, the idea of working at any particular hour of the day or night neither

1. Estimates of emergency night calls to doctors in general practice vary, but seem to average about two calls per doctor per week. See M. B. Clyne, *Night Calls: A Study in General Practice* (Tavistock Publications, 1961).

seems an unnatural way to live nor is completely foreign to their experience. Most of them have at some time known what it is to start out to work in the grey dawn, or to lie in late after a long evening shift. Manual workers are usually paid for the exact number of hours they have clocked in, or else on piece rates in terms of their precise output, and they tend to feel correspondingly less obligation towards their employers when they wish to take time off for domestic or even purely personal reasons: thus, as we have noted, it is not unusual for the working-class father to take a week off work when his wife has a baby; nor is it unheard-of for him to take the odd day in order to watch a football match or to go fishing – or even just for a rest, if the baby has been playing up all night. From the middle-class viewpoint, absenteeism is often condemned as an indication of a shiftless and work-shy generation, but it seems doubtful whether many workers think of this kind of practice in moral terms at all: it is just part of a way of life in which a man can now afford occasionally to choose not to work.

In terms of family relationships, what this seems to mean is that the working-class father feels that he has the right to be a part of the normal domestic scene, so that his wife must fit the domestic pattern round him. If he has to sleep during the day, it is the wife's job to see that there is peace and quiet in which to do so. The father's homecoming, at whatever time this may occur, is a major event demanding immediate activity on the wife's part, and the rest of the family time-table will be geared to this. However subordinate may be his position at work, in his own home he is the 'mester', at least in the sense that it is the wife's first duty to arrange her day to suit his comings and goings; perhaps it is not without significance that the stereotype of the henpecked husband is usually the clerical worker.

Professional and other white-collar workers usually work office hours, which not only are constant and predictable, year in, year out, but also fit fairly closely with school times, which are the other great pace-setters in a mother's day. In the middle-class home, therefore, the husband is more likely to be considered on an equal footing with the rest of the family for catering purposes; and any disturbance of her smooth, well-practised routine may even be resented by the wife as something which makes unnecessary work for her.

In an earlier chapter, we have emphasized the sense of partnership which is so often a feature of domestic family life for young married couples today. There are, however, various degrees of partnership and various patterns of co-operation between man and wife. Although two husbands may both undertake a wide variety of domestic chores in the home, for example, the roles assigned to them by their wives may still differ considerably. One wife may expect her husband to do these things as a matter of course, and complain when he does not; another may believe that the domestic work is really her responsibility alone, and that in helping her in the house her husband is demonstrating his devotion and kindness to her personally. These attitudes seem to be rather independent of social class, and must be determined both by the personalities of husband and wife and by individual circumstances such as the husband's total hours of work and the wife's own earning capacity. On the other hand, it seems to be generally true in our society that as one proceeds down the social scale the sex roles become more sharply defined and more rigidly typed. Perhaps this is partly due to the fact that in many of the socially lower occupations brawn still counts for so much more than brain; hence the distinction between 'men's work' and 'women's work' becomes increasingly obvious on simple biological grounds. It is true also that, while most of the professions are open to women as well as to men, there are a great many manual occupations which are exclusively reserved, by tradition, for men alone; and the principle of equal pay for equal work is much more nearly observed at the top than at the bottom end of the occupational scale.[1] Whatever the fundamental

1. In 1961, according to T. E. Chester ('Growth, Productivity and Woman-Power', *District Bank Review*, September 1962), the average earnings of adult male workers in all industries and services were almost twice as high as those of women: £15 6s. 10d. compared with

reason for this, it remains true that, as we move from white-collar to manual occupations, the father's work is more likely to consist of some activity outside the wife's own range of experience. It is also more likely to take him into exclusively male companionship and thus to become an area of his life from which the wife is fairly firmly excluded. Even in factories which employ both men and women, jobs at the manual level tend to be rather strictly sex-differentiated.

Within the family, these general social differences will find expression in the role in which the wife casts her husband. If he earns his daily bread by heavy bodily exertion, a man's sleep and food requirements are likely to be given a place of special importance, and the wife feels called upon to minister to these physical needs as a matter of first priority. For the man who works all day cramped at the coal face, in the hot vibrating cab of a heavy vehicle, standing at a clanging machine on the factory floor, or out of doors in all weathers, home is still primarily the place where he finds his creature comforts and can enjoy physical relaxation in congenial surroundings. The wife must recognize such needs as basic and urgent, and be prepared to accommodate to them. Her first function is to feed him. Whether or not the rest of the family is due for a meal, the manual worker expects his dinner to be ready on the table within a few minutes of his return home; if his hours are irregular, he will eat alone rather than wait. If there are grown-up sons living at home, the same treatment will be accorded to them, and if necessary the housewife will provide hot meals at regular intervals as the men come in; one informant told us, as an example of the very domineering behaviour of a neighbour's husband, that he insisted that his son, coming home from work half an hour earlier than himself, should wait that amount of time for his meal. The wife will often take pains also to protect the wage-earner from discomfort during his leisure

£7 14s. 6d. Mary Stott ('Women Talking', *Guardian*, 10 September 1962) points out that, on various estimates, women's wages rose by less than 8 per cent proportionately to men's during the hundred years up to 1941, and by less than 1 per cent during the following twenty years.

hours; when he is at home, she may deliberately avoid doing certain major chores, such as washing or floor-scrubbing, because she does not wish to upset the domestic environment while he is in the house.

Among the professional and managerial group, the wife's role is likely to be somewhat different. For one thing, she may well feel that her own duties as a housewife involve more sheer physical effort and drudgery than do those of her husband at work. With the growth of large-scale public and business organizations, many young men in this occupational class enjoy higher standards of material luxury and comfort in their working environment (in heating, lighting, air conditioning and quality furnishing, for instance) than they can expect to provide initially for their wives and families at home; furthermore, their wives are often quite well aware of this discrepancy. It may well be difficult for a woman to match her husband's status position at work by contriving a domestic environment which similarly enhances his reputation among friends and neighbours at home; and while she may privately blame this state of affairs on his financial inability to provide her with labour-saving gadgets or domestic help, she may still feel guilty if she fails, within her means, to achieve the kind of home which does him credit. Her efforts are thus likely to be directed less towards the husband himself than towards the home as his setting. She will wish as a first priority to make the house clean, presentable and artistically pleasing. She will take trouble to see that the children are well dressed by middle-class standards, and that they know how to behave when visitors come. And she will try to make sure that she herself is never caught with her hair in curlers.

In short, a middle-class wife is supposed to be a social asset to her husband, helping him to entertain his friends and associates and generally sharing in all his social activities. The arrival of young children inevitably restricts her horizons rather drastically to begin with; if she has aspirations to an active intellectual life, this may be a time of frustration and despondency, and at best felt as a temporary phase to be tolerated and lived through. Her dissatisfactions with the role of 'Mummy' can well be seen in the floods of letters from discontented young mothers, usually of better-than-average education, which periodically fill the women's pages of newspapers such as the *Guardian* and the *Observer*.[1]

To a far greater extent, the working-class wife must expect to find her major satisfaction in being the indispensable provider and minister to the needs of her husband and children. By way of compensation, the role of 'our Mam' is accorded high status value. Her children are thus a proud possession, a symbol of status in themselves, and an extension of her own personality. If 'the mester' is a king in his own home, 'our Mam' is certainly the queen, and in the ideal working-class family the roles are mutually supportive.

It seems to be generally true that many working-class women find the role of Mam highly satisfying in and of itself. She is the one person on whom the whole household depends for succour and comfort; the sure anchor to which husband and children cling. Even at work, the sandwiches made up by Mam will often be preferred to anything the canteen can offer; and children at school or in their first jobs will rush back to her during their lunch break for a quick cup of tea and a chat. The total helplessness and dependence of the young baby epitomizes her relationship with all the other members of the family; and, despite the disinclination towards breast feeding, her nurturant role is highly valued. Consequently, babies are for being picked up, petted and made a fuss of. They are to show off with to the neighbours, to be dressed up in their finery and pushed out in opulent and immaculate perambulators for all the world to see and admire. At the same time, the antics of babies are regarded as a rich source of potential amusement for other

1. For example, those which preceded and followed the series of articles by Elaine Grand, entitled 'Miserable Married Women', published in the *Observer* on 7, 14 and 21 May 1961. See also the correspondence in the *Guardian*, 26 February 1960, following an article by Betty Jerman on living in suburbia, which led to the formation of a national register of 'liberal-minded housebound wives' with fifty regional organizers.

adults. Thus they are often teased and stimulated in a way which would be looked at with disfavour by middle-class mothers. Many of these interviews were punctuated by the mother's efforts to put the baby through his repertoire of tricks and social graces, whether by tickling him, enticing him to walk, or by exciting him with the false cry of 'Daddy's coming!'

By contrast, the convention among middle-class mothers seems to be that one blatantly shows off one's children only to relatives and very intimate friends; on other social occasions, references to the child's virtues are made in careful understatement, and it is the visitor who is expected to initiate any admiration. In general, during a social call, the baby is left to get on with his own pursuits on the floor, and the mother ignores him unless he demands or provokes her attention. This is probably connected with the fact that so many middle-class mothers seem to see the period of infancy in particular, not as a time of fulfilment, but as an abnormal and in many ways deplorable interlude in an otherwise sane and well-ordered life: or at least, this is the impression which, again, it seems conventional to put forward. Ideally, the middle-class woman has a tasteful and well-run home into which it is possible to invite visitors at any hour. Once babies arrive, however, the reality frequently includes piles of dirty and malodorous clothes in the kitchen, toys all over the house, a rackful of steaming nappies hiding the fireplace and dribble (or worse) on the living-room carpet. Under these conditions she may find it difficult to reconcile her ideal self-image as a mature and sophisticated woman with her roles as a housebound baby-minder, nappy-washer and domestic slave. The resulting state of conflict and frustration may be shown in a variety of ways. She may live nostalgically in the past, remembering her early adult life, when she was still at work, as a time of gay adventure and unfettered freedom. Alternatively, she may see the humorous side of her present predicament, and put it to social use by telling funny stories against herself: how the elderly visitor, arriving unexpectedly, was guided deftly past the unemptied potty behind the front door, only to come upon the toddler admiring her naked stomach in the hall mirror; or how the cake for a party, collapsed when its baking was interrupted by the baby, was filled up with chocolate icing and passed off as a special new recipe. It is easy to understand why the young middle-class mother, in conversation with other adults, will often adopt a tone of mock callousness towards her children: 'I've decided I just can't stand babies', 'You can have mine any time you like', and so on. Publicly, at least, her aim is to get the babyhood stage over as soon as is reasonably possible, in order to return to the civilized state she fondly thinks of as normal.

For middle-class wives the ideal, often expressed, is to be able to keep up at least some outside interests despite having young children. As we have seen, however, very few of these mothers can today afford to have even a few hours of paid domestic help. The idea of delegating some of their responsibility for baby-minding to a resident nanny or even a part-time nursemaid, a real possibility for their own mothers, is nowadays only a fanciful dream. To relieve themselves from what many regard as the tedium of a purely domestic existence, they willingly accept help from the husband so long as this does not interfere with his career; and it may well be that, in modern middle-class families, a high level of father participation results initially more from the husband's wish to give his wife an occasional break than from any intrinsic desire on his part to enjoy the pleasures of handling a baby. Being able to ask the husband to baby-sit, however, offers no answer to the problem of how to share with him those outside social and cultural activities which may well have brought the couple together in the first place: occasions which can only be properly enjoyed when they can 'escape' together without the children. The only solution here is to have a baby-sitter; and in practice few couples with very young children can arrange to go out together as often as once a week.

It is clear from our figures that the extent to which husbands and wives do in fact go out together, at least sometimes, is a matter closely related to social class. The trend is shown in Table 27: more than twice as many white-collar and professional couples go out together sometimes (during the baby's first year) as do Class V couples. Paid baby-sitters are used so little that the ability to afford them does not seem a very important factor here; we would rely more on the impressionistic evidence which we have already discussed: that middle-class wives long to go out, that working-

TABLE 27

Couples who go out together frequently, occasionally or very rarely: analysed by social class

	I and II	III WC	III Man	IV	V	All Classes
	%	%	%	%	%	%
1 or more p.w.	21	17	23	22	19	22
Occasionally	54	47	35	36	22	38
1 or less p.a.	25	36	42	42	59	40

class wives are content with the television as their sole entertainment, and that working-class parents (fathers in particular) do not wholly trust their baby-sitters and therefore often stay at home on principle while the children are young. The class trend disappears when we consider only those who go out very frequently (once a week or more); the reason for this seems to be that, for many families, an arrangement of this kind only becomes feasible when there is some other willing and responsible adult living in the same house, a circumstance which is likely to be taken advantage of irrespective of social class.

We have seen that, in every social group, the father of today is taking a very large share in looking after his baby; but within this massive change in the masculine role there are certain class differences. The figures which appear in Table 28 are all those of the University sample; they are not strictly comparable with those of the Health Visitor sample, owing to a large number of cases in the latter in which the various activities of the father were merely ticked instead of being rated as 'often' or 'sometimes' (rating method described in Chapter 6). This meant that in these cases no distinction could be made between 'highly participant' and 'fairly participant' fathers. There is no other reason why differences should occur between the samples, and on the rating 'non-participant' figures do in fact agree.

TABLE 28

Participation in child care by fathers in different occupational classes

	I and II	III WC	III Man	IV	V
	%	%	%	%	%
Highly participant	57	61	51	55	36
Fairly participant	24	33	33	27	28
Little or no participation	19	6	16	18	36

The significant differences here occur between Class III (white collar) and the rest, and between Class V and the rest. Shop and office employees stand out as being exceptionally conscientious in helping their wives with the baby;[1] unskilled workers, while the majority of them will give at least moderate help, not only are much less likely to be rated as 'highly participant', but contribute twice as many as any other class group to the total 21 per cent of all fathers who do very little personally for the one-year-old. The reasons

1. It is worth noting that these findings are in direct contradiction to Dr Kenneth Soddy's statement (*Clinical Child Psychiatry*, p. 23, Baillière, Tindall and Cox, 1960) that 'Among ... office and shop employees generally ... family life will be very different [i.e. from that of skilled craftsmen] ... They are likely to have rigid ideas of roles ... For example, care of the baby until he can walk is commonly "the wife's job" and the husband takes no part.' Dr Soddy does not refer to sources of evidence for this assertion, but most of his other data comes from clinical case studies, and it may be that this very marked discrepancy is due in part to the differences between normal and clinical cases.

for these two groups appearing at the two extremes of father participation are not very clear, and we can only make very tentative suggestions in explanation. Perhaps shop and office employees fall between two occupational stools, as it were, in that they do not usually have the quantities of evening 'homework' which the young professional man must so often cope with, while at the same time their relatively light daytime work does not qualify them for the special attention and protection which the wife gives to the heavy manual worker; bereft of any excuse for escaping the practical duties of fatherhood, they therefore follow the general trend to its fullest extent. As for the unskilled labourers, it is possible that the men who make up this class do so partly *because* they are less well adjusted to society than others: opting out of the responsibility of acquiring a manual skill, they are also more likely to repudiate the domestic obligations which other young men nowadays so readily accept.

In this and the preceding chapters, we have been able to demonstrate a number of statistically reliable differences between the social class groups as we have defined them. Over and above this, in the total pattern of class differences, some general trends stand out. It is clear that, as we move along the social class continuum, differences between one group and the next are not very often of equal magnitude. There are certain very obvious points of discontinuity in the data: points in the social scale, that is to say, at which attitudes and behaviour are likely to change very rapidly. The locus of change will vary according to the area of upbringing under investigation, but it is particularly noticeable that some of the variables seem to distinguish mainly between the professional-managerial class and the rest of the population, some between the middle-class (white-collar) and working-class groups, and some between the unskilled section and the rest.

For convenience of comparison, Table 29 gives a general summary of the class differences in baby care. It will be seen that in nearly all cases there is a general trend running right

227

through the occupational groups. Where there are big differences in behaviour, the most obvious distinction is between middle-class and working-class attitudes; almost every area of behaviour shows a broad gulf between professional-managerial class practices and those of the skilled manual group which, it will be remembered, makes up about half of the general population. Of especial interest here is the white-collar section of Class III. When making the middle-class/working-class distinction in these chapters, we have included all white-collar workers together in the middle class; and it is clear that, on the criterion of child upbringing at least, we were not mistaken in dividing the Registrar General's Class III in this way.[1] Shop and office workers' wives behave in general rather differently from the rest of Class III; in some cases – the age at which they have their first baby, for instance, and their use of bottle or dummy beyond the baby's first birthday – they approximate more nearly to professional-class norms than to those of manual workers. In certain areas, however – notably in the use of smacking and the prevention of genital play – they are closer in behaviour to the skilled manual group, although even here they retain their position as bridge between manual and professional workers. The only case in which they really break out of rank, as it were, is in the participant role of the father. It is probably true to say that the wives of office and shop employees have aspirations to middle-class attitudes and behaviours, but that their limited resources, both financial and educational, determine a manner of living which in many ways is less unlike that of manual workers than they might wish.

The other main rift, between unskilled workers and the rest, can sometimes be linked with lower material or educational standards, as in the cases of inadequacy of diet or the baby's sharing its parents' room, but this does not always apply; and it is tempting to suppose some basic difference, in personality or in occupational ethos or in both, which makes

1. The 1960 *Classification of Occupations* (H.M.S.O.) does in fact make the distinction between manual and non-manual workers.

TABLE 29

Combined data on class differences

	I and II	III WC	III Man	IV	V
	%	%	%	%	%
Age 21 or less at first birth	24	25	40	46	53
Breast feeding: at 1 month	60	50	50	51	34
at 3 months	39	34	24	22	12
at 6 months	20	12	11	11	7
No bottle after: 6 months	10	9	4	1	1
12 months	50	47	29	21	15
Dummy: at some time	39	53	71	75	74
still at 12 months	26	38	55	57	46
Bottle or dummy to go to sleep	23	36	47	52	51
if wakes	24	36	40	47	42
Bedtime: 6.30 p.m. minus	47	31	29	24	31
8.0 p.m. plus	7	12	20	23	26
Sleeps in room alone	54	42	20	18	3
Diet inadequate	5	10	13	13	32
Potty training not started (12 months)	12	16	17	13	32
Of those started, never successful	36	38	46	42	79
Genital play checked	25	50	57	69	93
No smacking	56	38	32	42	35
General smacking	39	53	60	54	58
Frequent tantrums	9	8	14	15	23
Father's participation: high	57	61	51	55	36
little or none	19	6	16	18	36
Baby-sitting: once or less p.a.	25	36	42	42	59

the labourer so reluctant to help with the baby, and his wife so (comparatively) slow to start potty training, so extraordinarily unsuccessful if she does start, so apt to induce tantrums (or so ready to report them) and so very intolerant of the baby's genital play.

The reader may notice that the findings for Class IV are rather anomalous in that they sometimes do not fit in with what might otherwise be a well-defined class trend. A case in point is the use of bottle or dummy as a soporific. The reason is probably that Class IV is a rag-bag of occupations which have very little in common. They are all supposed to be semi-skilled, but in character and tradition they are very different. Some of the occupations included, such as hall porter, bus conductor and ticket collector, are partly clerical and offer secure and respectable, if poorly paid, employment; but the jobs of chemical process workers, iron furnacemen and tobacco workers, for example, are far heavier and dirtier, and there seems to be more possibility in these occupations of being laid off, put on short time or downgraded to labouring work. It seems reasonable to suppose that the semi-clerical jobs in Class IV attract men whose attitudes and general way of life have more in common with those of shop and office employees than of manual workers; and this would explain the inconsistent findings in this class.

The classless society in Britain is still a long way off. Men may be born equal; but, within its first month in the world, the baby will be adapting to a climate of experience that varies according to its family's social class. How far these experiences are built in to form a basic personality structure which is recognizably different for different occupational groups, and how far such structures are self-perpetuating in the following generation, we are not qualified to say; much, of course, must depend upon whether the basic structure includes among its characteristics the inclination to accept or to reject adaptation and change. The increase in social mobility offers rewarding opportunities for research here. It is not possible, with the data we have, to make a comparison between, for instance, first- and second-generation professional-class families; but the findings of Jackson and Marsden[1] on the attitudes of professional men born of working-class parents might lead one to expect such a group to adopt the stricter aspects of middle-class upbringing methods, while rejecting their more permissive attitudes. This is pure speculation; but it is an investigation which could be made, and especially at such a time as this when we know that both social mobility and class differences in behaviour are high. What we can never know is whether the different classes are closer or further apart in their attitudes to child care than they were thirty years ago. One would expect the former; better education combined with the middle-class trend towards flexibility and away from rule-worship would suggest a gradual rapprochement. Thirty years hence, we shall be in a position to make the comparison.

1. Brian Jackson and Dennis Marsden, *Education and the Working Class* (Routledge and Kegan Paul, 1962).

PART THREE

THE LONGER VIEW

CHAPTER THIRTEEN

THEN AND NOW

How far do the attitudes and the practices which we have described in this survey belong exclusively to the modern generation of mothers? To what extent, and in what ways, do the early experiences of our children resemble those of our own childhood? To answer these questions with any degree of certainty is very difficult indeed. We may find certain aspects of present-day child rearing surprising, or even shocking; but we can only be sure that modern mothers behave differently from their own mothers in so far as we have evidence about how most mothers actually did behave in the past. When looking for points of difference, it is all too easy to be misled by one's own personal memories of childhood; and, unfortunately, this is a subject on which we have very little reliable information. The main sources available to us are the baby books of twenty or thirty years ago, the memories of today's grandmothers and the picture of childhood which we find in autobiographies. We have already seen that contemporary baby books are a rather poor indication of what actually happens in the home; and since, according to the grandmothers, babies twenty-five years ago were nearly all fully toilet-trained by twelve months, retrospective evidence over two or three decades seems, hardly surprisingly, as suspect as that which looks back over five years. As for the autobiographies, while many of them are rich in evocations of a past world, and some are exceptionally successful in presenting relationships and happenings with the eye of childhood,[1] few are very illuminating on the

1. Of especial interest to the student of early childhood is James Kirkup's *The Only Child*, together with its sequel, *Sorrows, Passions and Alarms* (Collins, 1957, 1959).

subject of parents' attitudes to child upbringing in general
and baby care in particular: again, there is the taking-for-
granted that babies are really all brought up in much the
same way, the 'normal' way, until they reach eighteen
months or so. But, even if more information could be
gathered from autobiographies, the writers of books on
childhood hardly form a cross-section of society: most of
them are of middle-class origin, many were brought up in
rather exceptional circumstances or among exceptional
people (which is why they have written their books) and,
while we may be grateful for any sidelights which they may
give on parent–child relationships in individual families, it
can be dangerous to draw generalized conclusions from such
a source. The fact that 'ordinary' middle-class people are at
least more likely than 'ordinary' working-class people to
write their autobiographies, and also that it is the middle-
class mothers who read and are influenced by baby books,
does presumably mean, however, that we are on firmer
ground in discussing changes in child rearing among the
middle-classes than we are in speculating upon changes
which may have occurred further down the social scale.

Any conclusions which we may come to on this topic,
then, cannot be supported by statistical evidence of the sort
which we have used in previous chapters; we are forced to
rely rather heavily upon our general impressions based on
the mothers' own opinions, which must themselves be not
altogether reliable. Most of the statements which we shall
quote were made in response to the final question of the
University interviewer: [1] 'Would you say you are bringing

1. The interview originally ended with the question: 'How would
you describe . . . .'s character? What sort of little boy/girl
would you say he/she was?' While this served its main purpose of
bringing the conversation pleasantly to a close, the answers we received
were valueless in that mothers seemed to say 'Oh, he's lovely', 'he's
ever so nice', 'he's a little devil', more or less haphazardly. The question on upbringing changes was therefore substituted, but in the University sample only, since we considered the answers to be useful im-
pressionistically rather than statistically; thus their value was largely
dependent upon the use of the tape recorder.

up your children the same way as you yourself were brought up, or differently?' Thus the evidence we have not only compares present behaviour with remembered behaviour, but contrasts a mother's attitudes, seen from her own point of view, with her parents' attitudes *seen from the point of view of the child that was*. None the less, we believe that these opinions are valuable, not least because in many cases it was obvious that a mother's whole relationship with her children was built round the rejection of some remembered injustice or neglect of her own childhood.

The question was deliberately framed rather vaguely so that our informants could single out for themselves those changes which to them seemed especially significant; but we soon found a definite pattern of responses being formed. For some mothers, the great and obvious change was in material standards of living: they had been brought up in want, whereas their children knew hunger only as appetite. For others, it was the trend away from strict, and even harsh, discipline, and towards a greater flexibility, which was the salient feature. One aspect of this, so often discussed that it deserves a category of its own, was the greater freedom of speech between parent and child, occasionally deplored as 'cheekiness', but much more often welcomed as making for a relationship of real friendship between them. These were the major changes; there was a large number of mothers who remembered particular incidents or aspects of their own treatment in childhood and were determined to act differently themselves; and there were a few who had been brought up in unusual circumstances and who recognized in these the origin of some of their later attitudes towards their children.

The thirty- to forty-year-old generation is often castigated for lack of political fervour and for asocial self-interest. The Welfare State, say the critics, has sapped people's sense of responsibility: never having experienced the salutary incentive of mass unemployment, they take for granted the bread and butter for which their fathers toiled and were grateful, and have the impudence to demand jam on it. While it may be true that most people are now able to take as a right what once they had to beg for, the answers we received to our last question showed that memories of the 'bad old days' were still very much alive in the minds of working-class mothers; indeed, one of the most striking features of these quotations is the extent to which recollections of childhood are coloured by the social conditions which formed the background to family life.

Furnaceman's wife:

'No, I'm bringing mine up quite different. 'Cause when I was little we were very poor; well, I ain't ashamed to say it now, it's long ago; but we never had what they have nowadays, did we? I mean, sixpence or a shilling is nothing every day now, is it? And we never had more'n a ha'penny. We were a big family, you see, and of course wages were very poor then, weren't they, when I was small. And it was hard, very hard, to bring them up. I think everybody was the same – well, unless the rich people.'

Labourer's wife:

'I've noticed children don't eat the way we used to. I mean, they're faddy over food, they don't like this and they don't like that, whereas we – well, we'd eat what we was given, and thank God for it. That's it, I suppose – I mean, they get plenty now, they can afford to be choosy. Oh, it's very different now, isn't it? When we was young I can remember if we got two slices of bread to go to bed on we thought we'd had a party – specially if we got best butter on it! And you know you never see a kiddy with rickets now, do you? They're lovely, all of them. My sister had rickets, she had to have both legs broken for it. That's a thing you never see now. They say the cod-liver oil's for that – though mind you I've never given it to mine.'

Lorry-driver's wife:

'There was a big family of us. We had a *really* hard time, because my mother's always had bad health; and we haven't been able to have things that Sharon'll probably get. I mean, there's been Christmases when I haven't had a toy – when my father's been out of work, you know; and all those sort of things, well I don't think she'll ever have to go through that. She'll never be short like we were when we were kids. She'll have a bit better chance than what I had.'

A better chance: for many, this was the criterion of social progress, and it was a point that recurred again and again.

Miner's wife:

'Well you try to do a bit more for them, don't you? I always think you try to do just a bit more than you think was done for yourself.'

Postman's wife:

'I try to give these what I didn't have, you see – not just for that reason alone, but I like them to have it if I can afford it.'

Roundsman's wife:

'No, I'm definitely not. Well – I think – there wasn't the food, there wasn't the money, there wasn't the clothing when we were little. It was a harder way of being brought up – mind you, in the long run we was better off for it. Well, I think kiddies of today are pampered too much.'

(Do you mean you think your upbringing made you tougher?)

'Well, it hasn't made *me* tougher, it's made me softer. I think myself you give in to your own where you couldn't have it – you think to yourself, well I didn't get this, and I'll see that he gets it. I think that's the whole attitude of a lot of people.'

Window-cleaner's wife:

'So long as my husband can give the children more than he had, he's satisfied.'

Many other differences which the mothers mentioned were clearly related to this basic economic factor. It is widely recognized, for instance, that today children of every age enjoy a great deal more personal freedom in all sorts of ways than did their parents. Some of these mothers thought, however, that this was at least partly due to very practical considerations bound up with higher standards of living. Nowadays, parents literally can afford to let their children do more as they please. If a child has several changes of clothing upstairs, it matters so much less if, on occasion, he gets thoroughly dirty; and, when this happens, it is no longer necessary to put him to bed while his clothes are washed and dried again. Similarly, the cost of replacing clothes is no longer quite such a nightmare to most mothers, so that they are able to worry less about the damage and wear caused by crawling, climbing, and enjoying an occasional rough and tumble on the ground. When it is not quite so necessary to save shoes to pass on from one child to the next, scuffed toecaps are no longer a major calamity. Perhaps an additional factor in this freedom is that the general standard of children's clothing is so high that the difference between 'ordinary' and 'best' clothes is not now so great; nor should we forget that today's frilly petticoat is something to be worn every day, rinsed through and dripped dry over the sink at night, whereas twenty years ago it might represent half an hour's solid work in washing and ironing.

Scaffolder's wife:

'I'm bringing them up better. They used to stick to routine too much. They weren't allowed to have their freedom. You know, play and do things. I wasn't allowed to do things like playing with soil and things like that, like Lynn does – I wasn't allowed to ever get dirty. I was never allowed to make a mess.'

Dispenser's wife:

'Oh, my mother ruled us with a rod of iron; she did, we had to toe the line. I allow mine more freedom. Well, we used to be sent out like a bandbox on a Sunday and we were expected to come in the same way. Well, I send mine out respectable, and I do raise the roof if they come home looking as if they've been through a hedge backwards, but I do give them more way. And I give them more money – mind you, times are different – and I let them have their friends in, they're all over the house and they do what they want.'

Warehouseman's wife:

'They've got more freedom haven't they, today, kiddies have, than what we had. I mean, when I was young we didn't have so much money; and another thing, we had to go to Sunday School, I mean we *had* to go; I mean, it wasn't just put up to you, oh you please yourself, we'd *got* to go. On a Sunday you used to have your best clothes on, didn't you, and you used to have them on all day . . . I mean, we used to have to look after us clothes, but today they don't seem to bother, do they?'

Garage-owner's wife:

'We're a bit more free and easy; I mean, Sundays, when we were young, meant best clothes and no toys and sit still, but my children wear jeans on Sunday and we go up to the allotment and get really messy. They did go to Sunday School for a bit, but Brenda said "It's nothing but standing up and sitting down, we'd rather come to the allotment with you".'

Memories of harder times, now past, were also evident in the way so many of these parents took a conscious pleasure in being able to give their children more than the simple necessities of life.

Tobacco-packer's wife:

'There's so much more money these days, you can afford to be silly over your children, take them for holidays and that. I never saw the seaside till I was sixteen, my dad was on the dole all the time we was kids, but Janet went to the sea when she was four months, and she's going again next month.'

The changes in the strictness with which children are and used to be brought up were very frequently discussed, and there was general agreement that parents nowadays are not the disciplinarians they used to be. We heard much about harsh punishment which at that time was taken for granted, at least within the informant's immediate environment: 'In them days they was really strict towards you, you used to get a good hiding for the least thing'; 'When I was being brought up by my grandad, they could use the belt on you'; 'My father was a hard man, and we often had the stick'. Sometimes the recollection of punishments which seemed unjustified still rankled, even after twenty or thirty years.

Machine operator's wife:

'I used to get good hidings that I didn't deserve, and all like that, you know. Really, sometimes I think about it, you know.'

It was recognized, however, that social conditions might have some bearing on parental strictness. Mothers frequently made excuses for their own mothers' harshness, realizing that parents nowadays rarely suffer the very severe frustrations and anxieties which must accompany low wages and under-employment.

Tobacco worker's wife:

'Our mam was stricter, we got a lot of shouting at. Well, she was worried all the time about money, where the next meal was coming from and that. And we'd be asking, like kids do, "Mam, can I have a penny for this and a penny for that" – well, you're bound to get nasty if you haven't got it to give them. It gets on your nerves. Ours was a good mam, but it was the money you see.'

Railwayman's wife:

'I'm bringing mine up differently. For one start, we never knew where the next meal was coming from. My dad was out of work from the General Strike. Where my mother went wrong, I try to . . . you know . . . She always left us at night-time – she was working. Don't think I'm trying to blacken my mother, sort of thing, but . . . you know, we used to have two penn'orth of meat between us and a penn'orth of chips between six of us. Well, I thought to myself, my children will never be like that; and they never have been. Of course, conditions are different, but they've always got their meals on the table. My mother nearly killed me once for pinching a ha'penny off the shelf. She did, honestly – but then, you see, things were very bad then. . . . They were bad old days, I wouldn't like those to come back.'

Many mothers emphasized that, beyond the mere relaxation of discipline, there is a new warmth and companionship in the present-day relationship between parents and children; and it is possible that this trend, too, is the result of a more general change in the social background which makes it possible for families today to enjoy much more real leisure together. The advent of the forty-hour week and the tendency to finish the week's work on a Friday night mean either that the breadwinner can enjoy two clear days of domestic relaxation with his family at the weekend, or that he is making considerable overtime money, some of which will probably be spent on acquiring new labour-saving devices in the home. Again, in Nottingham, slum clearance and rehousing has proceeded at a reasonably steady pace during the last ten years; and, although it is fashionable (sociologically speaking) to deplore the dreariness and tedium of community life on modern housing estates, it should not be forgotten that the houses themselves are a tremendous improvement on the cramped, unhygienic and squalid slum terraces which they are replacing. With running hot water and a modern bathroom, simply getting the family clean is no longer the major operation it once was; and in a council-house kitchenette the modern mother probably completes her routine housework a good deal more quickly and efficiently than her mother could hope to in an old-fashioned back scullery. Leaving aside the washing machines and vacuum cleaners, which many mothers are still not able to afford, technological progress has benefited the housewife in a great many minor but highly significant ways: it is easy to forget what washing-up was like before the end of the war brought synthetic detergents to the general public, or how we managed before the great plastics revolution gave us cheap polythene kitchen utensils and wipable melamine working surfaces. Floor-scrubbing on hands and knees is out of fashion, and foodstuffs are increasingly available in a form which is easier for the housewife to prepare for the table. Modern conditions of work, both in the factory and in the home, have eliminated much of the drudgery in the lives of ordinary people in recent years; and a consequence seems to be that many young couples are now able to enjoy the simple pleasures of bringing up a family as never before. Whether or not one chooses to emphasize the economic and material factors here, it is generally agreed among these mothers that, in the space of a single generation, a great change has come about in parent–child relationships. Children these days, it is said, are able to 'talk to' their parents in a way which, for a considerable number, seems to have been quite impossible before. Partly this reflects a new feeling of equality between parents and child, which allows the parents to accept correction from the child and even to take pride in it; partly, it seems also a matter of frankness: a willingness on the parents' part to answer the child truthfully, without continually taking refuge on the parental pedestal.[1]

Driver's wife:

'I think there's a much closer relationship between parent and child – of course, I was one of a big family – but I notice it with my older children; they can talk to me a lot easier than ever I could with my mother – even though she was a real good mother, I mean she was a wonderful person really, but you just couldn't get through to them in those days, I don't think, same as mine do to me. I think they're better for it, they want to be able to confide in you now and again; mind you, times have altered – there seems to be a greater pace altogether these days, they grow up very quickly.'

1. The shrinking of this pedestal, incidentally, seems to be the salient (and rather shocking) feature of English life, according to a group of 'au pair' French, German and Swiss girls with whom we have discussed national differences in child upbringing.

Salesman's wife:

'I had a good home, a clean home, I had good food, I had a holiday every year, I was dressed quite nicely, I had my pocket money – BUT – I could never go to my Mum or my Dad and tell them any problem I'd got or any trouble I had – I couldn't go. I mean, Annette [fourteen] will come and tell me things my eyes open wide at, I mean she takes it as a matter of fact it's quite all right to tell us, because we discuss things with her. My mother's often said to me, "You let her do so-and-so? or say so-and-so?". I say to her, "Don't forget, Mum, I was working for five bob a week, and I didn't know half as much as Annette knows now; and *I've* told her, her *mother*; you never told *me*." "Oh, well, it was different in those days," she says.'

Shop manager's wife:

'Well, I think the best way I can tell you that is with Jennifer [eleven]. Now she's getting to the age when she is growing up, and she should know quite a lot of things about – well, different things, shall we say; well, there's not much she *doesn't* know about now. Well, when I was Jennifer's age I didn't know – I was never told – and I don't think that's right. I think they *should* know as soon as they start to ask anything – I mean they *ought* to be told. Same as when your periods start – well, when mine started, oh, I was frightened to death, I didn't know *what* was the matter with me; and of course I didn't tell my mother, until she found out. Well, Jennifer *knows*, and so of course she's *not* frightened. And also I've told mine – when I'm carrying a baby – they know where it is; and they know how it's born. Well, I didn't know – in fact, I don't think I really knew how a baby was going to be born until I started carrying Jennifer. I'd no idea where it came from or how it came away or anything! But I think you should tell them – because it can get them into trouble, especially girls.

'Well, as I say – she's just started, this week in fact, the first signs of it started; well, she came straight away and told me. Well, I don't think there's anything if she wanted to know she wouldn't come and ask me; and if it came to it, I don't think she'd mind telling her Daddy, if I wasn't here. You see, they *can talk*; we've never hidden anything from them; and I think that's how a lot of children do get into trouble when they first start going out with boys. I'm not saying she *won't* get into trouble, I mean she may do, but at least she will know what she's doing. . . . I hope there'll be more understanding between us.'

Machine operator's wife:

'I never had what you'd call – any love – from my mother. Now with ours I think that's the main thing, because even with our Patricia [five] – I'll put her on my knee and nurse her and love her, and she comes and asks me for it; well, I can never remember having any of that. I could never hold a conversation with my mother, well even now I can't – seems as though we're distant somehow, funny isn't it? Yet I think a lot *of* her, but I couldn't just talk to her like I'm doing you. We can't get near each other . . . I don't know if it's because of me being a bit timid of my mam, but my little girl has her say; I have to listen to her say, you see; and then I'm not right, you see, the little one knows it all, I don't know nothing!'

There was, unhappily, a rather large number of mothers who had felt themselves to be unloved in childhood; not un- naturally, this for them became the focus of differences in upbringing. One wonders how far affection in the home is something in which there has been a change from one generation to another, and how far it is a function solely of the individual personality. While it is clear that certain personalities find it easy and others difficult to *show* love to their children, there are some social factors which would seem to militate at least to a degree against the free expres- sion of affection. The mother who is anxiety-ridden because of poverty becomes highly irritable, snaps at the child when she would prefer to caress him: 'You're bound to get nasty if you haven't got it to give them.' Similarly, for the heavily over-worked woman a real effort has to be made simply to find time for the cuddling and comforting which a small child demands at odd moments throughout the day; and, while the physical helplessness of a baby ensures him at least a basic minimum of handling, the toddler, whose psychological need is probably greater, is likely, where time is in very short supply, to be pushed out to 'stand on his own two feet'. The old saying 'When poverty comes in at the door, love flies out of the window' may be true for the small child in the very practical terms of the attention and response he receives from his mother: which, after all, is his only means of measuring her love for him. The fact that parents nowadays do not feel so strongly the need to elevate themselves on to a different plane from their children, to *enforce* 'respect', must also help to foster the atmosphere of love within the home. It does not seem over-optimistic to hope that an investigation thirty years hence would arouse fewer memories of childhood loneliness and rejection.

Clerk's wife:

'My mother was stricter, and she nags a lot. And another thing: my children know I love them; I let them see I do, whereas my mother – she just wasn't that sort of person, she couldn't show she loved you. Well, I used to think she didn't love me. I thought she just didn't bother about me at all. I think children want to *know*, they want to *see* that you do. Well, I make sure mine know I love them, and my husband's the same.'

Twist-hand's wife:

'My mother always went to work and we never had the love – and – we used to come home to an empty house and – you know – everything was so different. I mean we used to come home and no mother there . . . I used to have to bring all my other brothers and sisters up, and you know – I've always had to do it, and I've always had to do housework from eleven. I never seemed to have no break . . . My mother was stricter than me – my mother *was* strict. I'm not strict, but I like them to do as they're told, you know what I mean – let them go so far, and if you get really cross they know. But with the baby, now – well, my mother'll tell me to give them plenty of love. My mother always says the first year they want plenty of love, she's always told me that, "always love a baby" – so I think she must have picked us up when we was real tiny. She did when we was tiny, but not later on when you could remember, you know.'

Factor's wife:

'I was spoiled – I had everything I wanted. What I *didn't* have was plenty of cuddling, and I make sure my children get that.'

Toolsetter's wife:

'No, I'm not bringing mine up the same, because, er – I don't think my mother had any love for children really, and children always know. I mean, to be quite honest, I didn't go in for my family [she has six] and I didn't want it; I think three's a nice family; but if you've got them, they're your responsibility, and it's up to you to share everything with them, sort of thing. Well, I don't think my mother actually did that really. We never seemed to be . . . she didn't starve us, we were well fed, and we were always clean and that; but it was always lacking that feeling of affection. Well, I hope that's not lacking here. I think I'm less strict with my children – well, I think that's just a movement of the times.'

(Do you think it's a good thing?)

'No, I don't *really*, but if the times move you can't stand still or go backwards. No, I don't really think it's a good thing, because I had far more discipline and I don't think it hurt me at all. I had far more smacks than these children *ever* get, but I don't think it did me any harm, it taught me manners and things like that, which I find it *very* difficult to teach children today. In fact, *I* can't teach it to them; I find that when they get to secondary school, then they *do* do that for the teachers, you see, which they won't do for you.'

'Times have altered'; 'that's just a movement of the times'; 'if the times move, you can't stand still or go backwards'. A good many mothers were very conscious of being caught up in social trends of which in some aspects they did not altogether approve, but which they found it difficult to withstand. An example often cited was the pressure towards the material indulgence of children. There does indeed seem to be a widespread social feeling that young children today are the most important part of the community, in whom is vested the communal desire for an even better life in the future; and it is difficult to gainsay the emotional argument that little children should be the first to enjoy the fruits of a more affluent society. Reinforcing the natural wish to 'give these what we didn't have' are the pressures of commercialism and the demands of the children themselves. Television advertising jingles replace nursery rhymes; supermarkets, by siting enticing packets at the child's eye-level, make use of him as an efficient agent in the wheedling of shillings from his mother's purse; and every council estate seems to have at least three ice-cream firms continually patrolling its roads. The chimes of these vans must be one of the most penetrating noises of modern living; few of our housing-estate tape recordings are without this interruption,[1] followed by an insistent 'Can I have an ice-cream?' from the older children. A refusal, of course, is met by 'Oh, but so-and-so's having one!' – for where so many mothers have the means to indulge, there will always be some other child who 'has what we haven't got' so that 'it isn't fair'. So, while many mothers give because they enjoy doing so, and many because it temporarily puts a stop to the demands, many are more indulgent than they think is right because they do not wish their children to feel hard done by in comparison with their playmates, or because they do not want to be thought mean by the other mothers; the old-fashioned moral arguments, which may still be subscribed to in theory, do not seem to help them very much in the practical situation of standing out against the prevailing tide. Thus a common complaint was that the mother felt compelled by the social ethos to behave towards her children in ways which she did not

1. Even as these words were written, an ice-cream van drew up a few yards from the house: the second of the morning.

entirely endorse. Sometimes she blamed herself for this; sometimes she blamed other parents; and often it was 'the times' which to her seemed out of joint.

Depot manager's wife:
 'I think we've given them too many things – toys and that – they don't look after things the way we used to have to.'

Miner's wife:
 'We didn't have the advantages, when we were kiddies, of what they have today; I mean, when we were kiddies we had a penny a week pocket-money: now mine come in every day, threepences and sixpences at a go – half a crown for the pictures on a Saturday; my little lad [eleven] wants a pair of flippers, two pound nine and eleven, for next Saturday – for the baths. Jim said, "I'll buy them if you can get them for ten bob." "Oh", he says, "I can get them for nine and eleven"; so Jim says, "Well, you can have them, then". But, "Oh", he says, "oh, they're not much good, I want to have what Kevin's got" – two pound odd! New bathing costume he wants, he wants a new bike, new pair of roller skates – when he gets them!' [she laughed].

There were some bewildered mothers (and fathers) who seemed to imply that today's children somehow differ by nature from children as they used to be: twentieth-century changelings foisted on unwilling parents not by the fairies but by modern times.

Bricklayer's wife:
 'Oh, children never hear anything these days. You have to tell them two or three times before they can hear you – in fact, you have to raise your voice. I do – they're not so well-behaved today as they were when we was young. They don't think so much of other people, of their parents, these days. I don't know – I think time changes and kiddies change with it, don't you?'

Dyer's labourer's wife:
 'When they get big they're very difficult, aren't they? they

seem to be more full of life than we was, I don't know if it's
the war that's done it or what. They seem to like their own
way a lot more, don't they? I don't know whether it's us
that's doing it or not.'

Unemployed labourer (disabled):

'When I got a pasting off my parents, I'd just sit down and
be quiet, you see – kind of mope; but these don't – they seem
to glory in it – like it more, you know – they seem to be
cheekier. Well, I think part of it's the food now, you know. I
mean, when *we* used to get home it was a slice of bread and
marge and that was it, you see. Well, you don't feel like being
cheeky with just a slice of bread and marge inside of you.
Now they get a good tea and a bit of meat, they've got something to be cheeky *on*.'

Perhaps this last explanation is not so fanciful as might at
first sight appear. It is a matter of common observation that
normally high-spirited and mischievous children may become pathetically docile and 'good' when they are off-colour
or sick. It is therefore not unreasonable to suppose that
undernourished children who are seldom in a really healthy
condition may come to depend heavily upon the goodwill of
their parents, and, as a consequence, become more amenable
to ordinary disciplinary control.

The quotations we have given in this chapter have in the
main shown the reactions of working-class parents to our
question; this is partly because more working-class than
middle-class mothers were interviewed, but mainly because
the social changes which we have discussed have been far
more sweeping for working-class families. This is obvious
where changes in material standards are concerned; but it is
probably also true, to a lesser extent, for changes in strictness and general discipline. A. S. Neill, Bertrand and Dora
Russell, Susan Isaacs and the psychoanalysts were writing
thirty years ago, and being read by forward-looking young
middle-class professional people; since that time, there has
been a steady percolation of educational ideas through the
social class structure. Thus middle-class mothers, especially

among the upper professional group, were more inclined than working-class ones to say that they were using much the same methods as their own mothers; the change towards greater permissiveness, and especially frankness, was noted by some; otherwise, the chief difference of which they were conscious seemed to lie in the increase of household chores in the absence of paid domestic help, coupled with a more vocal wish to escape from domesticity, either into the professional work for which they had been educated, or simply into the leisure which they had been brought up to expect. It is worth quoting again the Civil Service clerk's wife:

'Times have changed very much. I think my mother had a much easier time than what I've ever had. Well, mother had help, and I have no help – no domestic help, I have to do everything myself. My mother had a nurse to bring us up, things were very different – my mother did get out. We had a big house, I go there once a year. I find if you have help you have more time to amuse the children; I mean, in the morning I've got a *lot* of work to put in, and I want to be taking the children out instead. When I go up to Scotland, I do, I take the children to the seaside, and I mean the work's done when I come back, it's a great help, wonderful. My mother has a woman that comes in, and she does the washing and everything like that about three or four times a week, and it's a great help, and you're getting more pleasure out of your children.'

We have noted before that middle-class women whose mothers could afford to be relieved of much of the housework are inclined to feel somewhat resentful when, having achieved a comparable or higher social standing, they have to do most of their own chores themselves: even the best fully-automatic self-programming washing machine is not quite so convenient as a well-trained domestic who can be instructed to do the ironing too. An additional irritation is often that grandmother, in criticizing her daughter's child-rearing practices, fails to make due allowance for the fact that these days even a middle-class wife has to do most of

the cooking, ironing and heavy cleaning herself, and sometimes a good deal of the gardening and even the decorating
and maintenance as well.

Special circumstances

All these changes in upbringing have applied to rather large
groups of mothers; but there were some for whom individual
circumstances had induced a determination to achieve something very different for their own children. Of especial n-
terest are two patterns of circumstance which each occurred
several times: the first concerns childhood jealousy, the
second casual adoption.

Jealousy was mentioned by mothers of every social class;
and where it was mentioned it invariably took first place in
the mother's assessment of differences in upbringing. The
striking characteristic of these discussions was the bitterness
with which old memories were revived. Often it was clear
that these traumatic experiences informed the mother's
whole attitude towards her children; sometimes her very
conscious decision to avoid jealousy on their part seemed to
have become her chief principle in bringing them up.

Lorry-driver's wife:
' My children are much happier than I was. I was always
the odd one out; and that's a little – you know – *wall* between
my mam and me, you know, that I won't let one have anything without the other does – within reason – because I
don't want any of them to feel left out, you know; I won't
have it – I'll stop her coming if she does favour. She favours
my oldest one, you see, we've had one or two rows about it,
you know; I won't have it, you see. But you can't say anything without them taking offence; but I'll break with her
completely rather than have that.'

Office manager's wife:
' No. My children are being brought up much different.
Well, for a start, my daughter's fourteen, and she was
thirteen when David was born. Well, I was nine when my
sister was born; and from my mother getting up out of bed

after her confinement, I was made to push that baby around. I was only nine, I don't think I was really old enough to do, but I used to – I'd come home from school and I'd have to take that baby out from quarter past four till the six o'clock feed; and Sundays push her round for miles; and when she was older, say two or three, and she had a lot of little toys on wheels, I used to have to crawl up and down playing with her when I wanted to be with my own friends: well, I'd never expect that of Vanessa. And you know, even today, there's no love lost between us. And even when I was courting, you know, I had to have my boy-friend indoors so I could keep my eye on Margaret. I mean, she was eleven and I was twenty, and I'd just got my first boy-friend. I resent it to this day – my goodness, I resent it! I *do*. Because I don't think it was at all right. All at once she was born, and that was it – clean your own shoes from now on, and take yourself up to bed. My dad used to carry me up to bed *every* night, and he used to always play a game with me – he used to tuck me up, and then I had a lot of these stuffed toys, animals, and he used to stand at the door and throw them round – and that was a game we had, until my sister was born. Well, that just stopped. Well, that's not right, is it? But it's a good eye-opener, my goodness it is, it teaches you things.'

Of the sample of about 150 mothers who were asked about differences in upbringing, there were naturally some whose childhood had been rather abnormal. Several, for instance, had spent part or all of their earlier life in orphanages or with foster-parents; one or two had had very long periods in hospital; and a few had been brought up by relatives although their own parents were alive and often living only a few streets away.

It was this last type of upbringing which came to interest us especially. What first caught our attention was the very casual nature of these 'adoptions'. Usually it was the mother's grandmother who had taken her over – most often, it seemed, almost by accident; in one case the adopter was an aunt. It is, of course, not so very uncommon for an older woman to take over the illegitimate child of an elder daughter and bring it up as her own youngest child, knowing its true mother only as a sister; but our cases are rather different in that no deception is practised. Whether casual adoption by relatives takes place now to this extent (at least six mentioned, among about 150 mothers, and our information is obviously very incomplete on this point) we have no means of knowing: one would expect such a practice to be at least partly bound up with conditions of poverty under which a woman might be glad to be relieved of the expense of one of her children; certainly no middle-class mother mentioned such an arrangement. Sometimes the adoption had been initiated by a family crisis; Madeline Kerr describes such a thing happening in Ship Street, which closely parallels one of our own cases.

'Joe was brought up by his mother's mother. When he was about two he got pneumonia very badly. Granny took charge and took Joe over to her place. When he got well he remained with Granny. . . . She died quite recently. Joe continues to live with his stepgrandfather. Joe is now twenty-three.'[1]

For the sake of full anonymity, we withhold the occupations of the husbands of these informants; the first is married to an unskilled worker, the second to a skilled man, and the third's husband is semi-skilled.

'I was one of twins, I've got a twin sister. Well, when I was eight months old, she got pneumonia, and I was sent to my Granny's to stay. She kept me there for a fortnight, and then my sister was better and my parents came to fetch me back; but my Granny said, "Oh, let me keep her", she said, "just another fortnight". And they never came back for me. I stayed with my Granny till I was nineteen years of age; and they hardly ever came to see me all that time, and I didn't go to see them. And my sister only lives two streets away from

1. Madeline Kerr, *The People of Ship Street* (Routledge and Kegan Paul, 1958).

here, and I often see her; and my mother and father are always coming over to see her, but they never come and see me – two streets away! They've never seen the baby – well, they've never seen any of mine [four children] except just the oldest when he was a baby. But it doesn't bother me.'

(This mother's grandmother was visiting her at the time of the interview, and it was she who gave us this account):

'I used to have her a lot, and then when she went to school – she always wanted to come Friday night, and I took her back Sunday. Tuesday night her Mam would come up again with her, and I used to say, "Whatever have you brought her again for, you know what it is", I said, "and winter's coming on, and I shan't be able to bring her down"; because I lived on – I suppose you know Sherwood Vale? Well, I'd got that hill to go right down Winchester Street to take her to school. So I said – well, I didn't really mean it at the time, I just said it as it came in my mind, I said, "Well – if you want me to have her", I said, "you'll have to have her transferred to Walter Halls School". Anyway – when she came up next time she'd been and transferred her! And she lived with me then right up to being seventeen; and then I thought it was time she went home and appreciated her mother a bit, because, I mean, I was getting on; and I thought to myself, well, you know, she'll p'raps be better with her mother now.'

(The following semi-adoption is rather different, in that it was not complete, was the result of family discord, and was definitely traumatic for the child):

'Well, my mum had a lot, you see, children. Well, I was at my grandma's, brought to and fro, you see, with my mum being, er – I think she had milk fever over me, that was the trouble, you see – they was always fetching me to and fro; then my mum used to fetch me back. I was there when I was born from about ten days old till I was about ten month old, then I came home, then I used to go back for months at a time, you see – it was more of a family argument, really;

when my dad used to have an argument with my mum, I'd be packed in a pram and my dad used to take me to his mother's, and then I'd be nicely settled there, cause I loved it there; and I'd be fetched back, and I'd be heartbroken, and then when I cried at my mum's I used to get a slap for crying – oh, I can remember that right up till I was thirteen – I can remember it ever so plain; and then in the end I went to my grandma's when I was sixteen for good – and I still go. Well, what I mean, she's more like my mother, like, kind of thing – it's as if *she's* my mother, not my own mother – funny, isn't it? That's why I've always tried to give these . . . I mean, I shouldn't want it to happen to these.'

Apart from these last two sets of quotations, which are very much the result of individual experience of less usual conditions, it can be seen that most of these mothers took their childhood as being representative of their generation and their own children's upbringing as normal for the modern age. Their answers to what was in fact a very personal question thus made some attempt to generalize from particularities: many were consciously groping for words in which to express the essential difference between two worlds. So some emphasized material standards, some linked these with the relaxation of discipline, some went on from this to the psychological closeness which they felt to be characteristic of the relationship between parents and children today. Perhaps a further step towards the centre of the change was taken by our oldest mother, who chose 'interest' as the key.

'I think we're more *interested* in the children. I remember them singing to us after our baths, but we never had interesting *conversations* with our parents, the way I do with my children.'

But the last word must be given to Mrs West, whom we have quoted before (notably on temper tantrums), and whose whole discourse showed *in excelsis* that 'thinking' which she regards as the essence of modern baby care. In her reference to the more intropunitive attitude of the younger generation of parents, we believe she has reached the heart of the matter.

'People nowadays think more about what's good for the children, from the children's point of view. Everything I do with him, I try to do the best thing *for* him, I'm *thinking* about that all the time. I'm careful about his food, and I hold him on my lap after his bottle so he won't have a tummy-ache, he's inoculated so he won't catch diseases, later on I take them to the dentist so they won't get toothache: I'm thinking in advance for his comfort all the time. I know there's some people leave their children and go to work now, never mind what happens to the children so long as you get the money, but that's just a few – most people think more of their children's good. It used to be just the higher classes that did that, but now I think that that ... thinking ... has spread right through the general classes.

'Nowadays, if they don't turn out right you wonder where *you*'ve gone wrong, don't you? It used to be, they made you do this and do that, and you did it, and if things went wrong it was the child's fault, not the parents', they could never be wrong. I think we're not so happy about *ourselves* these days, we blame ourselves, not the child. I do, I know. I wish I didn't sometimes.'

In this, our final chapter, we have been ranging further afield, and discussing broader aspects of child rearing than the practices adopted in the first year of life with which this survey is primarily concerned. We have concentrated on the baby's first twelve months, not necessarily because we believe that such matters as breast feeding and toilet training are the most important factors in the development of the personality: naturally we have our own opinions about the various techniques which are used by parents in different situations, and naturally, in our dealings with our own children, we apply or attempt to apply those methods which we believe to be best; but what criteria we may employ in judging this 'best', beyond those of humanity and common sense, it is difficult to be sure. So we have been motivated in our explorations, not so much by a desire to study breast feeding and the rest *per se*, but rather by the realization that very little factual information is at present available about how children in general are being brought up, that information of this sort is indispensable as a basic prerequisite for any theory of personality development – and that we have to start somewhere. This survey is itself only a part of the general trend towards a psychological ecology in which psychological problems are studied less in the laboratories and the clinics and to a far greater extent in the natural habitat of the human animal. In the childhood of *homo sapiens*, the first year is only the beginning: so it will be, we hope, for these investigations.

AIMS AND DESIGN OF THE INVESTIGATION

General aims

In planning the investigation, and in designing the questionnaire which was eventually used when interviewing the mothers, we set out to obtain evidence concerning a number of special aspects of infant rearing. It is a consideration of each of these questions in turn which occupies the major part of this book. For example, we wanted to find out what sorts of things most mothers in fact do, irrespective of what they are told to do. We wanted to discover how their babies normally behave, and what is the range of variation in such behaviour as, for example, sleeping. We hoped to find out whether there are consistent social class differences in the way mothers handle young babies. And so on. A glance at the table of contents will give a fair indication of the other major areas of interest which we had in mind. There were, however, quite a number of detailed minor questions which it would be difficult to fit into any coherent overall pattern, and these are each considered in what seems to us the most appropriate place.

The design of the investigation

The way in which the investigation was planned and carried out may conveniently be described under three main headings: first, the sample; secondly, the interview schedule; and, thirdly, the interviewers. These will now be considered in turn.

The sample

Our survey was carried out in the English Midlands, within the boundaries of one city, Nottingham. This city, which is not far from the geographical centre of England, is a fairly typical modern industrial conurbation. It is the eighth largest city in England, and has a population of about 312,000. Today it is a prosperous

1. Appendices One and Two appeared as the first two chapters in the original edition.

city, and over the few years preceding the survey there had been little unemployment. Apart from the coal-mining industry, the three biggest employers of labour are a manufacturing pharmaceutical firm, a cycle works and a tobacco processing works; in addition, there is a large number of light industrial firms, mainly concerned with the traditional textile trade of the city, with a special emphasis on hosiery and lace. A direct result of this emphasis is a tradition of the large-scale employment of women workers, which includes the provision of special evening shifts for married women and a fairly extensive system of 'home-work' for women who prefer to do such jobs as making-up and finishing in their own homes.

The city is reasonably well separated from neighbouring conurbations, and may be regarded as a self-contained community in which all social classes and most occupations are represented. Altogether the area seemed well suited to an investigation of this type.

The sample itself was entirely drawn from records kept by the City of Nottingham Health Department. These records refer to all children born in the City of Nottingham and resident within the City boundaries between birth and the child's fifth birthday. The records are more or less complete and accurate for children from a few weeks old. They depend upon information returned by midwives, doctors and hospitals in the first place, and are subsequently confirmed by a notification from the Registrar of Births and Deaths. Later the records become a little less accurate because of the movement of families both into and out of the city, and because of local movements within the city itself. However, a considerable effort is made to keep continuous track of the movements of families, and the health visitors are asked to notify the Department of all removals which they may discover in the course of their attempts to visit families in their homes. Health Departments in different parts of the country also notify each other of movements out of their own areas. In view of the circumstances, the available records of children by the time they reach their first birthday would seem to be as complete as can reasonably be expected.

The total interviewing programme was spread out over a period of two years, but the mother of each child was interviewed within a fortnight either way of the child's first birthday. In order that the samples should be as up to date as possible, batches of names were drawn month by month.

During the first stage of the project, we took a random sample from the records until we had a total of 500 completed interviews. At the second stage, we began by drawing random samples, which were then passed to the health visitors who were able to tell us, from their own records, the occupation of the father of each child. Occupations were then grouped according to the Registrar General's classification of occupations by social class.[1] In this way it was possible to increase the overall representation of those groups which were not well represented numerically in the random sample. Thus at stage two we interviewed according to a plan for stratified random sampling, using social class as the basis of stratification.

Our original aim was to have 700 completed interviews. In fact, during the second stage of the project, 209 interviews were completed. Thus the total number of completed interviews for the whole project is 709.

Exclusions

In planning the study we were primarily interested in normal babies in ordinary family situations. For this reason we deliberately excluded from our sample a number of cases which did not fall into this category. All illegitimate children and all children known to have gross disabilities were excluded at the outset. For obvious reasons, we omitted children who were not in the care of their mother, although we included in the sample those whose mothers were in full-time work, and who were therefore 'daily-minded' by grandmother, neighbour or day nursery. Children whose parents were recent immigrants to this country were also excluded. While some of these groups, such as the growing population of West Indians in Nottingham, are of considerable interest and might repay special investigation, we decided that for the purposes of this study the picture could only be confused by their inclusion.

Losses

In order to obtain 709 completed interviews, it was necessary to attempt 773. Thus in 64 cases we were in fact unsuccessful in obtaining an interview. This represents an overall loss rate of 8·2

1. General Register Office, *Census 1951: Classification of Occupations* (H.M.S.O., 1955). We have modified the original classification by the introduction of a 'white collar' classification in Class III (see pp. 152–3).

per cent. There were various reasons for these losses, and some kinds of loss are more likely to distort the overall results than others. In Table 30 we have analysed all the losses by dividing them into a number of broad categories.

TABLE 30

Losses from the sample

Reason for loss	No. of cases	Percentage of 773
		%
1. Mother or child seriously mentally or physically ill	15	1·9
2. Moved out of the area	21	2·7
3. Unable to contact	11	1·4
4. 'Unsuitable' problem families[1]	5	0·6
5. Refusal of the interview	12	1·6
Total, all reasons	64	8·2

Losses of this kind tend to distort the overall results of a survey only in so far as they represent cases which are likely to differ from the rest of the sample. Clearly, we would expect categories 3, 4 and 5 of Table 30 to be most important in this respect. The only actual information which we tried to obtain about these mothers was whether they were out at work. We discovered that at least three of them were working part-time, and at least seven full-time. This definitely represents a higher proportion than is found in the rest of the sample.

However, a certain number of losses is inevitable in a survey of this sort, and, as a loss rate of approximately 10 per cent seems to be fairly normal in work of this kind, the results may be considered satisfactory. We were pleased to find that outright refusals accounted for only a small fraction of the total losses, and for less than 2 per cent of the total sample.

THE INTERVIEW AND THE INTERVIEW SCHEDULE

Getting the mother's cooperation

Mothers of one-year-olds tend to be busy people. More often than not, they have older children as well; some even have

1. These were cases which a social worker had specifically asked us to exclude in order not to disturb a delicate relationship.

younger babies. They almost always have a home to run, meals to prepare, nappies to wash, shopping to do, and a host of other responsibilities. Moreover, in these days of consumer research, housewives probably have to suffer more interviews per head than any other single section of the community. We therefore felt it necessary to restrict the scope of our interview to what could be accomplished in a single visit.

In practice, it was sometimes possible for the interview to be completed in just over half an hour. But some mothers had a lot more to say than others – for some it was obviously an opportunity to 'let their hair down' to somebody not personally involved with themselves – and often the interviews were punctuated throughout by a series of unavoidable, and sometimes lengthy, interruptions. Thus some interviews took well over two hours. In any case this was not the sort of interview which could be undertaken on a doorstep, and interviewers were instructed to make an appointment with every mother beforehand, either by calling on her to explain what was wanted, or by sending a letter.

On the whole, it was not very difficult to get the mothers interested; indeed, few mothers can resist the invitation to talk about their own children, uninterrupted, and for as long as they wish. This was a subject on which they could not help being authorities: mothers really do *know* something about how they bring up their own children, and most of them appeared to welcome the opportunity of explaining what they felt about it, and how they had learned from their own mistakes. In asking for their cooperation, we tried to explain to them that we were seeking their advice and not expecting to give advice ourselves; and many of them seemed to appreciate not being on the receiving end for once.[1] In general, then, there was very little problem in establishing rapport in the interview situation.

The design of the schedule

In the study of human behaviour, bald facts are of little value without interpretation, and interpretation involves understanding the underlying motives and values which human beings attach

1. Extract from interviewer's report: Mrs Sturgess poked her head round the door, glared at me and said, 'I know how to bring up me children thank you, I don't want any advice from you'. I said, 'I don't want to give you advice, I want *you* to give *me* some'. She stared, then opened the door, saying, 'Come in, duck – I'm just making some tea'.

to most of their actions. Certain factual information was essential; but in addition we wanted to know what the mothers felt about various questions of child upbringing, what their attitudes were, whether they felt guilty in doing certain things, whether they did some things on principle, and whether they kept rigidly to those principles; and so on.

The construction of a questionnaire thus involves a great deal more than thinking up a few likely questions and running them off on a duplicating machine. To the social scientist, a properly constructed interview schedule represents a delicate research instrument specifically designed to reveal the subtle kinds of information in which he is really interested; and, where this information concerns behaviour between people, the truth may not be amenable to the direct question. As in other spheres of investigation, the ultimate quality of his work will depend to a large extent on the quality of the research tool that is used.

The interview schedule was divided into various sections according to the main topics which we wished to discuss. A deliberate attempt was made to arrange the various topics in a natural order so that the whole interview would run as smoothly as possible. From the mother's point of view, we hoped that the interview would resemble a natural conversation as far as possible, and we particularly wanted to avoid the impression that we were simply getting answers to a list of direct questions. We believe that we were fairly successful in this, since mothers would frequently begin to discuss questions in the next section of the schedule just before the topic was broached by the interviewer. Incidentally, this also served to keep interviewers on their toes, simply because it is embarrassing to find oneself asking a question to which one has been given an answer only a minute before.

All interviews can be placed somewhere on a continuum between the completely structured and the completely free. At the one extreme, the questions are such that they can only give rise to a few possible alternative answers which are already known, so that the interviewer simply has to put a cross in the appropriate box. At the other extreme, the interviewer decides for himself how to put his questions, and he may even make the decision as to what kinds of questions he will ask. This is no place to discuss the relative merits of these two extreme approaches, but it will be seen that, while ours was a fairly well structured interview on the whole, there were instances in which we left the method of introducing a question to the interviewer.

With regard to the form of the answers required, our methods varied from one question to another. Thus, for some questions all that was necessary was to underline one of a set of alternative responses. An example of such a question is: 'Does he ever wake during the night now? Most nights/more than twice a week/less than twice/very seldom or never.' For other questions, we wanted not so much the mother's direct answer as a rating of her attitude to the problem. This type of judgment was best made by the interviewer herself (all our interviewers are female), in the actual situation, where she could appreciate all the subtle nuances of voice, inflexion and gesture which always play such a large part in true conversations between one individual and another. An instance of this sort of question is one on toilet training: 'Are you taking trouble to get him trained at the moment?' From the mother's tone, from her facial expression, and from the tense or relaxed quality of her reply, as much as from her words, the interviewer judged whether she was 'very concerned', 'mildly concerned' or 'unconcerned' about the general topic of toilet training. In some open-ended questions where we were particularly interested in individual comments as well as in the mother's attitude, the interviewer was asked to record the mother's reply verbatim. The main question for eliciting attitudes to birth was of this type: 'How did you get on? Did you have a good time?'; so was the question designed to find out whether children were smacked: 'How do you punish him when he's been naughty?' In addition, there were of course many factual questions, such as 'Did he wake during the night last night?' for which it was only necessary to ring YES or NO.

One problem in the investigation of this sort of behaviour is to avoid questions which are likely to elicit meaningless or conventional responses. The difficulty is that mothers realize that nearly everyone holds strong views on some of the subjects we wished to discuss, and there is a strong temptation to say as little as possible, either out of a sense of politeness, or for fear of censure. Thus it was important to establish a permissive atmosphere from the start of the interview, and the interviewer had to be careful not to reveal her own feelings, nor to act in any way which might imply criticism of the views held by individual mothers. In addition, it was necessary to resort to various devices in drafting the questions themselves. One such device was to follow a series of factual questions with a more informal one about the mother's feelings; an example is the birth attitude question already quoted, when a number of routine questions about family structure, place of birth and birth weight was followed by the much more intimate one: 'How did you get on? Did you have a good time?'

Another device was to ask an opening question and to follow it by a whole series of probe questions so that the interviewer could approach the topic from several angles and thus be more certain of arriving at the truth. For instance, in discovering how responsive the mother was to the child's crying and how far principle was involved in her attitude, the initial question 'What do you do if he won't sleep, or cries after you've left him?' was followed by the series: 'And if he goes on crying? Does he ever wake during the night now? What do you do if he wakes during the night (or what would you do)? Does anybody else ever go to him in the night? Do you think it does a child of this age any harm to be left to cry? How long would you let him cry if you thought there was nothing wrong with him?'

One further device was to include 'shock' questions which were likely to prove directly provocative to mothers with a particular attitude. The question mentioned earlier, 'How do you punish him when he's been naughty?' is such an item; apparently rather heavily loaded, it in fact serves a double purpose as 'shock' question for the non-punishing mother and 'permissive' question for the punishing mother. The direct question 'Do you punish him?', while it would elicit the true answer 'No' from the non-smacking mother, might well draw a politely false answer 'No' from the smacking mother, who may feel slightly guilty about smacking a one-year-old. When the question was asked in its more loaded form, the smacking mother was able to reply truthfully to a questioner who seemed to assume that one-year-olds *were* naughty and had to be punished; while the permissive mother was shocked by this very assumption into a rather definite declaration of her attitude. Thus we obtained the typical opposing answers 'I just smack his legs' and 'Oh! Oh *no*! He's not naughty, he's only a baby yet', each of which has the ring of truth. In using the shock question it is of course especially important fully to explain its purpose to the interviewer, to whom, if she is herself permissive, there is a strong temptation to alter or qualify the wording in order not to draw the permissive mother's disapproval upon herself; in such a situation, the mother's effect upon the interviewer must be thought out beforehand with as much care as that of the interviewer upon the mother.

In summary, our general approach to questionnaire construction was eclectic and pragmatic. We were prepared to use any device that worked in practice. This meant trying out possible versions of questions on all kinds of mothers in order to find out which of them worked satisfactorily. As a result, our whole questionnaire went through several revisions before we arrived at the final draft, and even then it was necessary to include a few additional instructions as the work proceeded. Of one thing we are convinced: however good his interviewers, it is essential for the research planner to experience for himself the practical use of his own research instrument; only by himself entering the interview situation can he really get the feel of what he is working with and discover with a full understanding where the faults lie. We do not pretend that our questionnaire is a perfect one, or that the methods we employed were necessarily the best. We do believe, however, that in this kind of investigation each research worker has to fashion his own tools to meet the purposes he has in mind.

The interviewers

Social survey interviewers need to have a pleasant manner and a certain skill in persuading cooperation. A rather high degree of persistence and conscientiousness is also required. The interviewer may have to call back several times to the same address in order to obtain an interview, and she must be capable of getting a satisfactory answer to every question on the schedule, however far from the point her informant may stray. Our interviewing programme obviously demanded these basic qualities, but it also demanded special skills related to the particular subject we were investigating. It was clear at the outset that we could use only women interviewers; but they also needed to be reasonably mature and intelligent people, able to discuss the intimate details of birth and child rearing without causing the mothers too much embarrassment. After all, it may not be easy to discuss such matters as breast feeding and toilet training with someone you have only just met for the first time.

A full-scale project only really became possible when the City Health Department offered to let their health visitors undertake a large proportion of the interviews. This solved many of our problems. The health visitors are a fully trained and widely experienced body of professional social workers, and they are deployed in an interlocking network of districts which covers the entire city. Furthermore, they already have access to the very homes in which we were interested, and they have generally been visiting the mother regularly since the baby was two weeks old. Health visitors are also experienced interviewers; they are frequently asked to assist in the inquiries into the social aspects of illness which are organized on a nation-wide basis. Thus they met all the requirements for interviewers outlined above.

There is, however, one serious difficulty. It is part of the job of a health visitor to give advice to mothers on many of the subjects that we intended to discuss with them. Health visitors also wear a uniform and, as members of the nursing profession employed by the local administrative body, they undoubtedly represent, to some mothers at least, an alien authority and part of the 'Them' which is officialdom. It is true that much of their training is designed to overcome this handicap. They have no *right* of access to people's homes, and the service they provide is purely advisory. Their continued usefulness must depend to a very large extent on the tact and discretion which they employ when giving advice to mothers. But, despite this, the very fact that the mothers know that health visitors do give specific advice on various topics such as scheduling, weaning and potting means that they may not be entirely frank in answering their questions about these matters. For this reason, then, we were worried that the use of the health visitors as interviewers might produce a certain amount of bias or distortion in our overall results.

We attempted to deal with this difficulty in two different ways. In the first place, we decided to interview an independent control sample of 200 cases ourselves, so as to be able to compare the health visitors' results with our own. The majority of these interviews was conducted by Elizabeth Newson, but a small number (16 in all) was undertaken by one or two other university people who had been interested in the survey from its inception and who had volunteered to help in this way. All these interviews were discussed with us as soon as possible after their completion.

Secondly, the health visitors know that their relationship with some families is a difficult or delicate one. A few families resent their visits and actively obstruct their attempts to work with them. In some cases, the visitor, while she is tolerated, is only received with a polite hostility. In such circumstances we asked the health visitors to notify us before approaching the mother, and we then wrote to the mother asking her to take part in an inquiry being conducted by the University; that is to say, we did not give any indication that the health visitor or the Health Department were involved in any way. One of our own interviewers would then undertake the interview. All interviews of this sort were included as part of the health visitors' sample.

Our total number of 709 interviews is thus composed of two separate samples: the Health Visitor sample and the University sample. Each of these two samples comprises a certain number of cases drawn at random and an additional number of cases sampled selectively according to the father's occupation. The relationship between these different subdivisions of the total sample is shown in Table 31.

TABLE 31

Breakdown of total sample of 709 completed interviews

	Health visitors	University	Total
Random sample	365	135	500
Selected sample	144	65	209
Total	509	200	709

THE EVALUATION OF EVIDENCE

The total investigation was designed to produce two kinds of evidence upon which we could base our final conclusions. In the first place, all the answers which the mothers gave to specific questions were classified so that the results could be analysed statistically. As this involved a great deal of cross-classification, the information from each interview schedule was transferred to a pre-coded punched card, and these cards were used for all further numerical sorting.

In the second place, all the interview schedules included some answers in the mothers' own words; furthermore, most of the University sample were recorded with the aid of a portable tape recorder, and in these cases we were able to make verbatim transcripts of whole interviews. All this provided an important additional source of evidence which we have used throughout to help us in the interpretation of the statistical findings.

The use of the tape recorder in interviewing is sometimes criticized on the grounds that it makes for self-consciousness and lack of ease on the part of the person interviewed; and, indeed, we ourselves expected difficulties of this sort. Our experience, however, was quite otherwise. Probably because the topic was one on which most mothers are extremely fluent, the recorder seemed to be no barrier to free and natural conversation. The machine used was small and unobtrusive, similar in size and shape to a large handbag with shoulder strap and powered by batteries. It was, of course, used quite openly, and was never switched on without asking the mother's permission; in a very few cases, the mother preferred not to have her voice recorded, and here we used pencil and paper. Our impression was that, once the interview was under way, the tape recorder was quickly forgotten; indeed, at the end of the interview a number of mothers remembered with surprise that they were being recorded when the interviewer leaned over to switch off.

The reason we gave for using the tape recorder was simply that it avoided the labour of writing down answers; in fact, of course, the advantages extended much further than this. Often a mother will talk at some length, elaborating and qualifying her answer to a direct question, or going off at a tangent to discuss some aspect of child upbringing which the interviewer has not asked about. From this free flow of talk we may obtain much valuable information concerning a mother's attitudes and difficulties, and many useful sidelights on the general problems of child rearing; yet if the interviewer attempts to take it all down manually she necessarily destroys her role of sympathetic listener. In addition, it has been of special value to the non-interviewing half of the research team to be able to hear the entire course of the interview; this, of course, would be much more important for those investigations in which the planning team takes no part in interviewing. Often, the possibility of listening again to the mother's tone of voice as she gave an answer has been useful in the assessment of her attitude on some point. And, finally, the fact that we have been able to quote verbatim, often at length, without fear of inaccuracy or distortion, has allowed the subjects of this report to give it some sense of immediacy by speaking for themselves.

The reader will gather that we are fully persuaded of the virtues of sound recording, for this type of interview at least; and, if further evidence is necessary of the mothers' lack of constraint before the microphone, we may call attention to the accounts which we include elsewhere of very intimate and private feelings, of illegal activities such as attempts at abortion, and of other things for which, as Mrs J. said, 'I could get into trouble, you know, if They got to know'.

The statistical analysis, generally speaking, proceeded in two stages. For any particular question we first compared the results obtained from the Health Visitor sample with those obtained from the University sample. To make this comparison it was, of course, necessary to 'correct' the proportions from the stratified sample to equivalent random sample proportions. If after correction both samples yielded much the same result, they could then be combined to give a result which was correct for a total random sample.

Sometimes, however, the results from the two separate samples differed to a significant extent. This occurred, for example, when mothers were asked whether they had ever given their child a dummy.[1] When asked this question by a health visitor, only 63 per

---

1. For a full discussion of this, see pp. 57–61.

cent of all mothers admitted having done so. When they were asked by a University interviewer, the percentage rose to 72 per cent, and the difference is statistically significant. It is fairly easy to interpret a difference of this kind, and the fact that it exists can be taken as evidence that many mothers believe the health visitors to be less permissive about the use of dummies than they are themselves. In general, indeed, the emergence of a discrepancy between health visitor findings and University findings can be taken as a useful pointer to those areas of child rearing in which mothers believe themselves to be at variance with clinic teaching: where, in practical terms, they feel some embarrassment at telling the health visitor what they actually do with their children. On the other hand, the discrepancy in this case makes it difficult to give a very precise estimate of the extent to which dummies are in fact used. As a mother is hardly likely to say that she uses a dummy when she doesn't, it seems probable that the higher estimate is nearer the truth; although, since the mothers may be 'idealizing' their behaviour to the University interviewer also, though to a lesser extent, the true figure may be higher still. Thus we have here drawn a tentative conclusion that dummies are used by at least 72 per cent of all children during their first year. In the circumstances, any such estimate must be a rough one: but it is worth noticing that, if our entire sample had been interviewed by health visitors, we might have been tempted to accept the apparently precise estimate of 63 per cent without question. It will be remembered that other surveys of this sort have in fact used health visitors as interviewers[1] without any non-medical check: and this may provide some explanation for the areas in which their findings differ markedly from ours.

Where discrepancies are found between the University and Health Visitor samples, they tend to be in the direction which one would expect if the mothers were trying to please (or at least not to come into conflict with) the health visitors. This in no way reflects upon the health visitors' work, or upon their ability as interviewers. It has long been an accepted fact in investigations of this kind that the interviewee tends to have a placating attitude towards the interviewer, as indeed happens in most casual social relationships: the well-dressed interviewer finds a greater propor-

1. Notably those reported in Population Investigation Committee, *Maternity in Great Britain* (O.U.P., 1948); and J. Spence *et al.*, *1,000 Families in Newcastle upon Tyne* (O.U.P., 1954).

tion of Conservative voters, the sallow-skinned finds less expression of race prejudice, and so on. Where the interviewer's opinions are known, or thought to be known, there will almost inevitably be a certain amount of avoidance of controversy.

In all cases in which such a discrepancy between the two samples exists, we have at least noted the fact. Furthermore, in any subsequent analysis we have kept the two samples separate. Not infrequently, when we have done this some further trend still shows up quite clearly in both samples, and we can then give a final overall estimate of its significance.[1] Thus in the case of the use of dummies there are consistent social class differences found in both the samples, and we therefore feel justified in going on to discuss these, even though the two samples differed initially.

1. For results of statistical tests of significance, the reader is referred to the original edition, pp. 253–6. The text of the interview schedule and of the instructions for using it have also had to be omitted from the present edition: these are the only omissions.

A NOTTINGHAM GLOSSARY

words and phrases used in everyday speech

against:
by, beside, next door to; as in 'I sat against a lady', 'she lives against the Co-op'.

baba!:
warning interjection, to a child being naughty or about to be naughty. Also 'It's a baba!' Used in many different situations.

bits and bobs:
bits and pieces. Of solid food: 'He's had bits and bobs ever since he was three months old.' On the interviewer's departure: 'Have you got all your bits and bobs?'

bobbo:
exactly equals 'gee-gee'.

bobby:
faeces (childish); also used as verb.

bothered:
used in various related senses: 'I'm not bothered' – 'I don't care for it much'. Of child and Welfare orange juice: 'She's not ever so bothered' – 'She's not very keen on it'. But 'It doesn't bother me' – 'It doesn't worry me'. Compare 'fussy'.

catch for:
become pregnant with. 'We'd only been married four months when I caught for Susan.'

crib:
full-size wooden cot, not a tiny baby's basket.

duddoos:
sweets (childish).

entertain:
frequently used in the sense of 'tolerate': 'He won't entertain the potty'; 'She won't entertain her Daddy'. It is also used in the sense of 'amuse', however: 'We don't go out, the children are our entertainment.'

fast:
stuck, caught. 'It's fast!'; 'If he gets his toys fast anywhere'.

fetch:
commonly used instead of 'bring'; 'We fetch her downstairs', or even 'My mother fetched me up different' (see 'road'). Also used often in the sense: 'She was fetching her first two teeth'; cf. 'she's after her teeth at the moment'.

fussy: the nearest equivalent seems to be 'enthusiastic'. 'She's not fussy about orange juice' – meaning she *is*, i.e. she doesn't like it. 'My husband's not very fussy about small babies.' Another example – 'She'll pull her ears when she's really fussy' – was elaborated to show that this happened when the baby was really happy and pleased over a situation.

Mam: usual for 'Mother', 'Mum'.

mardy: grizzly, whining, cross, spoilt; making an (unnecessary) fuss. See pp. 80–1.

mester: man, gentleman; as in 'Look at that mester'. Also, husband: 'How's the mester?' – 'How's your husband?'; 'Mester's not at home' – 'My husband's not at home'.

missus: woman, lady; 'Missus next door said . . .'; 'I ask missus up the terrace'.

Nan, Nana: Granny, Grandma.

nasty: much used meaning bad-tempered. 'It makes me very nasty when she keeps on crying for nothing at all'; 'She's sometimes very nasty when she's teething'; 'You're bound to get nasty if you haven't got it to give them'.

not: used for 'won't', 'doesn't'; 'It not matter'; 'My husband says don't stop him, it not harm him'.

pods: baby's woolly bootees.

rip: used for tearing, however slight: 'She found a tiny little rip in her dress'.

road: commonly used instead of 'way'. 'Any road' – anyway. 'Not that road' – not that way, not like that. 'You try to fetch your children up the right road.'

same as: used often for 'like', 'as', 'for instance'. Same as these mothers said: 'Same as I say'; 'You couldn't get sat down to proper meals and that, same as you should do'; 'She gets up to mischief – same as when I'm washing the pots and she'll tek a cup. . . .'

swill: for getting rid of breast milk, not by pouring it away but by medication: 'I asked the doctor for tablets to swill it away.'

starved: chilled. 'He was in his pram and he looked starved to death' – he looked frozen. The Concise Oxford Dictionary says that this use is 'now rare', but it is common in Nottingham.

tabs: ears (children are told not to use this word; it is considered very 'rough').

tap: smack, blow, hit (either verb or noun). 'That mester gi' me a tap on the tab'; 'I just tap his legs, quite gently'; 'I'd give her a real good tap for that'.

tata: time of it. Of a child waking every night: 'He gave us a proper tata.' 'I've had a terrible tata with her over that potty.' The word implies activity to cope with the problem.

tegs, teggies: teeth (childish); possibly short for toothy-pegs, but we have not heard this used as it is in the south.

time: added to a statement of time of day, denotes 'approximately'. 'Half past two time' means 'about half past two'. Similarly, 'About last August time'.

toffee (toofi):   sweet – *any* sweet, not necessarily the chewy, caramel sort. Thus 'toofi-fags' are sugar cigarettes.

us: our. 'We had us tea.'

what's going off?   equals 'what's going on?' – most often used of trouble or mischief afoot.

whittle: worry, fuss; 'My milk goes, I whittle too much, you know.' Also in the sense of gentle grizzling: 'Perhaps sometimes he'll whittle a little while, but then he'll drop off.'

LIST OF REFERENCES

Bateson, Gregory, and Mead, Margaret, *Balinese Character: a Photographic Analysis*, New York Academy of Sciences, 1942.

Bronfenbrenner, U., 'Socialisation and social class through time and space'; in E. Maccoby, T. M. Newcomb and E. L. Hartley, *Readings in Social Psychology*, third edition, Henry Holt and Co., N.Y., 1958.

Chester, T. E., 'Growth, Productivity and Woman-Power', *District Bank Review*, September 1962.

City of Nottingham, *Eighty-fifth Annual Report of the Health Services*, 1957.

Clark, F. Le Gros, 'The Weaning of the Human Child', *Nutrition*, Summer 1953.

Clyne, M. B., *Night Calls: a Study in General Practice*, Tavistock Publications, 1961.

Consumers' Association, *Which?*, 1960, 1961.

Cranbrook Report, Maternity Services Committee, H.M.S.O., 1959.

Crawford, W. S., Ltd (Market Research Division), *The Foods We Eat*, Cassell, 1958.

Cuthbert, Anne, 'Babies Should be Happy', *Housewife*, February 1960 (Vol. 22, No. 2).

Davis, A., and Havighurst, R. J., 'Social class and colour differences in child rearing', *Amer. Sociol. Rev.*, XI, 1946.

Davis, A., and Havighurst, R. J., *Father of the Man*, Houghton Mifflin Co., Boston, 1947.

Dingwall, E. J., *The American Woman*, Duckworth, 1956.

Douglas, J. W. B., and Blomfield, J. M., *Children Under Five*, Allen and Unwin, 1958.

Dykes, R. M., *Illness in Luton*, Leagrave Press, Luton, 1950.

Gibbens, John, *The Care of Young Babies*, fourth edition, Churchill, 1955.

Good Housekeeping, *Baby Book*, twelfth edition, National Magazine Company Ltd, 1959.

Gordon, I., and Elias-Jones, T. F., 'The Place of Confinement: Home or Hospital?' *British Medical Journal*, 1, 1960.

Grand, Elaine, 'Miserable Married Women' (series of three articles), *Observer*, 7, 14, and 21 May 1961.

Heardman, Helen, *A Way to Natural Childbirth*, E. & S. Livingstone, 1954.

Hoggart, Richard, *The Uses of Literacy*, Chatto and Windus, 1957; Penguin Books, 1958.

Jackson, Brian, and Marsden, Dennis, *Education and the Working Class*, Routledge and Kegan Paul, 1962.

Kerr, Madeline, *The People of Ship Street*, Routledge and Kegan Paul, 1958.

Kirkup, James, *The Only Child*, Collins, 1957.
    Sorrows, Passions and Alarms, Collins, 1959.

Kleitman, N., *Sleep and Wakefulness*, Chicago, 1939.

Kleitman, N., and Engelmann, T. G., 'Sleep characteristics of infants', *Journ. Appl. Physiol.*, 6, 1953.

Kok, Winifred de, *Milestones in the First Four Years*, British Medical Association (*Family Doctor* booklet).

Liddiard, Mabel, *The Mothercraft Manual*, sixth edition, Churchill, 1928; twelfth edition, Churchill, 1954.

Mellander, O., Vahlquist, B., and Mellbin, T., 'Breast Feeding and Artificial Feeding', *Acta Paediatrica*, 48, 1959.

Ostermilk Book, Glaxo Laboratories, Ltd, 1957.

Population Investigation Committee, *Maternity in Great Britain*, Oxford University Press, 1948.

Radio Doctor (Charles Hill), *Bringing up your Child*, Phoenix House, 1950.

Read, Grantly Dick, *Revelation of Childbirth*, third edition, Heinemann, 1955.

Registrar General, *Statistical Review of England and Wales for 1960*, H.M.S.O.

Registrar General (General Register Office), *Census, 1951: Classification of Occupations*, H.M.S.O., 1955.

Registrar General (General Register Office), *Classification of Occupations*, 1960, H.M.S.O., 1960.

Ross, A. L., and Herdan, G., 'Breast Feeding in Bristol', *Lancet*, I, 1951.

Nesbit, E., *The Story of the Amulet*, T. Fisher Unwin, 1906.

Sears, Robert R., Maccoby, Eleanor E., and Levin, Harry, *Patterns of Child Rearing*, Row, Peterson and Co., N.Y., 1957.

LIST OF REFERENCES

Shapiro, Pauline, 'The Unplanned Children', *New Society*, 1 November 1962.

Soddy, Kenneth, *Clinical Child Psychiatry*, Baillière, Tindall and Cox, 1960.

Spence, J., *et al.*, *1,000 Families in Newcastle upon Tyne*, Oxford University Press, 1954.

Spock, Benjamin, *Baby and Child Care*, Bodley Head, 1958.

Stott, Mary, 'Women Talking', *Guardian*, 10 September 1962.

Whiting, J. W. M., and Child, I. L., *Child Training and Personality*, Yale University Press, 1953.

Widdowson, E., Slater, J., and Harrison, G. E., 'Absorption, excretion and retention of strontium by breast-fed and bottle-fed babies', *Lancet*, II, 1960.

Wilkinson, R. T., 'How much sleep do we need?', *Listener*, LXV, No. 1659.

Wimperis, Virginia, *The Unmarried Mother and her Child*, Allen and Unwin, 1960.

INDEX